William Watkiss Lloyd

Christianity in the Cartoons

referred to artistic treatment and historic fact

William Watkiss Lloyd

Christianity in the Cartoons
referred to artistic treatment and historic fact

ISBN/EAN: 9783741156502

Manufactured in Europe, USA, Canada, Australia, Japa

Cover: Foto ©Lupo / pixelio.de

Manufactured and distributed by brebook publishing software (www.brebook.com)

William Watkiss Lloyd

Christianity in the Cartoons

CHRISTIANITY IN THE CARTOONS

REFERRED TO

ARTISTIC TREATMENT AND HISTORIC FACT.

BY

WILLIAM WATKISS LLOYD.

WILLIAMS AND NORGATE,
14, HENRIETTA STREET, COVENT GARDEN, LONDON;
AND
20, SOUTH FREDERICK STREET, EDINBURGH.
1865.

ADVERTISEMENT.

In abandoning this work to the world, I am not aware that it is necessary to guard against more than one misconception. In the body of it will be found various coincidences with the newer views of Dr. D. F. Strauss in his 'Leben Jesu für das deutsche Volk bearbeitet,' which, to the readers of that noble book, may appear strangely unacknowledged. The explanation is this: the present book was already printed, and indeed in the hands of Dr. Strauss himself,—his cordial recognition of it I value in the place of any decoration,—some weeks before his own issued from the German press; finished in 1862, it was printed in 1863, and from that time to this present, the pages as they follow hereafter have been content with whatever appreciation they might find among the few to whom they were addressed by the limitary epigraph, appropriate no more,—AMICIS.

I take the opportunity of appending some not incongruous illustrations of "the Spirit of the New Testament within the Old," that have been denizens of my desk from a date some twenty years earlier.

10, *Hereford Street, W.*
1st September, 1865.

PREFACE.

THE title of this work briefly but sufficiently defines its purport, namely, the appreciation of the Cartoons of Rafael as works of Art, accompanied by a critical inquiry into the value, as history, of the narratives furnishing his subjects. The criticism of Art and that of the New Testament story thus run on side by side; and the pregnant selection of incidents by the painter, has enabled me to comprise in the historical inquiry, with but occasional and moderate divergence, an illustration of the origin of Christianity, and its development through the most important epochs of the Apostolic age.

In the combined treatment and in the relative space given to my associated subjects I have been guided exclusively by the degree and kind of interest they have created in myself, and I have written without consideration, and am still quite unaware of the extent to which any number of persons will care to take up and linger upon the same points of view.

I do not, however, put this work into the world without being conscious how widely my processes are divergent from those of critics of established influence and merited fame at home and abroad; though I have preferred to take the ground of exposition rather than of controversy. I am quite aware that I have assigned a certain value to evidence that by the canons of Mr. Grote and Sir Cornewall Lewis would be cast aside as unworthy of attention, on the ground that where the doubtful or the false is mixed with truth beyond a certain proportion, it is labour thrown away to attempt analysis; and that it is shorter and safer and sufficient to disbelieve all, rather than to commit belief to the results of an illusory process of discrimination.

Still, it is in discrimination that criticism has its function and being; and I am of opinion, that where evidence exists of a certain voluminousness and of a certain diversity, cross-examination will at last elicit truth. "Expedit reipublicæ ut finis sit litium" is a good maxim, no doubt, in literature as socially; but discussion, endowed with still more tenacity of life than even litigation, is not to be got rid of by denial of appeal or by arbitrary shutting up of courts, however exalted.

I have still a serious objection to anticipate from another side. The critics of the German school, which takes its name from Tübingen, and of which the English public possesses so excellent an account in the recent work of Mr. Mackay, have never been chargeable with despairing of an ultimate reward for critical labour on the New Testament; they have indeed followed up worthily the great opening made by Strauss, and have largely succeeded in restoring the colours and outlines of the living men whose varying bias gave changeful forms to the incidents that fell into their hands for record or compilation. Nevertheless, it seems to me that they have still written—I will not say overmuch in the spirit of the party of attack, but I will rather say, as though they had enough to do to work out and to complete the case and the arguments susceptible of being brought forward to put the history and its documents on their defence. The defence has still to be fully heard on whatever new ground so complete, so candid, so critical an attack may have obliged it to fall back upon. The adherents of this school, if they indulge me with a glance, will probably wonder at my denouncing but coldly large alloys of falsity, while I am lingering to store the scarce grains of well-attested truth; but I stand confidently on my results;—they have been gained in earnest search for a reply to the inquiry—When we have utterly and heartily given up whatever in the New Testament is fairly convicted as unhistorical, what facts remain for us unimpeached after all the questioning, and what is the series, the significance, the connection of these cardinal facts in the story of human civilization, which have thus come thrice tried through the fire?

CONTENTS.

INTRODUCTION.

		PAGE
I.	THE SISTINE CHAPEL	1
II.	THE ORDER OF THE CARTOONS	18

CHAPTER I.—THE CALLING OF PETER.

I.	THE CARTOON OF THE CALLING OF PETER	24
II.	THE CRANES IN THE CARTOON	30
III.	THE SEA OF GALILEE	40

CHAPTER II.—THE CHARGE TO PETER.

I.	THE CARTOON OF THE CHARGE TO PETER	54
II.	THE TWELVE IN RELATION TO JESUS	66
III.	THE APOSTLES AFTER THE CRUCIFIXION	75

CHAPTER III.—THE MIRACLE AT THE BEAUTIFUL GATE.

I.	JERUSALEM AND THE TEMPLE	86
II.	THE CARTOON OF THE MIRACLE AT THE BEAUTIFUL GATE	107
III.	THE FIRST EXPANSION OF THE GOSPEL IDEA	125

CHAPTER IV.—THE DEATH OF ANANIAS.

I.	THE CARTOON OF THE DEATH OF ANANIAS	139
II.	THE CONTINGENCIES OF COMMUNISM IN THE CHURCH	151

CHAPTER V.—THE STONING OF STEPHEN.

I.	THE TAPESTRY OF THE STONING OF STEPHEN	157
II.	THE GOSPEL AS ACCEPTED BY HELLENISTIC JEWS	160
III.	THE SCATTERED CHURCH: THE RESIDENT APOSTLES	183

CONTENTS.

CHAPTER VI.—THE CONVERSION OF ST. PAUL.

	PAGE
I. SAUL THE PERSECUTOR	198
II. THE TAPESTRY OF THE CONVERSION OF ST. PAUL	213
III. THE RECEPTION OF PAUL THE DISCIPLE BY THE CHURCH	220

CHAPTER VII.—GENTILE CHRISTIANITY.

I. THE PRIVATE COMPACT OF PAUL AND PETER	235
II. THE PUBLIC ALTERCATION AT ANTIOCH	243
III. THE APOSTOLIC DECREE OF COMPROMISE	247

CHAPTER VIII.—THE HISTORY OF THE CHURCH IN THE BIOGRAPHY OF JESUS.

I. THE PHARISEES OF ANTIOCH IN THE GOSPELS	257
II. THE EXPANSION OF THE CHURCH IN THE PARABLES	267
III. PETER, JAMES, AND JOHN AT THE TRANSFIGURATION	275

CHAPTER IX.—ELYMAS STRICKEN WITH BLINDNESS.

I. PAUL AND BARNABAS IN ROMAN CYPRUS	292
II. THE CARTOON OF THE REBUKE OF ELYMAS	304

CHAPTER X.—THE SACRIFICE AT LYSTRA.

I. THE MYTHOLOGY OF OVID IN ACTS	312
II. THE CARTOON OF THE SACRIFICE AT LYSTRA	328
III. TIMOTHY OF LYSTRA, AND ACCOMMODATION	333

CHAPTER XI.—PAUL IN PRISON AT PHILIPPI.

I. THE CHRISTIAN APOSTLE IN ORPHIC THRACE	339

CHAPTER XII.—PAUL PREACHING AT ATHENS.

I. THE CARTOON OF PAUL PREACHING AT ATHENS	356
II. CHRISTIAN PROMISE AND GREEK CULTURE	371
III. THE HARMONY OF THE REVERENTIAL AND THE RIGHTLY REASONABLE	384

LIST OF ILLUSTRATIONS.

		Page
1.	PORTRAIT OF RAFAEL (*to face the Title*).	
2.	THE SISTINE CHAPEL	1
3.	THE CALLING OF PETER	24
4.	EMBLEMATICAL CRANES (*Otto Venius*)	31
5.	THE CHARGE TO PETER	54
6.	PLAN OF HEROD'S TEMPLE (*Fergusson*)	90
7.	THE MIRACLE AT THE BEAUTIFUL GATE	107
8.	THE DEATH OF ANANIAS	139
9.	THE STONING OF STEPHEN	157
10.	EMBLEM OF THE WELL OF SAMARIA (*O. Venius*)	193
11.	THE CONVERSION OF ST. PAUL	214
12.	THE TRANSFIGURATION	282
13.	THE REBUKE OF ELYMAS	304
14.	THE SACRIFICE AT LYSTRA	328
15.	EMBLEM OF DIVINE LOVE AND THE SOUL (*O. Venius*)	352
16.	PAUL PREACHING AT ATHENS	359

THE SISTINE CHAPEL.

From Fergusson's 'Modern Architecture.'

CHRISTIANITY IN THE CARTOONS.

INTRODUCTION.

I. THE SISTINE CHAPEL.—II. THE ORDER OF THE CARTOONS.

I. THE SISTINE CHAPEL.

THE Sistine Chapel of the Vatican was commenced for Pope Sixtus IV., by Baccio Pintelli, a Florentine architect, in 1473, one year before the birth of Michael Angelo, and ten before that of Rafael. It was embellished with frescoes by the most celebrated painters of the time, and, no doubt, was designed with reference to the reception of their works, and for the general enrichment becoming the private chapel of the Popes. Most of these paintings were left by Michael Angelo as he found them, and so they still remain; in subject as in position they fall happily between those with which he adorned the ceiling, and the series of tapestries, from the designs by Rafael, that were one day to hang below them.

The plan of the chapel, of which the exterior is perfectly plain, is an oblong of three squares, 150 feet by about 50 feet; it is 60 feet in height from pavement to ceiling. The unpierced wall-space below the window-sills is crowned by an entablature that was originally returned at each end, and is divided by a string-course into two nearly equal horizontal bands; the lower of these is painted with elaborate representations of hangings. It was for actual tapestries that should cover this space,—for two-thirds of the length of the chapel, the proper sanctuary,—that Rafael made the designs which we know as the Cartoons. The subjects are taken from the New Testament exclusively, and have especial reference to the mission of the Apostles.

Upon the band above this and immediately below the windows, the earlier painters had left represented the lives of Moses and Jesus, in a succession of parallel incidents, advancing in historical order from the altar end of the chapel to the door.

Above the entablature of the wall space on either side are six round-headed windows, and originally there were two more at each end. The window arches spring from a string-course, which is continued from window to window, but broken intermediately by that of a narrow pilaster, on which descend the spandrils formed by intersection of the coved ceiling, by the transverse coves to the semicircles over the windows. On either side of each pilaster are painted niches, with figures of sainted Popes, twenty-eight in all. The entire and varied surface above the line of the pilasters was covered by the work of Michael Angelo, executed by his single hand: the flat part of the ceiling from end to end; the descending triangular spandrils; the lunette coved to right and left above each window; and the flat space between the concentric semicircles over it. The Cartoons of Rafael for the tapestries were designed by him within a year or two after the completion of the decoration of the ceiling by Michael Angelo, namely, about 1514. A quarter of a century more was to elapse before the great Florentine put his hand to his seven years' labour upon the vast picture of the Last Judgment; it occupies the entire end wall, where he obliterated the two windows that were over the altar, and the horizontal string-courses, to make room for it. The opposite end wall, on either side and above the chief entrance, was destined by him to receive the 'Fall of Lucifer,' for which he had prepared designs, but the picture was never executed. This subject, left till the last and deferred until too late, was the first in historical order of the grand series which made the enrichments of the Papal chapel an epitome of the Christian conception of the scheme of the world, its history and destiny.

The Fall of Lucifer was a fable felt to be sufficiently grand, remote, and indistinct to be propounded as an explanation of the origin of evil, of misery, and sin. It has the same significance in the Sistine Chapel as in the opening movement of England's epic of 'Paradise Lost.' To this succeed, again with a parallel in the poem, the great scenes of cosmical creation. In the first great compartment on the flattened ceiling, God divides light from darkness; and in the associated smaller compartments he places in the firmament, between the upper and the lower waters, the greater and the lesser lights—rulers of night and day,—and creates the general life that is to occupy the land and water.

The next large design presents the creation of a common ancestor of mankind; the ensuing shows his transgression and fall; and in the small compartment between the two, which is the very centre of this series, we see the origin from his own side of Woman, the immediate instrument of Lucifer in luring him to his destiny, and ancestress also of his ultimate Saviour.

The series terminates, as it commenced, by a single large compartment between a pair of associated smaller ones. The consequences of the Fall are shown in the Deluge, provoked by incorrigible sin; and the mingled disposition and fortunes of the world thereafter appear in the Thanksgiving of the miraculously-rescued Noah, and the instance of his speedy lapse in inebriety,—the second fall of man's second ancestor.

If variety of interpretation were conclusive, the painter would be chargeable with obscurity in the three first compartments of his design; but the charge must recoil upon ourselves for dulness, unless in so far as we may be cleared by pleading the obliteration of traditions once lively and familiar. Michael Angelo here is as frugal of secondary intimations of subject as Phidias himself, who not alone withheld inscriptions, but only admitted established symbols when they were too absolutely fixed in men's associations to be excluded, relying on the sensibility of the spectator to expression, and on his perception of the appropriate, to identify god or hero, their occupations, and surroundings. To exceed the modesty of these limits was to approach and to impute the underbred,—a damage and an insult similar to what the dramatic poet endures when the actor, officious or unfortunate, thinks it necessary to emphasize indications of character of which the point resides in their unconsciousness.

I give my own interpretation at my own peril. In the large compartment the Deity is introduced in two personifications, and, by the ingenuity of the painter, without any incongruity. In the Deity, who sails forward on supporting cherubim, and with expanded arms, I see the Creator of light in the primal distinction of day and night. In the second personification, of which the retiring aspect is given, the introduction of a tree and land less prompts us than confirms us in discerning the Divine agency fructifying the dry land by herb and tree, by seed and fruit. To those who prefer, in the first agency, to see the division of the land and the waters below the firmament, I have nothing to object; though, for myself, I would prefer to regard this act as implied in the second epitomized representation.

A significant contrast again occurs between the Deity of either of the small accompanying compartments; in the first, he looks and reaches upward; in the second, he as manifestly hovers or descends, and sheds his influence below. Therefore it is that I regard the first as the creator of the lights of heaven ruling the day and night, and the second as the distributor of the germens of life, animal life, in the waters and over the broad earth. The interpretation, as I have given it, follows the order of the epochs in Genesis, and marks the natural sequence of attention in the spectator of the design.

The triangular compartments, by which the coved ceiling descends upon the piers between the windows, are occupied by Hebrew Prophets and Heathen Sibyls alternately, the recognized prognosticators of the great Deliverer, of the descendant of Eve by whom all mischief was to be retrieved and the power of Lucifer finally quelled.

These are the largest figures in the whole work, and it is by very happy management that they are brought next to compartments that keep them remote from the smaller figures of the designs on the flat. They are without rivals in the whole range of creative art.

> "Dies iræ, dies illa,
> Solvet sæclum in favillâ,
> Teste David cum Sibyllâ."

Pious fraud, at an early date, had put Messianic prophecies into the mouths of Sibyls in spurious verses with sufficient dexterity to satisfy or deceive St. Augustine. But there is more in it. Through the Pollio of Virgil, and the pastorals of Theocritus, we can track the course of the fiction until we look over the shoulders of Hellenistic Jews, busy fabricating sibylline prophecies out of Hebrew materials, and sending abroad in this form the same anticipations of a Saviour-King that had cheered their ancestors when down-trodden by Assyria or Egypt. Largely by machinery of this nature the Roman world, even before the reign of Tiberius, had become habituated to the theory of a coming Deliverer of some sort: it was a prophecy that went begging for a fulfilment first, and then had its choice from a series; and in the race of competition, the interpreters who applied it to the Nero who was to return from beyond the Euphrates, lost the race to the enthusiasts who could persuade generations of miserable slaves that, in a sense of their own, and the best sense of all, it was fulfilled by Jesus of Nazareth who had come already.

Howbeit, in pictorial symbolism, an expression for the

common yearnings of Pagan and of Hebrew is invaluable; and, sooth to say, the Hebrews would have been as much surprised by the sense posterity chose to apply to rhapsodies in which they anticipated a revived Hebrew kingdom, under a descendant of the conqueror David, as any sibyl of the series, supposing her to have existed, could be at the ascription of words, not to say meanings, never uttered by her at all.

The prophet Jonah is introduced upon the space that is over the end wall, and not without intention and reference to the subject which his very position proves, that Michael Angelo had already assigned to this position. The story of the durance of Jonah for three days in a whale's belly is interpreted in Matthew as typifying the sojourn of Jesus for the same space of time, but ill made out, in the grave. Oblivion of this text has betrayed some commentators, who will blush if they read these remarks, into the honesty of denouncing the combination for a puerility. Certainly it is by several degrees more fantastic than the painter's whim of giving to the tossing drapery of the prophet a capricious resemblance to the head of a sea-monster.

Certain sections, if we ought not to say certain ages, of the human race have shown an inaptitude, at this day present almost inconceivable, for appreciating the connection of cause and effect. Of such minds it is characteristic to be anxious and curious, not for causes but for signs; resemblances disconnected, but still premonitory. The arrival of a swallow to these is a sign that spring is coming, not an effect of its approach; and hence no incident is too trifling, no analogy too remote to be charged with the weightiest significance.

Whatever may have become of science, imagination and poetry, at least, have often flourished under such a dispensation; nay, under it faculties of the most refined class have even attained to reject sympathetically the accidental and the paltry, and to attach themselves to those indications which bespeak identity in nature and character, and guide us truly and more wisely than we know. We shall find examples as we go on.

Four subjects from the history of Israel occupy the corner-soffits of the ceiling. Two of them are deliverances of the nation by the courage and favour of its daughters; Judith slays Holofernes, and Esther compasses the ruin and death of Haman. These antique heroines are intermediate figures of that deliverance, by crushing the serpent-type of evil, that is promised in Genesis to come through woman. In the deed of Judith there is even a parallel recognized to the warning, " She shall bruise thy head;" and in a certain sense, no doubt, both Judith and Esther had become traditionally accepted, with whatever incongruity, as types of the Virgin Mother.

The two other subjects are equally significant; Moses gives health and healing to the people by lifting on high the brazen serpent; and here again tradition had been prompted in its vagaries by Scripture averment of a sensible type of the redeeming Crucifixion. As the story stands in the Old Testament, Moses is clearly making a forced concession to an idolatrous craving of a disheartened people; then we find the idolatrous symbol dedicated in the temple of the God that denounces images; then it is destroyed in pious anger by a king who would be holier than Moses; and, lastly, it reappears as a type of all that is sacred, supernatural, divine.

There is a certain antithesis between the saving cross of Moses and the vile cross of the pernicious Haman.

Here then Moses is introduced,—the great Old Testament type of Jesus, as was interpreted on the faith of the words, "A prophet shall the Lord your God raise up like unto me, him shall ye serve:" words that the original writer, whatever his age, and whoever he might be, probably intended should designate Joshua,—certainly not Jesus of Nazareth, to whom, by the mouth of Peter, they are applied in Acts, with many a curious result both in literature and art.

The last of these subjects is the decapitation of Goliath by David; again antithetical—a bruised head—to the fate of Holofernes, subdued by a woman, as Goliath by a boy. The choice of an exploit of David has a peculiar force, as it is upon the restoration of the glories of his reign that Messianic anticipations so constantly turn, and as he is that one of the long chain of ancestors of whom the Saviour is emphatically designated the Son.

The stem of Jesse is a favourite type in old symbolical art; and we are presented constantly, in correct arborescent form, with a series of heads of the representatives of the pedigree of Jesus. The representation is often crude and quaint enough. Michael Angelo has given an equivalent of the indispensable type,—the chain of descent which was to unite the subjects of his ceiling with those that decorated the walls; he has done so in the charming domestic groups that fill up the lunettes and spandrils that were still vacant.

The names inscribed show that the painter followed the genealogy traced in Matthew up to David and Abraham, not that followed by Luke with less of national restriction, and by somewhat different route, up to Adam and God, but asserting, no more than Luke, other parentage for Jesus than Joseph the carpenter; and here, as so often, we shall ask in vain, whether he could help observing the divarication, and what in the world he thought of it.

The alternations of sibyl and prophet are so arranged that not only is each prophet followed on the same side by a sibyl, but is opposite to a sibyl on the corresponding pendentive of the other side; the number of pairs of pendentives however is uneven, namely five; and in consequence, the plan involved the necessity of having an unequal number of male and of female figures on either side. The right-hand side as we face the door has three sibyls and two prophets only, and on the left-hand of course the numbers are reversed.

The two pendentives at the opposite ends of the ceiling are both assigned to Hebrew prophets, and thus in the expression of the grand commissure of Semitic and Indo-European religions, preponderance is preserved for the race that gave the master-movement to the union. Jonah and Zechariah, to whom these conspicuous positions are assigned, are usually reckoned the earliest and the latest among the seven prophets who are introduced; but neither chronological order nor canonical will account for the sequence of the rest. Subjects were painted on the disks over the head of each which might be illustrative if we had an account of them.

<table>
<tr><td></td><td>Jonah.</td><td></td></tr>
<tr><td>*Libyca.*</td><td></td><td>Jeremiah.</td></tr>
<tr><td>Daniel.</td><td></td><td>*Persica.*</td></tr>
<tr><td>*Cumæa.*</td><td></td><td>Ezechiel.</td></tr>
<tr><td>Esaias.</td><td></td><td>*Erythræa.*</td></tr>
<tr><td>*Delphica.*</td><td></td><td>Joel.</td></tr>
<tr><td></td><td>Zechariah.</td><td></td></tr>
</table>

I await better instruction as to the theory of these combinations, and would prefer to listen to discourse rather than to proffer it on what I can see is a rich theme,—the artistic management of harmonious blending and contrast between every figure and its opposite, and at the same time also its lateral associates.

The particular motive of each grand figure and its relation to its secondary companions in the background, also afford scope for fine remark, for which I can but send to search elsewhere.

To the imagination of one who only knows these figures from engravings, they are apt to seem to the full as much works of sculpture as of painting. Indeed it is curious to remark how the elements and theories of composition which Michael Angelo at the commencement of his career designed to realize in the frustrate monument of Pope Julius, welled up again in his mind, and found place and purpose in the Sistine ceiling. Of that mausoleum, the grandest ornaments were to have been statues, of colossal magnitude, of prophets and apostles, paired alternately with ethical and philosophical abstractions in feminine personification; Paul and Moses with the Virtues of Active and of Contemplative life, and so forth.

Again, in the sketch that remains to us of the monument (Agincourt) we see the same architectural framework of the seated figures united with decorative infantine forms, supporters of piers and salient entablatures; and yet again another series of figures, subordinate in expression and intermediate in scale, but aiding by happy adjustment in both these respects to give relief and force to the centres of idealized thought.

The pairs of boys that support the salient cornice on either side of the several thrones, are painted, like pier and cornice, to appear as if sculptured in white marble; the larger figures that singly surmount these piers represent bronze, and are composed with reference to the large seated prophet or sibyl, whose throne they pertain to. The perspective of the piers and their cornices is independent for each niche or throne. Each has its own vanishing-point, as if the spectator stood exactly opposite to it. The boys below that support the name-labels are painted in natural colours.

I will notice one more point of treatment. I have said that the subjects painted on the compartments of the flat ceiling commence from the end nearest the altar; they do so, and they are so composed that the feet of the figures in each scene, the ground on which they stand or lie, is at that end. Shall we then say that the series was so adjusted in order to be viewed most favourably from this end of the chapel? Scarcely; in effect it will be found, if we hold any picture above our head, that we only comprehend it readily and comfortably when turned in such a sense that the heads of the figures are in the direction of our station-point and the feet more remote. Looked at the reverse way, the groups are unintelligible or seem to be upside down.

The ceiling therefore, I should suspect, is seen most favourably when the face is turned towards the grand altar, and the altar-piece of the Last Judgment. And this would not in any way interfere with the perusal of it in natural order, as from above downwards.

If it is the case that when the work and colours were fresh the whole design could be appreciated from a station not very remote from the doorway, we may have an explanation of the smaller scale of the figures in the designs from the history of Noah. The nature of the subjects rendered numerous figures all but indispensable, and as these pictures were considerably nearer to the spectator, his eye was not called upon for an exertion beyond its power in this place.

So much must suffice from me on this immortal work of Michael Angelo Buonarroti, to which I only intended in the first instance to advert cursorily, as leading to the subject I have chiefly in view,—the illustration of the Cartoons of Rafael, and of New Testament history by the suggestions of the Cartoons.

The same consideration demands yet a few observations on the series of pictures that form the immediate sequel, though dating from an earlier period; the frescoes below the windows.

The life of Jesus is seen depicted on our right, as we advance to the altar, and that of Moses on the left. The numerous figures are on too small a scale to be seen favourably at such a distance. Each series of subjects follows historical order, commencing, like those on the ceiling, from the altar end of the chapel and advancing towards the door. The opposite designs, from the Old and New Testament, have always a certain reference to each other, often of pregnant significance, often on the other hand barren enough, as will appear from a comparative enumeration.

In this contrast of designs on opposite walls I am irresistibly reminded of the paintings of Polygnotus on the opposite walls of the Lesche at Delphi, with subjects from a very different fund of mythology, but parallel at least in being directed to enforce, as if of equal sanction, a priestly dogma and a code of moral duty. The peril of neglecting initiation and of infringing apostolical authority, are texts in all essentials identical. Not less resemblance is there in some of the modes of treatment; the superposition of groups by Polygnotus must have had much the same effect as the combinations of several moments of time in the paintings of Sandro Botticelli. Polygnotus, however, did not repeat the same personage in the way that Sandro paints Moses, first as removing his sandals, and then again within a few inches kneeling unshod before the burning bush. On the other hand, I suspect the Greek was less skilful or less particular in indicating distance and diminishing remote figures. I refer to my account and restoration of his work, in the 'Classical Museum.'

The intention of this series is most salient in the incidents from the life of Jesus, which are selected to give emphasis to the epochs of Redemption in the first instance, and then to the appointment and authority of apostolical hierarchy. The scheme and order are on this wise:—

1.

Finding of Moses. (Or, Moses in the Bulrushes.)	Assumption of the Virgin.	Birth of Jesus. (Jesus in the Manger.)

(These three, by Pietro Perugino, were cancelled by Michael Angelo to make space for the Last Judgment.)

ALTAR.

Moses attacked by God at the Inn; Moses and Zipporah; the circumcision of their son.	2.	The Baptism of Jesus; in background Jesus preaching; also John; at a distance Jerusalem.
Moses at burning Bush; repels shepherds from the well of daughters of Jethro; smites the Egyptian. (Engraved in Eastlake's Kugler, p. 201.)	3.	The Temptation of Jesus (overcoming Satan); Service and sacrifice at the Temple in front.
Moses and Israelites by the Red Sea after passage; the song of Miriam; the host of Pharaoh struggling in the waves.	4.	The Calling of Apostles by the Lake.
Moses receives and delivers the Commandments from the Mount; the punishment of the people for their apostasy.	5.	Jesus Preaching on the Mount. (Engraved in Eastlake's Kugler.)
Punishment of Korah, Dathan, and Abiram; and also of the sons of Aaron; Moses before the Altar; in front Roman triumphal arch in the scene.	6.	Jesus gives the keys to Peter; in background architectural comparison of Solomon and Sixtus in inscriptions on buildings.
Last injunctions of Moses to Joshua; Moses reads to the people his last Psalm of praise.	7.	The Last Supper; in the background the Agony and Crucifixion.
Michael rescues the body of Moses from Satan. (Jude ix.)	8.	The Resurrection.

The last pair of subjects are on either side the doorway. Wherever these comparisons appear forced, the violence is in the Mosaic incidents on the left-hand side. The agreement obtained is sometimes but a happy accident, presenting itself with tolerable obviousness, as of the bulrush-basket of the foundling Prophet, and the manger of the destitute Jesus.

In the second pair, Baptism and Circumcision are the respective rites of initiation of the Old and New Covenants.

In pair three, the discomfiture of Satan has a typical importance assigned to it, as the same proof of arms between the originator and the destroyer of Evil, that makes it the turning incident of the 'Paradise Regained.' Against this are set exploits of rescue of Moses; and the incident of the burning bush is added, I believe, on suggestion little more forcible than the scene lying also in a wilderness.

So, in the fourth pair, the value of the parallelism rests to rather a childish extent upon the agreement in water-side locality; albeit, in one case by salt-, and in the other beside a fresh-water sea. I must, however, speak cautiously, as import may be helped by some secondary groups, as—possibly, the walking on the waters, of which the epitome I use makes no mention.

In the fifth pair, the parallelism extends beyond common locality of a mount, to the moral position of the prophets. There is considerable appearance that the delivery of the moral code of Jesus, like that of Moses that it so largely superseded, from a mount, was not a mere coincidence. Whether we admit that such a sermon was so delivered, or rather infer that to a sermon of Jesus, whether ever really delivered or not, such a scene was invented or came to be ascribed, the influence of a feeling for parallelism and competition would be one and the same. This is in Matthew; in Luke, the substance of the same speech is put into the mouth of Jesus at a later date, not on the mount, but expressly on a plain; and, instead of standing to deliver it, he is seated. I fear it is vain to investigate which version was the original. One is the view favoured by a Christian writer, disposed to contemplate with pleasure the resemblance of Jesus to Moses; the other is the view of the teacher, or convert, who rather took pleasure in insisting on the contrast of the dispensations, and would pursue the contrast not only in essentials but in accessories.

On the delivery of the keys to Peter in pair six, I shall have much to say when I arrive at the Cartoon; it was the typical installation of the Papacy. The parallel subject gives force to its significance,—edge and point. Korah, Dathan, and Abiram were victims of a premature attempt to assert the evangelical equality of the laity, but of course are adopted here as the impersonations of sacrilege, blasphemy, and impiety.

The purport and correspondence of the two concluding pairs are self-evident.

The painters employed were Pietro Perugino, Luca Signorelli, Sandro Botticelli, Cosimo Rosetti, Domenico Ghirlandajo, Cecchino Salviati. The superintendence was given to Sandro, and to him we may probably ascribe the selection of the subjects. One asks, with vain curiosity, whether he had also a plan for the decoration of the ceiling, and how far it may have afforded a hint to Michael Angelo.

However this may be, the designs on the ceiling lead

c

directly to the subjects on the walls by both ethical and historical sequence. The chain of Scripture history was then further carried on through its Apostolic section in the tapestries of Rafael; and, lastly, the mighty design of the Last Judgment, by an extra-Scriptural excursion, closed all the movements of Scripture and of the world with an outburst of awful magnificence, answering to what doubtless would have been before us as their opening act, had it been allowed to Michael Angelo to realize his conceptions of the fall of Lucifer.

II. THE ORDER OF THE CARTOONS.

The tapestries executed after the Cartoons by Rafael, and that are still preserved at Rome, are ten in number; of the original Cartoons seven are in England, the remainder have perished. It is certain that they were intended to be placed along the walls, as already described, under the horizontal courses of pictures from the Old and New Testament, and so to cover up and supersede, for the occasion, the imitative hangings. There is considerable difficulty, however, about their precise order and distribution, and no tradition survives at Rome that renders any assistance.

The ground-plan of the chapel was divided into two unequal parts by a transverse white marble colonnade, consisting of four columns on either side a central entrance, with entablature and high stylobate, and ironwork in the intercolumns. Four out of the six windows were included in the inner division, or presbyterium; and as the wall paintings were spaced under the windows, and the designs on the tapestries were divided by representations of pilasters, fancifully decorated, we are justified in assuming that they ranged with the pictures and windows above, by the same division which governed the ordination of the ceiling.

There were thus eight spaces on each wall, and the number is increased to ten, the original number of the tapestries, if we include the two corresponding spaces that were on either side the altar previously to the changes made to accommodate the requirements of the Last Judgment. This seems satisfactory enough, the more so as the subjects of the tapestries fall naturally into two sets of five each; the first having reference to the history of Peter and the ante-Pauline Church, the second to the history and labours of Paul.

But difficulties presently occur. The second space to the altar's right is diminished one-third by the Pope's throne, which has attachments to the wall; and the fourth space on the opposite side is still more seriously interfered with by the gallery for the choir, and both throne and choir appear to have belonged to the original arrangements.

It is true we have certain tapestries of either set of diminished size, which permit us to cover the spaces in the way of arrangement of upholstery; and this process has been carefully worked out by Bunsen, and it has been rested in as satisfactory. It would be vain to contest his arrangement without details of measurement that are not forthcoming; and it must suffice to say that while the order he adopts confounds the historical sequence, it does not vindicate itself by any artistic or ethical principle, and scarcely pretends to do so.

The following is the series of subjects in their historical order:—

1. [1] The miraculous draught of fishes, and calling of Peter.
2. [2] The charge to Peter and delivery of the keys.
3. [4] The miracle of Peter and John at the Beautiful Gate.
4. [5] The death of Ananias.
5. [3] The martyrdom of Stephen and complicity of Paul. (Cartoon lost.)
6. [6] The conversion of Paul. (Cartoon lost.)
7. [7] The rebuke of Elymas. (Only the upper half of the tapestry exists.)
8. [8] Paul and Barnabas at Lystra.
9. [10] Paul imprisoned at Philippi; the earthquake. (Cartoon lost.)
10. [9] Paul preaching at Athens.

The numerals in brackets indicate the arrangement arrived at by Bunsen. The Martyrdom of Stephen is a very small tapestry compared with the others; and the Earthquake at Philippi is again much smaller, only 4½ feet broad, and hence the transpositions to suit the limited spaces.

The order of time is the first most obvious principle of arrangement, at least by way of trial; there is, however, fair ground for modifying this on an appearance of systematic contrast and parallelism in the subjects of the designs, and this is not wanting.

If we regard first the Petrine series, we have before us displayed, on Biblical authority, in pointedly selected scenes, the origin and the pretensions, the functions, authority, and destiny of the Apostolical hierarchy. To Peter, the predecessor and representative of the Pope, called by special miracle, are assigned the charge of pastoral tending, and the authority to bind and to loose in heaven and on earth. The functions of mercy and of power, rescue and severity, are provided with all sufficient illustration in the healing of congenital deformity at the Beautiful Gate of the Temple, and the striking down of Ananias and Sapphira for a lapse in matters of temporalities; while Stephen the Martyr shows the spirit of the Church in affliction, and opening heaven that is its reward.

This last subject, by the presence of Paul, forms a transition to the parallel story of the great Apostle of the Gentiles. The conversion of St. Paul, if indeed it occupied the right-hand side of the altar, would form the fittest pendant to the calling of St. Peter on the left.

The miracle of the associated Paul and Barnabas, at Lystra, answers in its spirit of benevolence to that of Peter and John at the Temple; and the rebuke of Elymas testifies to a claim and confidence in authority almost as distinctly as the destruction of Ananias.

Stephen stoned, and Paul imprisoned, may be held, without violence, to give common illustration of the endurance of persecution and its reward.

Thus far well,—thus far, I think, unquestionably; we are now left, however, with the charge to Peter, and the sermon to the Athenian philosophers as its pendant. Certainly it is in this scene at Athens that Paul appears most positively in that function of Apostle of the Gentiles, in which he claimed to be co-ordinate with Peter, mighty with the circumcision. On this shadow of parallelism, however, I do not insist, but prefer to regard the Athenian Cartoon as independent, and as the closing expression of the final position of Christianity, that rising in a province among the obscure and the illiterate, struck so soon and so boldly for a position in the very centres of education—of intellectual subtlety and culture.

While therefore we recognize a practical and philosophical analogy between the double series, we may hesitate to infer that the most decided parallels were really arranged antithetically. Were such indeed the case, it would be preferable to place the Petrine series in historical order and sacrifice that of the Pauline; but I believe that in the painter's thought historical sequence was regarded as much in one as in the other, and as of importance in both.

The foot of the tapestries has a representation of an architectural socle, with designs imitative of bronze; and on the Pauline series, we have here the secondary incidents of the Apostle's career, following on in historical order, with the grander designs, and thus making another protest against disruption. Below the other series, are incidents from the life of Cardinal Medici, Leo the Tenth, adjusted with a certain reference, as clear as can be expected, to the Apostolic career above. The election by the conclave, for instance, is subjoined to the calling of Peter.

I find it difficult, therefore, not to believe that the tapestries were planned and intended by Rafael to follow on in true historical and chronological order, though I am unable to explain away the difficulties of the interrupted spaces with the information that is at present accessible.

It seems, on every ground, appropriate that the earlier incidents of the history of Peter should be placed on the right-hand wall looking from the altar, as it is on that side that the earlier histories commence above. To commence the new series on the same wall on which the old concludes, upon an upper line, would have the harshness of a *boustrophedon* archaism.

Peter, as the apostle of Judaism, comes fitly upon the side of and under Moses.

Rafael was occupied with the Cartoons in the years 1515, 1516; he was paid for them 434 gold ducats. The tapestries arrived in Rome in 1519.

In Waagen's 'Treasures of Art in England,' vol. ii., will be found a copious collection of technical notes and observations respecting the Cartoons, their execution, and the sketches, engravings, and tapestries that are connected with them. For such references in general I refer to the book. I content myself here with setting down a few disconnected extracts.

The Conversion of St. Paul has been engraved by M. Sorello, etched by Louis Sommerau; *The Prison at Philippi*, etched by Louis Sommerau; a sketch of the giant that personifies the earthquake is in Charles Rogers's collection of prints. The original sketch of *the Death of Stephen*, which has some differences from the Cartoon, is in the collection of the Archduke Charles at Vienna; it has been engraved by A. Bartch, lithographed by Pilizotti.

The Cartoons are painted in size-colour on paper. It is a good observation, that the proportions of the figures, which far exceed the size of life, are in favour of effect in tapestry, which, from the thickness of the threads, would give coarseness to smaller figures and features. The broad character of the folds of the drapery is also an advantage in a design that was to be executed in wool; colours of dresses were adopted with like foresight, and hence the frequent introduction of shot materials, and of treatment which allowed high lights to be executed in gold thread, besides a certain number of draperies that were to be executed in gold almost entirely.

CHAPTER I.

THE CALLING OF PETER.

I. THE CARTOON OF THE CALLING OF PETER.—II. THE CRANES IN THE CARTOON.—III. THE SEA OF GALILEE.

I. THE CARTOON OF THE CALLING OF PETER.

THIS cartoon represents the calling of Simon chiefly, and then of his brother Andrew, and of James and John, from the state of fishermen on the Sea of Galilee to be fishers of men,—Apostles.

The boats are near a strip of land, occupied only by cranes; but we see that they have put well out from the shore, where the crowd, whom Jesus had been teaching, is still lingering. The miraculous draught has declared itself; Simon's boat is full of fishes, while his partners or mates in the other boat are still straining to raise the overcharged net. At the end of the right-hand boat is seated Jesus, and before him Simon is on his knees in an agony of mingled enthusiasm and terror: "Depart from me, O Lord, for I am a sinful man;" behind him Andrew, with more elastic action, and an expression rather of single adoration, bends as he moves hastily forward, and in his expanded arms we see the movement of devotion that prompts the sacrifice to leave all and follow the Master.

It is impossible for any description to do justice to the feeling of these faces and gestures; here, if anywhere in the Cartoons, we have the very hand of Rafael himself, in finish as well as in design. Jesus raises one hand—the right, with a tranquillizing movement, to calm the excited, if not trembling Simon.

James and John, in the next boat, are less immediately participant, though marked already by the prefiguring nimbus of Apostleship. John, the nearest to Andrew, is recognized by his unbearded youthfulness; his attention is already attracted, and, with his body yet unlifted from his labour, he turns his head to observe. One hand is already released from the net and rests on his knee to permit this movement, and with the other he rather holds the net for the moment than drags it; while the stalwart arms of his brother James, more mature in age, are in the full tension of undiverted toil. Zebedee behind, still more remote, seems engrossed with the balance and management of the boat, which the heavy strain on one quarter threatens to disturb.

The movement of John is scarcely more than may be due to his notice to the sudden movement of Andrew, but it is sufficient to blend the expressions of a pair of groups which here, as we shall find in other Cartoons, are at once combined and contrasted. In one boat already the brothers are by far more apostles than fishers; in the other they still remain rather fishers than apostles, yet not without an intimation of their coming change.

The muscularity of the sons of Zebedee is strongly emphasized, and the limbs and hands of Simon and Andrew also have the largeness and massiveness befitting their occupation; the hand and figure of Jesus receiving peculiar delicacy and slightness by the contrast. But it was evidently the painter's aim, and he succeeded, to give force to the spirit of his incident by showing that these cumbrous forms might be the vehicles of sentiments that become and that constitute the saint.

The gradation of movement and expression in these groups, so eternal are the inspirations of the highest art, have wonderful analogy to the dispositions of Phidias; as, for instance, in his group of the triple Fates, aroused by the marvellous epiphany of Athene.

The horizon of the picture is high, as in all the Cartoons. The line of water against the sky marks it exactly; the chief group is thus relieved against the light waters of the lake as a background: the broken line of coast is so distributed as to clear the heads and follow the lines of the groups. Only the head of Andrew is slightly backed by a margin of landscape, a variation which gives to the scheme a happy and accidental air.

A sketch in the hands of Mr. Dyce, which may easily be or represent an original, shows the landscape background much lower.

The flying birds are introduced ingeniously to soften the suddenness of transition, in the background, to clear sky and level reflecting lake.

A light breeze moves the hair and beards of the figures, and gives pressure and movement to the drapery, with assistance to the free open-air effect. It is noteworthy how the flying drapery of John unites the groups, and still more so is the manner in which Andrew's right hand is relieved upon the mass, light upon dark, as his left hand is as definitely relieved by darkness against the light free background. The disproportion of the boats, or punts, has always been a subject of remark; and why, it has or may have been said, did not Rafael dispose of any pictorial superfluity of boat by an arrangement of foreshortening, by carrying the ends of the boats clear out of the picture, or by making one boat cover up the greater part of the other?

It is not for me to say; I can quite conceive that the disproportion may be due to an oversight of the painter; such lapses have happened to the best, and it is possibly due merely to familiarity that the disproportion does not now seriously damage the main effect of the picture. On the other hand, considering the independence and value of this effect, who will venture to say but that Rafael may have admitted the incongruity deliberately as even in some way, patent to himself, advantageous to the expression of the miracle.

Of the significance of the cranes in the foreground I shall have more to say presently; pictorially, they have great value in breaking the formality with which the figures in the boats are repeated by reflection in the water. Zebedee's chest is reflected, and the full face of the figure next to him is seen in the water, though, as he stands, he presents only his profile to the spectator. The legs of Andrew, the body of Peter, the wooden boats,—all are discernible in duplicate with much more minuteness than is indicated in the engravings. The birds are so introduced as to relieve, while they do not interfere with, these duplications.

The drapery of John is red, the colour he usually is distinguished by as an Apostle; his hair is almost flaxen.

The drapery of Christ is now white in the Cartoon, though the reflection in the water is red. Either the colour has faded, as is most probable, or the indications for the tapestry workers were otherwise conveyed. In the tapestries it appears red.

I have spoken of the figure of Jesus as raising the right hand, and as seated in the right-hand boat, thus following the engravings of Dorigny, which reverse the positions of the groups, as seen in the Cartoons. Dorigny, in fact, in this reversal agrees with the tapestries; and there is not the slightest doubt that Rafael anticipated and allowed for this reversal, and that he designed the left hands on the Cartoons with regard to their ultimate transference into right. Following the tapestries, we shall find that Christ consistently delivers the keys to Peter with his right hand. Peter, in accordance with the text, grasps the right hand of the lame beggar; the Apostles denounce Ananias with right arms, free from the encumbering robe which is cast over the left shoulder; while Sapphira enters, counting her money from her right hand into her left. The friend of Sergius has station at his right-hand, the lictors on his left, and the knotted togas give like indication. Mercury at Lystra holds his caduceus in his right hand, and the fellow-statue of Ares at Athens grasps spear with right hand, and carries shield to the left. The tapestry of the Conversion of Paul, no doubt, reversed the Cartoon that is lost, and it shows figures with swords hanging on appropriate side.

This scene on the lake is a calling of Apostles,—the summons from daily struggle for daily support, by coping with the coarsest material forces of wind and water for animal prey of the least noble order,—to become fishers of men to set the end of life in gaining trust and conviction; to strive in unselfish endurance; and endeavour to give to others the privilege of regenerate life and ardent faith and the self-devotion that looks above, and fain would look beyond the world. Such is the subject of the Cartoon, and being such, it is most wondrously expressed in fundamental contrast and secondary associations by every line of treatment and shade of vigorous expression.

The change for the fishermen, at least as represented, was from the wild of water and open cope of sky to the crowded haunts of wretchedness and wrong; and the city on the horizon is no insignificant gloss in the exposition.

Peter and his brother are already visibly well advanced in years, and the prescribed transference of his activity involves almost a transformation; it implies a regeneration of energy in himself that guarantees the resources with which nature waits to second his regenerating labours upon a world engrossed with bodily exercise and appetite, and showing signs of growing cowed and cankered by accumulated prejudice and age. Peter is here type of the capacity of society for regermination from an obscure but a vigorous root.

The soul of an Apostle in the case of a fisherman! Opportunity in daily labour for the exercise of powers and proof of dispositions that constitute a calling above the honours of earthly potentates! Such, it seemed to the recorders of the paramyth, was the truth of the world.

And this was the ideal of morality and the manifestation of God in the world that Rafael reinforced, and made visible as well as legible for all ages, and displayed first in the high chapel of corrupted Christianity before priestly potentates, who claimed title and succession from Peter, and reversed the very spirit and process of his calling. What less can be said of plotters for sinister attraction of worldly pelf by quasi-spiritual function, by employing the mask of apostleship to embezzle the living of the needy, the haul of industry, and to starve them body and soul?

Corrupt patrons were to the inspiration of Rafael and Michael Angelo but as dirty rags whereon to wipe paint-brushes,—steps to stand on while they wrought divine marvels that were thenceforth to endure and operate independently.

The Cartoon of Rafael, then, albeit he gives halos to saints, sometimes omitted by Protestant engravers, was the artistic culmination of that same development of the mind of Europe that was at this very time giving a vernacular translation of the Bible to the poor with a purpose as honest, however more liable to be misconstrued in process, and to reproduce original mischiefs, —the weed seeding with the corn.

II. THE CRANES IN THE CARTOON.

The design on page 43 of the Emblems of Divine Love of Otto Venius, illustrates the theme that the claim of God to our affections supersedes even the claim of our parents. The design itself might be enigmatical enough but for the elucidation of its purport in the texts from Scripture and comments of the Fathers of the Church in Latin, the Spanish triplet, and the verses in Flemish and in French that garnish the opposite page.

The most significant text is from Matthew x. 37, "Whoso loveth father or mother more than me is not worthy of me." The French verses are thus translatable, "We are accountable to God for a love stronger and more zealous than we are to our parents, by whom we were born wretches subject to death, whereas his death delivers us from it; since, therefore, he voluntarily died for us, we are bound to live here for no other end but to cherish him wholly in heaven."

In the picture, accordingly, Divine Love is leading the Soul towards an altar, and points to a crucifix, which is placed upon it, the representation of the death of Christ; the Soul, the usual personification of the book, accompanies with willing step, and with eyes fixed on the crucifix to which she advances, while her hand is extended sideways, with a gesture of renunciation, towards an emblem that must necessarily symbolize the duty of children to earthly parents; necessarily, for only thus can the gesture be accounted for, and the symbolism of the picture be completed in agreement with the text. The emblem is quaint, but, when explained, apt enough; and as the text does not drop any hint as special aid to explain its aptness, I conclude that it was a well-known and accepted type. This type is a stork standing erect, with another stork couchant on its back. The filial piety of the stork—*ciconiæ pietas*,—is proverbial, at least in poetry, both Greek and Latin, and in the natural histories, at least, of the ancients. In the work of the Abbé Crosnier on Christian Iconography, St. Ambrose and St. Basil are cited (p. 319) as authorities for symbolizing filial piety by the stork (*cigogne*). (See Birds of Aristophanes, v. 1355; Sophocles, Electra, v. 1058; Ælian, Hist. Anim. iii. 23, and x. 16; Aristotle, Hist. An. ix. 14, 1; and Pliny.)

The pious office usually ascribed to the stork is the feeding its infirm parent; whether it was said also to extend its dutifulness to carrying its helpless parent I am unable to say, but could almost suspect that it was so. The smaller size of the carried bird indicates, however, that the standing bird here is the parent; swans and some other birds carry occasionally their young on their backs; this may suffice as an illustration of the device of the ingenious Fleming.

But the explanation thus obtained carries light, where light is more welcome and more interesting, as displaying a symbolical appropriateness for the cranes introduced by Rafael in this touching Cartoon of the calling of Peter, Andrew, and the sons of Zebedee. It now appears that there was a further motive for the introduction of the birds,—whatever the variety of the genus they may be, whether storks or cranes,—than their avidity for fish, which would scarcely alone explain their prominence and conspicuousness.

Rafael chiefly followed the third Gospel in his representation of the calling of these Apostles; there we find the miraculous draught of fishes, and there the gesture and exclamation of Peter, and the astonishment, the θάμβος, of the company. In the first Gospel, however, (see Strauss, 'Leben Jesu,' xi. 68, on the incompatibilities general and detailed, and the sources of them,) we find the mention of Zebedee as present; he can be no other than the elder figure in the second boat, who is exempt

from the excitement that in various gradations is animating the four. While, again, the third Gospel simply says, "they brought the boats to land, and left all and followed him," the first with emphasis, or with a susceptibility of emphasis that was not lost sight of, says that "they straightway left the boat *and their father*, and followed him." The word *left* is scarcely strong enough to represent the Greek ἀφέντες; it should be rather, *gave up*, renounced, or even *deserted*. So Peter appeals later, "Have not we given up everything and followed thee?"

The second Gospel says that James and John "left their father Zebedee in the boat along with the hired servants, and departed after Christ."

I think the proof is sufficient that on the strength of the expressions given in the first Gospel, the quitting of Zebedee by his sons at the call of Christ was recognized in the middle ages, and both before and afterwards, as a typical instance of the duty to prove worthy of Christ, by not loving father or mother above him,—that Rafael, in the cartoon in question, did not neglect this aspect of the incident, and that he conveyed his appreciation of it by his introduction of the cranes, types of filial duty, which probably told the tale all the more easily from being long established in the function, and as little requiring then an interpretation in so many words, as they received afterwards when they reappeared among the Emblemata of the master of Rubens.

In Matthew (iv. 18-22), Jesus first calls Simon and his brother Andrew as they are casting their nets, which they leave at once to follow him and become fishers of men. Then going further, he finds the brothers James and John, in a boat with their father Zebedee, *mending* their nets; at a summons these also follow, leaving both boat and father. This double calling of two pairs of brothers is repeated in Mark (i. 16-20), with such coincidence of words as to prove that the same record was the source of both narratives, whichever may be nearer to the original. The one variation of consequence is that already noticed, the mention of the servants; and I am of opinion that it proves Mark's edition the later, and that it was derived from a record corresponding with that of Matthew at this point. The hired servants seem introduced from a feeling that the desertion of Zebedee to utter loneliness, with nets unmended, and a boat on his hands to take care of, was unfilial,—the later editor missing the true significance of the anecdote; in fact, his version fails to emphasize, as required, the giving up of the boat, the means of livelihood; and would almost bear the interpretation, that the sons left Zebedee and the servants in the boat to take care of it while they were absent only for a time with Jesus.

The third Gospel omits the presence, and therefore the desertion of Zebedee, rewrites the entire circumstances, and introduces a miracle. The two callings are made one, the two pairs of brothers being partners, and a distinctly leading part is given to Simon Peter. Is it possible that the miraculous draught of fishes that breaks the net, may have been partly suggested by the double occupation of the pairs in the other versions of the story?—some casting the nets for a draught, the others repairing nets.

Everything is changed again in the fourth Gospel, unless we should say, that not a change but a substitution is in question. The Baptist directs the attention of two of his disciples to Jesus as the Lamb of God. Andrew, one of these disciples—the other is not named, communicates to Simon, probably his brother, the Messiahship of Jesus, and then Simon is brought to Jesus, and receives the surname Peter. This narrative lowers Simon, by making his calling only intermediate, and by superseding his acknowledgment of the Messiahship of Jesus. This is again done, but in favour of John, in the last chapter of the fourth Gospel. The connection of Andrew, and hence, probably, of Simon with the Baptist as a disciple, is however highly probable, and agrees with the dating of the new movement by Peter in Acts from John's baptism.

In the fourth Gospel again (chap. xxi.) we find what must be regarded as another version of the miracle on the lake, but marvellously changed in detail, and dated after the resurrection: it has no significance relatively to the Cartoon, and none of its own that is easily within ken. It reads, indeed, like a fabrication of the simplest puerility, yet may prove hereafter, in the hands of some acuter analyst, the key of an historical mystery, that but for its aid were hopelessly locked: for him I leave it.

It is necessary and important to notice that whatever may be the historical value of the hints that are given of the social position of the Apostles now in question, they all tend to raise them above that of labourers for hire, to the possessors of, at least, the apparatus of their own industry, and to independence consistent with sufcient education.

The calling of the Apostles in these narratives corresponds in several respects with the calling of Elisha by Elijah, 1 Kings xix. 19. In this incident there is no immediate miracle; Elisha follows Elijah at the simple signal of a mantle being cast upon him; but as we are led to understand that the purport of such a sign was understood, so it is also consistent with the story to assume that the person and office and miracles of Elijah were known generally, and to Elisha as to the rest of the world. The devotion of the disciple at his sudden calling is expressed by his quitting oxen and plough in the midst of the work, and his readiness to leave father and mother with just one farewell kiss. The narrative almost implies that this proposed leave-taking is given up at a check from his master, as though it were a sign of slackness; and that without thinking further of his parents, without turning homewards for a moment, Elisha sacrifices the oxen on the occasion of his new profession, and there and then departs at once to serve and minister to his spiritual parent. In this incident, a mixture of authoritative and fascinating power is ascribed to Elijah, and the same reappears in the tone of the New Testament callings of the Apostles. This parallelism does not in itself prove that the New Testament anecdotes are inventions or myths modelled or modified by that of the Old; such transcription, conscious or unconscious, would, it is true, be quite natural to a Jewish biographer of a contemporary prophet who was regarded as modern representative of Elias; but on the same principle, the prophet himself who should aspire to be such representative, who should believe himself destined to fulfil the functions of the prophet, and even of Messiahship, would quite as naturally adopt the style and affect the authoritative ways of his prototype. Again, the sympathetic insight into character is no unnatural suggestion, independently, from the very idea of prophetic character and the proprieties of a supernaturally gifted teacher; we find the like ascription to Pythagoras.

I am inclined to think that the calling of Simon and Andrew, as related in the first Gospel, originally stood alone, a simple duplication of the calling of Elisha, and therefore emanating from the Jewish disciples among whom Peter was so mighty. These brothers are letting down their nets, but leave the unfinished labour at the summons of the prophet, as Elisha left his oxen and his plough mid-furrow.

Of this form the sequel is a reduplication; the pretensions of James and John to equal dignity with Peter, of which we have a trace in the ambitious petition of their mother to Jesus, as well as in the incidents of Acts, are asserted in this supplement; they also, it is now averred, followed to the call of Jesus as unhesitatingly as the other brothers, and they gave a still more decided evidence of devotion by leaving, not merely boat and labour, but,—the suggestion of this also is in the story of Elisha,—the ties of family, their father Zebedee.

To the author of neither of these records was there any deficiency of motive in the incident as related; the familiar precedent of Elisha made the instant acquiescence of the summoned disciples the most natural, the only natural result, as the simple summons the only natural antecedent.

With the third Gospel it is different; the author of the version of the anecdote here, besides combining the two callings into one, with a feeling for poetical grouping and effect, supplies, in a miracle, a motive for the sudden devotedness of the future Apostles, and thus betrays his unconsciousness that the point of the incident, as modern repetition of ancient prophetry, lay precisely in the absence of any such special incitement. Here therefore we seem to have a less decidedly Hebrew origin, as well as, it would appear, a modification of the story on deliberate principle. Many verbal and some incidental diversities of the first and second versions may easily have been due to the laxity of transcribers, the slips of memory between the glance at the copy and the new manuscript, of a writer intending and desiring to copy exactly; and this, I think, is an explanation very largely applicable to such diversities. Certain it is that the texts constantly run more minutely parallel than would be the case as between recorders writing down from memory what both had heard at the same time, or as between translators each translating the same text independently. But the re-making, in the third Gospel, of the calling of the Apostles, as related in the first and second, is too extensive and elaborate to have ever grown up out of a series of errors and misconceptions.

In fact, I am of opinion that it was a designed expression, in conscious allegorical form, of the relative activity of the several and associated Apostles, in the great revival of the sect, after the death of Jesus; the success surprising, even alarming to himself, that followed the exertions of Peter, mighty with the circumcision; the secondary aid rendered to him at the crisis of his difficulties by the brothers, "who seemed to be pillars," James and John.

Indulgence in composition in this form does not necessarily involve deception; the original anecdotes, and many another like them, might be too palpably or notoriously factitious for any scruple to be felt in giving point to the narrative or improvement to the moral.

At the same time, they who invent and elaborate such anecdotes, with party feeling and purpose, are just in the position which tempts them to deceive themselves at the same time that they deceive others, and then almost as easily and readily to deceive others without deceiving themselves.

It were illiberal towards the inventors of these apologues, to impute that they must have given circulation to them as facts and with set intention to deceive; it were equally illiberal towards the critics of these inventors, to deny that such may easily have been the state of the case, whether the aim were low, respectable, or lofty,—to promote self-interest, self-importance, to advance a party in the church, or to enforce a moral and save souls.

There are epochs of controversy when it will not be easy to find, even among conscientious men, the virtue of stating imaginations or conjectures with guarded explicitness, whenever it is foreseen that otherwise they must soon, without further complicity of the promulgator, be found in full currency as matters of fact.

III. THE SEA OF GALILEE.

The Sea, or, as the third Gospel more correctly styles it, the Lake of Tiberias,—of Gennesareth,—of Galilee,—is made the scene of many of the incidents in the life of Jesus, besides the calling of his Apostles. He is active at Capernaum and Bethsaida, cities on its banks, and crosses and recrosses it, and is represented as causing wide excitement throughout the district on its borders.

The district, in fact, contained peculiar elements of excitability.

The lake continues the line by which the Jordan, that passes through it, divides geographically the region of Galilee westward from Gaulonitis on the east, but the distinction was evidently rather geographical than social. We observe from the narrative of Josephus, that the borders of the lake were occupied by a busy population for whom its waters furnished the easiest of high-roads for intercourse, as well as a source of wealth and subsistence in productive fisheries. It is significant of the sympathy that united the people on either side of the lake, that Judas of Gamala, whose agitation, anterior to Jesus, had such serious political consequences afterwards, is spoken of indifferently as the Gaulonite and the Galilean, and his influence survived importantly among the mariners of the lake.

Galilee and the borders of the Lake of Galilee had been vehemently agitated by some of the most exciting phases of the Messianic hope long before the appearance of Jesus; and that it continued to be so through the period which comprises his career, and quite independently, is strikingly manifest in every page of the history of the revolt against Rome, long after the personal career of Jesus was closed. Galilee was the great centre of the assertion of the unlawfulness of Jews paying tribute to Cæsar, of the resolution to own no mortal lord and master and to strike boldly for freedom, in reliance that a Divine interposition,—the Deliverer or Saviour promised in both Law and Prophets—would only thus, and thus surely, be successfully invoked. The hope and the anticipation of Messianic deliverance may be considered as universal among the Jews; but it was a great and terrible day, which had two different aspects, for the apprehensive and the sanguine; the circumstances of it were variously read from various texts of prophecy; and opinions varied as importantly as to the course of conduct by which Israel could hasten or defer it. One enthusiast recoiled from the idea of the desecration of the Temple, which he found in prophecy was to introduce this great day, and, with whatever inconsistency, he shuddered at an announcement of it, like the judges of Stephen, as at blasphemy. To another, the prospect of escape from the unholy and intolerable yoke of Rome, made any eventuality welcome, any peril indifferent. According to school or sect or temperament, the Jews, all equally believing, were either content to await, or eager to hasten a triumph, or to defer a catastrophe for the sake of peace in their time; all, equally enthusiastic, were disposed variously to have faith for the result they wished, in ceremonial puerilities, in more spiritual purification, or in the valiant wielding of the sword of the Lord and of Gideon.

It was this last idea that was most deeply planted in the Galilean mind anterior to the ministry of Christ, and that bore its bitter and desolating fruit before the generation he himself addressed had departed.

The commencement,—the commencement of the end, for the sentiment was chronic,—was on the occasion of the assessment of properties in Judæa by Cyrenius under Augustus Cæsar. The measure was carried through without any outbreak, notwithstanding the repugnance of the Jews, who deferred to the authority and the reasons of Joazar, the High Priest; but the sting remained. Judas, a Gaulonite of Gamala, associated with Sadduc, a Pharisee, was zealous to bring about a revolt, and at least laid a sure train for it. His sect, says Josephus, coinciding in other respects with Pharisaic notions, have an irremovable affection for liberty, and for leader and master (ἡγεμόνα καὶ δεσπότην) admit God alone. He appealed forcibly to all the motives of manly pride and independence, and urged the doctrine, moreover, that the Divinity would only co-operate with their desires on the condition and in case that they entertained noble designs, and themselves shunned no labour, pain, or peril. Josephus refers to their endurance of pain and persecution under Gessius Florus rather as obstinacy than heroism, but in terms that avouch how highly strung was their confidence and their resolution.

The sons of Judas persevered in their father's purposes, and were crucified about A.D. 45-6 by the Procurator Tiberius Alexander. From the connection in which the historian relates their death, it seems probable that they were concerned in the demonstration of Theudas, an aspirant to Messiahship, who had come to grief shortly before. Having as much confidence in himself probably and in his mission as he inspired in his followers, Theudas sallied forth, leading a multitude of people, who, as for a second Exodus, took their possessions with them, and expected that, as a prophet "like unto Moses," he would divide Jordan, and give them a passage across. The horsemen of the Procurator Fadus intercepted them, and Theudas, taken alive, was beheaded, and his head carried to Jerusalem.

The complicity of the sect of the Gaulonite with the Pharisees as mentioned by Jósephus, is consistent with its tendencies and nature as a wide popular movement. The Jewish population at large, the Galilean in particular, was Pharisaic; the multitude were adherents of the Pharisee, the accurate and scrupulous interpreter of the law and of the unwritten traditions, the ostentatiously ascetic, the asserter of angelic natures and of the revival of the soul for immortality in hell or in happiness. The Pharisees were as popular as the Sadducees were the reverse; and they used their influence as far as they dared,—sometimes further than was prudent,—to tighten round the mind the web of minute and puerile ceremonialism. The exaltation of theocracy, it is clear, was quite in harmony with their doctrines and pretensions. Doubtless there was insincerity and inconsequence enough. Josephus himself is a Pharisee, who tells us frankly how he adopted the profession for the sake of power and position, and, with many another of his class during the Jewish revolt, ran with the hare to hold with the hounds, and saved himself by betraying a cause which he knew to be hopeless, but could not help taking part in. Still the theory of the Pharisaic sect was theocratic, and the hope and the promise that they cherished was not less for the revival of the Jewish kingdom than for the resurrection of the dead. Long before the time of Judas, six thousand Pharisees had refused to take the oath of allegiance to Herod and Cæsar. Through female protection at court, they did not suffer by the fine that was imposed; but the sword of Herod was brought down by the discovery of intrigues which turned upon their promise of a Messiah to be born under very extraordinary conditions of paternity. Some ruthless deed on this occasion may easily have been the historical root of the tale of a later murder of innocents.

The mingled religious and political antipathies which beset the publican, the agent of obnoxious tax-collection, in the midst of a Pharisaic and Gaulonitish population, are readily to be understood; the hatred of the badge of tribute went along with the hope of a Messiah; and Pharisaic tendencies in themselves, therefore, rather predisposed to reception of any Messianic pretender, who held out promise in any form, or could be supposed to do so, of political deliverance.

Having said thus much of the Gaulonite agitation when it commenced, I will add some lines for the echo of its despair, when it was extinguished in blood at Masada.

When the outbreak against Roman authority actually arrives, we find the sailors of the lake associated by Josephus with the poorer classes of Tiberias as the strength of the faction most eager in the cause. Josephus, as emissary of the Sanhedrin at Jerusalem, was negotiating for access to Tiberias, on the pretext of a commission to clear the palace built by Herod, of the abomination of forbidden images. This faction prevented his simulated zeal, and the demolition and plunder of the palace was followed by a massacre of the party obnoxious to them. The world has had enough experience of revolutions to make the hardest words of Josephus probable enough; the more probable, because the half-intentions and double-dealing that he avows on his own part are ever, by force of inevitable polarity, the immediate cause of such reactions.

The capture of Tarichew by the Romans in the war made them masters of the entire circuit of the lake, while vast numbers of the Jews sought refuge in the craft afloat on its waters. Vespasian hastened to attack them with vessels constructed from abundant materials at hand, and by wreck and slaughter destroyed them all. The lake and its shores, the earth, the air, and waters of the lovely and fertile region that the historian had described with enthusiasm were polluted by the blood and putrefaction of innumerable corpses, by sights and stenches hideous even to an enemy. The captives of Tarichew were passed into slavery after the old and ineffective had been disposed of with breach of faith by massacre in the stadium.

After Jerusalem and its Temple had been taken and desecrated, and all Judæa pacificated by the peace of desolation, Eleazar, a descendant of Judas the Gaulonite, still held out at Masada. This was a fortress adjacent to the Dead Sea in a remarkable natural position, which had been strengthened and provided by Herod the Great as his last reliance in case he were ever reduced to extremity.

Urged by the Roman besieger, depressed by an accident fatal for the defence after deceitful promise, Eleazar resolved on self-immolation, and the entire garrison shared the self-sought fate. Josephus has speeches for him on the occasion, which may have no possible authenticity of even remotest hearsay. They are, however, remarkable compositions, and there is a depth of feeling in them too profound to be the promptings of the imagination of Josephus; and we must credit him for reproducing a better effect than he could have invented, from memory of mingled regrets and complaints that he had been in the way of hearing abundantly and at his ease.

"Long ago," are words given to Eleazar, "we determined, valiant comrades, never to be servants to the Romans, nor to any other but to God, and now the occasion has arrived to make good our resolution by deeds. We were the first of all to commence the revolt, and we are the last who have continued fighting. Where now is that great city, the metropolis of the entire Jewish race, so built, so fortified, so garrisoned? Where the dwelling of which we had believed that God himself was the occupant? The sole monument of it is the camp of its destroyers laid out among its ruins. Some old men crouch upon the ashes of the sanctuary; a few women are reserved by our enemies for shame and dishonour. Verily I would that we had perished all, before witnessing the ruin and profanation of the city and the temple. But since a hope, not ungenerous, beguiled us, that peradventure we might be able to take vengeance for the ruin upon our enemies, and this has vanished, and left us alone in our necessity, let us make haste and die nobly while we may."

Such were the links that united Pharisee, Gaulonite, and Galilean; such were one class of the elements of ferment at work when Simon and Andrew, James and John, were toiling with boats and nets on the Lake of Galilee.

But the banks of Jordan, and all the country round, were, soon after the date of Judas, to be the scene of another popular excitement, also turning upon Messianic anticipations, but essentially at variance with the spirit of the bigoted Pharisee and fighting Gaulonite.

John the Baptist attracted multitudes to his exhortations, of which the purport was, that the kingdom of Heaven, the salvation or rescue of God, was indeed at hand. He announced, if we may rely on records that are very self-consistent, the approach of a Messiah who would deal vengeance and reward by no ceremonial standard, by no mere regard to favoured descent from Abraham, but according to moral deserts. He summoned all his countrymen therefore to repentance, and he sealed their pledged resolution by a baptismal rite.

His costume and habit of life were those ascribed to Elijah, the great prophet; and his ascetic retirement in the desert was in accordance with other teachers of influence, like the Banus to whom Josephus resorted; like Banus, he probably would be regarded as an Essene, and have the advantage of the exceptional tolerance for wide divergence in practice, which made the Essene of Judæa, so similar in position to the modern Friend.

His exhortations were evidently seasoned with that tone of severity and sound of alarm that are effective with a devoutly-disposed populace; and his simple rite, already recognized in Jewish conversions, had all the value that we have witnessed in our own day attaching to the temperance medal and blessing of Father Mathew.

Whether he denounced Pharisaism or not, his principle was, above all things, anti-ceremonial, as well as alien to the violent injunctions and theories of the Gaulonite; and it is easily conceivable how it happened, as we find it represented in the Gospels, that the leaders of the Pharisees did not believe in him, at the same time that their usual followers resorted to him in crowds.

The impulse was permanent and diffusive; late in Paul's career, if we may trust the record, we meet with an instructed Jew of Alexandria, Apollos, zealous in promoting it at Ephesus. He spoke and taught perseveringly about the Lord,—the Messiah, preparing his way as John had urged to prepare it, and only conversant with the baptism of John. "He began to speak boldly in the synagogue;" that boldness was required in order to enunciate John's doctrine to Jews, agrees with what we have observed of the opposition that it involved to technical Pharisaism, to the magnifying of privilege, form, tradition.

Here also is betrayed what might be inferred independently, that the personal recognition by John, of Jesus as the Messiah, can only be treated as fabulous; his sect continued without any such recognition. But the Christian movement was, in fact, in direct affiliation to that of John, and hence it was in natural sympathy with it; the process by which Paul annexed, or is said to have annexed, the disciples of Apollos is illustrative of the tendency of a hardier and more progressive sect to overpower the earlier; and in the motive to forward a coalition, in which the Christian element should be the dominant, we have the key to the tone and details of more of the anecdotes respecting John, Jesus, and their families, than can now be entered upon. The motive is rife in the idyllic history of the infancy incorporated by Luke, and peeps out in such expedients as turning the so-called descent of the Holy Ghost into a baptism, in order to cap the water of John with a baptism of fire.

That Jesus himself was baptized by John, and that it was from John's rite and doctrine that he received the original inspiration of his career, his claim to the Messiahship, his connection of the advent of salvation with regeneration of the heart and not with conjurations of ceremony, is the most obvious inference from the story, as it is told with many enrichments in the Gospels. There is also every probability that his earliest adherents were disciples of John in a certain sense,—the same sense in which he himself was,—and came to him in virtue of this discipleship, though by no means from any particular indication by the Baptist.

According to the fourth Gospel, Andrew positively, and Simon by implication, were disciples of John the Baptist. This is in accordance with Peter's ascribed practice of baptism by water in the case of Cornelius, and agrees with the views, expressed in his proem on the same occasion, of the relation of the two movements: "The Gospel of peace through Jesus Christ; even what was spoken through all Judæa, beginning from Galilee, after the baptism which John preached." (Acts x. 37.)

There may be some fair ground for the imputation

that the Christian doctrine was only too strongly impressed by its character as a reaction from the spirit of rebellion of the resolute Judas; the inculcation of political submission which has made it so often a byword, as a "doctrine of patience and pusillanimity" (Gibbon), would thus be derived from its very origin. There are certainly some strong words of Peter, that may be cited on the other side; but they are precisely those which, taken along with a certain readiness in resorting to his weapon, have made me suspect that before being a follower of either Jesus or John he had received a tincture of the disposition of the Gaulonite.

If we now look again to the scene depicted in the Cartoon, what do we see on the broad and fair and yet unpolluted expanse of the Sea of Galilee? A party of fishers are out away from the shore still in commotion with the crowds that a companion they have with them has been addressing. His words have enforced a moral already diffused by the Baptist, but probably with still greater urgency, as to the immediate proximity of the kingdom that was to be conquered for the Jew by personal repentance and amendment and purification of the heart. The fishers had apparently taken draughts from the same well-head of doctrine as the new young teacher, who came fresh from the workshop of the carpenter, to reinforce an impulse that the imprisonment and execution of John might easily cause to languish outwardly, however self-collecting and concentrating within. We conceive of the crowd about the region of Tiberias and Taricheæ visible in the horizon, as the hotbed of the agencies that were to work the ruin of Judea, and also to remodel the dominant character of the leading sections of progressive mankind. There are knotted the Gaulonitish enthusiasts, unconvinced by any exhortation that would keep the sword in its sheath, and appealing to the Pharisaic mass and to the ostentatious Pharisee himself, to abet their machinations and make or prepare for the venture, that, with the God of Israel to aid, would not hesitate to try the hand-grapple with Rome and all her legions. There are the meeker and ascetic disciples of John, who avert their eyes in disgust from selfish faction and licence, and from Pharisaic ceremonialism and spiritual pride, and, relying on Scripture, read by lights of their own consciences and coloured by their speciality of hopes and inclinations, would wrest from the Priest and the Pharisee their honester following, by convincing that the kingdom they hoped for would come indeed, but would come only for happiness to them, and only be hastened, by regeneration of the heart and that moral purification of which baptism was but the outward type and expression.

The Cartoon declares that it was already in Galilee, and at the time of personal attachment of Simon to Jesus, that the claim to Messiahship was recognized. This is the aspect of tradition one way; but in another, as we must interpret it, the earlier ministry of Jesus was carried on independently of any such overt claim, save with his immediate followers, and then it was as a secret of the very core of the sect that it was recognized. There are then indications that it got about in a covert manner, and brought and attached adherents who held it conscience to suppress, for the safety of the leader, the expression of the zeal they had at heart. Thus it was that devout and wealthy women,—the distinguished

Salome, the regenerate Magdalen,—brought service and substance to support the Lord and his society; and when the wave of popular excitement had gained full head, he at last started on the progress to Jerusalem, with the confidence, and probably under promise that there the salvation of the twelve tribes, for whom he had provided twelve presidents, should be revealed, and there the manifestation, of which he recognized the failure at last in the bitter words, "Eli, Eli, lama sabachthani!"

Of the revival of the sect, and the reproduction of his Messiahship in another form afterwards, there will be more to say. In this revival the Apostles of the Cartoon, and Simon especially, were leading instruments; its course and history bore the impress of their character, for good, and also for evil and abuse.

We see in the expression of the kneeling Peter a mixture of devotion and qualifying alarm; and this is but prefiguration of the timidity that so importantly affected his course. His zeal was equalled at last by his courage, but in the first instance outran it, and in the interval he was unprotected.

The powers most inimical to the spirit of his Master found entrance at the breach. The friends of Pharisaic ceremonialism grafted it on the new sect, and found opportunity to shield themselves by the inconsistencies, which were appealed to as the authority, of Peter. The worst abuses of the devotional tendency of mankind, that the doctrines of John and Jesus seemed to have been designed, and certainly most naturally tended to destroy, found a metropolis at Rome, and flourish there to this day, under the name of Peter, supreme over the Gentile world.

What chance was there, then, that the original root of these mischiefs would be extirpated in the original race? Let the landscape of the Lake of Galilee again suggest the reply.

Tiberias, that we see in the distance, rose out of the desolation of the wars with Rome, as the secondary metropolis of Jewish superstition when excluded from Mount Moriah by the victors, in vain anticipation that it was a vitality conditional on a consecrated site. The dispensation of Moses had much about it of the majestic; the establishment of Solomon, at least symbolized a united and independent nationality, mighty and magnificent. The domination of the Rabbins, that ripened at Tiberias, was the vile and vulgar tyranny of craft and stupidity the most mischievous, over craft the most stupid and superstition the most besotted. And so, for Jew as for Gentile, narrow-minded subjection to reliance on the conjuration of holy meats and holy days and rites, and consecrated vestments, gestures, and, worst of all, on the intervention of consecrated men, was as far and remains as far from extirpation as ever.

Still, the better movement of the incident we have studied has not been without an outcome; and what there is best in the world of civil and religious liberty, must give the incident this Cartoon typifies,—allegiance to truth at sacrifice of all interests and all ties, the national as well as the domestic,—a leading line in its annals.

CHAPTER II.

THE CHARGE TO PETER.

I. CARTOON OF THE CHARGE TO PETER.—II. THE TWELVE IN RELATION TO JESUS.—III. THE APOSTLES AFTER THE CRUCIFIXION.

I. THE CARTOON OF THE CHARGE TO PETER.

AGAIN, in this Cartoon, we stand with the Master Jesus and the Apostles, by the Lake of Gennesareth; but between this moment and the former lies a lifetime of instruction, of institution, and of suffering; the life's work is finished, and the subject of the picture represents the very instant when, the personal agency of Jesus having come to an end, the world was to be left to make what it could of the germs of development with which his career had endowed it.

The bight of the lake in the background fixes the scene; and the end of a fishing-boat, that extends into the picture, is reminiscent of the origin of the fishers of men.

The Apostles are eleven in number, the traitor being gone; and the appearance and costume of the Saviour declare that the incident is subsequent to his passion and resurrection. The scars of the cross are visible upon hand and foot, and perhaps also in the side. The ample drapery that is thrown round him is now white, but was originally roseate or symbolically golden; there is something of clearness and majesty in the flow of its lines, that gives it the air of an idealized investiture, contrasting with the Apostles' raiment of use and habit; the same effect of independent superiority is enhanced by the absence of the under-garment or tunic, worn by all the other figures, leaving chest and shoulder exposed. In the tapestry in the palace of Milan the drapery of Christ is a light-pink enriched with golden stars; this particular tapestry is wretchedly ill-executed. In the corresponding tapestry in the palace at Mantua, the robe again is pink, but with no stars; and indeed this set, which is very fine and much better preserved than that in the Vatican, was executed without the employment of gold in any part. The robe of John in the subject of the Death of Ananias is a delicate rose-colour, which has vanished from the Cartoon. I do not doubt that the present white appearance of the robes both of John and of Jesus in the Delivery of the Keys as well as in the Miraculous Draught, is simply explainable by the fugitiveness of the same pigment.

The white robe of Christ, as it shows in the Cartoon at present, is very ineffectively relieved upon the white fleeces of the sheep.

Christ, then, is before us, in the aspect and array of a revelation, an apparition, an ὀπτασία,—the significant New Testament term for his reappearances. He stands entirely apart and disengaged from the group of his disciples, in a manner to remind of the warning to Mary —" Touch me not, for I have not yet ascended to my.

Father;" and a tranquillity of pose and moderated symmetry of gesture, complete the dignity of a conception as grand as it is appropriate. Tenderness and love are in his eyes, as he appeals to Peter's profession of love to himself as warranty that he can have loving care of the flock committed to him.

The scene, the time, and the leading circumstance of the picture, are taken from the last chapter of John; but the text is made subservient to a broad general treatment, which enabled the painter to combine a wider range of expression than belongs to the particular incident as there narrated. In the neighbourhood of the lake and the fishing-boat, and in the presence of disciples, Jesus appeals thrice to Peter whether he loves him, and receives three assurances, not given without pain at the repetition of the inquiry; and thrice the commission is given, "Feed my sheep;" so far and in the detail that John, the disciple whom Jesus loved, is following upon Peter during the colloquy, the painter is content to take his outline from the Evangelist. But the significance on which he was interested to insist, was the assignment to Peter of a certain primacy over the Church and the Apostles. He therefore assembles as witnesses all the other ten Apostles, instead of merely those enumerated in the text, "Thomas, Nathanael of Cana, the sons of Zebedee, and two other of his disciples;" he suppresses all indication by costume of "fisher's coat," of that resumption by Peter of his occupation, which is so incongruous in the text. He arrays them all with a dignity that comports with the full establishment of their office. He then transfers to this occasion the committal of the keys to Peter, the power

to bind and to loose on earth and in heaven; and in displaying the effect which this produces upon the other Apostles, he finds the means to give expression to all the intimations which are scattered through the Gospels and Acts, of the workings of feeling and temperament among their community.

Peter, with crossed arms, embraces rather than clasps the keys, which seem to have been just delivered to him with intimation of the control that they symbolize; he is humbly on his knees, as in act of homage, but his attitude presses forward, his foot is visibly not yet inactive, and the entire figure breathes out the zeal and sense of responsibility, and the ardour that had so readily professed that though all others might be faithless he would never fail, and that grieved at the renewed requirement of avowal of love, either simply or as greater than that of others.

The keys and the browzing sheep are realized figures of speech, which support each other harmoniously, and continue into this Cartoon the spirit of symbolism which in the former suggested the introduction of the cranes. By these happy inventions, incidents from the life of Christ seem to be brought into sympathy with that very tendency to apologue and parable that characterize his teaching. This treatment also conduces not a little to give to the two designs in which the Saviour is introduced, the same ideal air that establishes a certain contrast between the narratives of the Gospels and the greater naturalism of the Acts of the Apostles and the Cartoons from the Acts. This is a gradation which always reminds me of that by which we are conducted from the beginning of the Iliad to the end of the

Odyssey. The kneeling position of Peter on this the great occasion of his preferment, signifies something in addition to fitting deferential homage to the Saviour; it is in accordance with the terms of Christ's rebuke to the disciples after they had disputed by the way which should be greatest in the kingdom of heaven, and when they were told that he that was eldest among them was bound to be as the younger, and he who should be leader of all to be as a servant.

The spirit indicated in that discussion finds full expression in the general group, and is indeed the key of its chief contrasts.

Immediately behind Peter, John, conspicuous by youth and grace, presses forward with eyes of devotion fixed on the Saviour, and with countenance and hands composed to warmest sympathy and adoration. The air of his head, the lines of his drapery, bent knee, and foot are in immediate harmony with those of Peter; and the four Apostles who are grouped with him most closely, share in various degrees his sympathetic impulse.

On the other hand, the spirit and liveliness of his action finds a contrast in the most advanced figure of the group remote from the Saviour, where the germs or the remains of different feelings are equally evident. This figure, which in its suspended pose shows less action than any other in the picture, was probably intended for Thomas, representative of a disposition, not to denial, but to doubt. With head poised in steady attention, he stands quite upright, and his ample robe slips directly downwards from his shoulder, as his right hand—reversed as usual in the Cartoon—drawn back upon his breast, seems to keep down the slightest movement to enthusiasm. The left hand has a movement to collect the cloak which is neglected by the unconscious right, and the left foot could be prompt for advance but that the right is so entirely quiescent,—altogether the most complete embodiment conceivable, of absorbed attention and most equivocal suspense, of coolness and hesitation.

Expression the most decided is declared in the Apostle behind him,—a marked antithesis to the cordiality of John. Repugnance, if not protest, is seen in his profile and in his movement in a direction away from the chief incident. He is of somewhat smaller proportions than his companions, the flow of his hair partakes less of free luxuriance than of the negligence of the unkempt student, not to say ascetic; in the folds of the cloak that he huddles round him, we see that his hand grasps a book.

This Apostle, I do not doubt, was intended by Rafael for James; not the brother of John, but the James who appears in Acts, occupying a position in the church at Jerusalem, where his influence rivals, if it is not opposed to, that of Peter. The counterworking is intimated or asserted in Acts, and in Paul's Epistle to the Galatians, as hinging on the influence of James over the communistic church,—the poor saints at Jerusalem,—and his protection of those who would enforce upon the free converts the fetters of Judaism in law and tradition. Both these characteristics have contributed to the ideal formalist in the Cartoon, who is recoiling from an authority which might be superior to a code that he clings to as a talisman.

The Apostle who is visible between Thomas and John is pressing forwards with zeal displayed in both hand and step, and turns at the same time to address both looks and words, I think of expostulation, to the uncordiality of James. He thus becomes the intermediate link by which, with some assistance from the indecisive Thomas, the sentiment of one group blends with the other.

Here we have an example of one of the pictorial *schemata* which Rafael perhaps invented, as he often repeated and always varied it. By this, figures that are visible on either side of one intermediate and nearer, are observed to exchange glances across the vacant space behind it. We see this in the picture at Bologna, where St. John and St. Augustine appear to the left and right of St. Cecilia behind her, and are exchanging looks at least, if not words. In the School of Athens, the youthful pupil of Pythagoras communicates in this way with the female associate of the philosopher, and other instances lie near to hand. It is a stratagem that gives wonderful lightness and openness to composition.

Behind James, three Apostles stand by themselves and close together, with a similarity of pose that associates them in feeling,—a feeling of questioning at least, if not of discontent. Two of them are the oldest of the eleven, and therefore naturally jealous of being superseded; or as it may be more fitly put, two of these Apostles who represent the sentiment of discontent, are appropriately made by the painter much older than the rest, and thus provided with a motive, if not excuse, for reluctance in admitting a superior. That the face of the last figure of all is not visible leaves open an expressive possibility as to how much further dislike may not have deepened. Certainly an end of projecting robe has the appearance of being thrown out by a gesture of sudden folding up and tightening round of drapery of one who has to submit with ill grace to an arrangement that he would fain, but cannot, protest against.

We have still to remark on the individual figures of the foremost and more sympathetic group.

The first figure, with venerable beard, has an expression of seriousness and awe, and raises his hand in admiration at the grave event. I regard him as Andrew, the brother of Peter. Joy and admiration appear to me to characterize the next head visible in the background. If we please we may call him Philip, who is next in the enumeration of the Apostles after Peter, Andrew, James, and John, and is said to have been, like Peter, from Bethsaida. Between these two the head of John composes, and gains great force from contrast with their distinct expressions of joy and veneration that in his own blend harmoniously as reverential love.

Behind John, in the same line, is another Apostle, sedately sympathetic. I think we may regard this as James, the brother of John; induced partly by proximity and partly by a certain resemblance in cast of the hair as well as of features, to his brother.

It is impossible to over-estimate the force, facility, and invention which are exercised by the genius of Rafael in this wonderful composition. The most contrasted feelings are blended by gradation, the finest lines of modified sentiment are rendered with complete distinctness. The manner in which the expression of the heads of John and Thomas are defined by contrast with those that appear on either side of them respectively, is illustrative of the principle that pervades the condensed apposition of gestures, and the play of line and flow of draperies, throughout.

The very marked break in the general group of the Apostles, cut into deeply in the midst, is suggestive and expressive of moral liability to schism. The level light of early morning, the time given by the text and observed, I think, by the painter, is taken advantage of to render the division more distinct; and while it meets full the placid brow of the Saviour, it throws exactly half his figure into shade, rendering conspicuous the glow of the raiment, symbolical of his risen state.

The two keys are most naturally interpreted as being keys respectively of heaven and of hell; but though doctrine might assign a double wardership, there was a difficulty for the painter, who could scarcely admit proximity of the two portals. Italian painters and poets usually distinguish the keys as one gold, one silver; the golden being taken to symbolize the divine authority of priestly absolution, and the silver, the learning and discretion requisite for the office. Another view is given in the line of Milton,—

"The golden opes, the silver shuts amain," (*Lycidas*,)

in a passage which always conveys to me the poet's familiarity with this design. It was after the date of this poem that he went to Italy,—could he have seen copies of the tapestry in England, or the cartoon itself in the gallery of Charles I.?

The perspective diminution of the heads of the Apostles, to agree with distance into the picture, which in strictness would be considerable, is somewhat neglected, —a neglect which may share whatever explanation shall be adopted for the small boats of the former Cartoon.

It will be noticed how the line of the natural horizon rises in order to provide harmonious background for the isolated figure of Christ. On the other side it is broken by a mighty tower, at the foot of which is a conflagration comparatively insignificant; I could almost think we have here a suggestion of the Church founded on a rock,—the rock of Cephas,—"and the gates of hell shall not prevail against it."

A study exists for the group of the Apostles,—the figures are in Italian costume.

It would be poverty of spirit and weakness indeed, to turn away scandalized from the truth and beauty of this design, on the ground that they subserve the false pretensions to authority of the corrupt head of a corporation of modern priests. As truth and beauty they must be right and good; and reason is the rather that we should claim them for the right and vindicate them from false appropriation.

What Rafael read in the Gospels and what he painted, was in the first instance a special appeal to the peculiar affection and attachment of Simon to his Master, and a consequent committal to him of charge and pre-eminence over weaker brethren,—weak though he himself might be,—brethren who witness the charge with not uniform cordiality. This incident he partly chose and partly made up from evangelical intimations, and painted it moreover as typical of the dignity and office of the admitted head of the Church and occupant of the chair of St. Peter, as was held, in right succession. A certain Pope was not, Popes in general are not apt to be, endowed with zeal and love like Peter's, and apart from these have no claim to his authority; this may be, but the essential verity as depicted holds good nevertheless. It is spirits that are finely touched that are so to fine issues; and assuming that the contemporary chief of the Church had not the qualities ascribed to Peter, the tapestry simply hung up before him in his false enthronization, an ensample and a reproof, the most vivid exposition of an ideal that shamed his shortcoming and invalidated his title.

It is the natural theory of every church that the qualifications of its actual chief are those of the ideal, as the laws of a state assume in the central power the qualities essential to sovereignty; on their own heads, on the heads of rulers and of teachers be the penalty, in case these qualifications are falsified; and it is one of the best mementos of their obnoxiousness to such penalties, that the original circumstances and conditions of their delegated power, should be set forth pictorially, and set constantly before their eyes.

Lofty duties and pre-eminence in sway do pertain of right and of fact to the highly gifted teacher, relatively to the inferior and to the large general body of disciples, who,—such is humanity as recorded hitherto,—are scarcely disposed to be or capable of ever being more. If Peter were so qualified, any dignities assigned to him would not be abrogated because disqualified modern priests claim succession as of right; and if such pretenders bespeak a pictorial exposition of their title, they only provoke, as in this case, a record of reproach, and in place of commendation, a satire.

Rafael painted, and only could paint, the truth of nature unimpeached by the gloss of false interpretations, and moreover, transcending observance of the literal accuracies of history. This truth would remain, though Peter had never lived nor been supposed to have lived; it would be none the less valid though the illustrative anecdote were an incident from an avowed romance, instead of being, as we shall find it, a myth involved in a too liberally accredited history.

So much for the relation of Peter to the other Apostles, antitype of relation of Pope to Cardinals, of bishop to a church or laity, that seem typified as silly, imitative, tractable, irrational sheep. The Apostles in the scene however are both teachers and disciples, clerical and lay; and the sheep, alas! are inevitable type of the large herd of helpless, that are destined in the best times and for many a long day to make up the majority of the devotional. These are they who wait for even the most ordinary spiritual nourishment on the dispensing will of their superiors, pastors, and masters, appointed or self-appointed; they who by nature and habit can have nothing but what they are taught by others,—the children, too many women, too many men child-like and woman-like. Such is the flock that lends itself, if it does not proffer itself, for guidance; and the quality of the guidance tendered to which is the test of teaching minds, and the verity of their commission. It is the authorized function of the genuine mediator between intelligence and dulness to turn one key, like the ideal Peter, to open the display of truth; and to turn the other to confine condemned and condemning error; and to be conscientious alike in liberal admission of the inquiring, and in guidance of the submissive who can be no more, to the enjoyment of the best that inquiry has obtained.

II. THE TWELVE IN RELATION TO JESUS.

The appointment of twelve chief disciples is one of the very best authenticated incidents in the career of Jesus, and also one of the most significant. The testimonies of the Gospels and the Acts are confirmed by the unimpeached Epistles of St. Paul. From such confirmation, it is probable that we may even assume the title 'Apostles' to be original, or equivalent of the original. To recover its primary import may seem more difficult. It cannot have been given by Jesus as expressing a commission to go forth and teach all nations, etc.; for this view of their functions, with the text that declares it, was certainly an after-growth. The Apostles, as a corporation, are found very steadily fixed at Jerusalem, waiting and watching for the kingdom of God,— a Jewish kingdom, and in the interest of the conservation of the ceremonial law. If they move, it is under the compelling force of persecution or for short excursions,—to Samaria, to Antioch,—to take possession of the harvest sown by more adventurous and dispersive missionaries.

The narrative of their appointment, however, supplies a sending forth during the lifetime of Jesus, which sufficiently explains their title, and illustrates at the same time his wide anticipations. Their number was, no doubt, fixed with reference to the twelve tribes,—a point which in itself is expressive of the strictly Judaic limits of his own theory of his Messiahship. When we collect the scattered traditions which are dispersed through the records, that consistent with this theory are inconsistent with the more metaphysical theory that afterwards obtained, and with hints of which they are jumbled, the result is as follows.

In the regeneration, the twelve who had given up all to follow Jesus, have promise that all broken domestic ties shall be replaced manifold, all sacrificed possessions restored hundredfold; they shall eat and drink at the Messiah's table in his kingdom, and sit on twelve thrones judging the twelve tribes of Israel; and to them generally is given the power, restricted in one statement to Peter, to bind and loose both in earth and heaven. "Know ye not," says St. Paul, "that the saints shall judge the world?" Paul, coming a little later, extends the privilege to Gentile Christians of a world-wide Church; but the author of the Book of Revelation, writing a little later still, in the short interval between the death of Nero and the fall of Jerusalem, only knows of Gentile Christians to be in antagonism to them, and finds his millennial ideal in a new Jerusalem of sealed Jews under the tribal presidencies of the Twelve.

The devoted attachment of this number of immediate personal followers is expressive of the influence of the character of Jesus, and the aggregative power that he exercised in common with certain other movers of the world's ways of feeling and thought, as Pythagoras, Socrates, Epicurus, Mahomet.

To the same effect—the height of his pretensions considered,—is the attachment to his sect, of his own mother, and his brethren, her other sons. Jesus, it is distinctly said in one text, was the eldest of a family, and may probably have been so, though we may not rely too surely, as a mystic motive soon crept in to prove that he was necessarily a first-born.

The Greeks in historic times could fable to much the same tune and tenor in favour of Macedonian Alexander or of Plato. A precedent or a parallel in Judæa is supplied by Josephus, who knew not, or did not venture to declare, or did not think it necessary to do more than intimate, all its significance. It is the story of king Izates. I give Whiston the responsibility for terms of translation: the Muse of history has not the option of fastidiousness. "Monobazus, the king of Adiabene, fell in love with his sister Helena, and took her to his bed, and begat her with child. But as he was in bed with her one night, he laid his hand upon his wife's body and fell asleep, and seemed to hear a voice, which bade him take his hand off his wife's body, and not to hurt the infant that was therein, which by God's providence would be safely born, and have a happy end." The child is the second son by the same wife, yet is called by Josephus "only-begotten." May it be equivalent of "single-parented," as with the only-begotten Athene of Hesiod? The sequel of the story of Helena and her son betrays an aim to bid for the Messianic *prestige*, and I do not doubt that, by a more exact rendering of the original tale, Monobazus would have been warned off, like Joseph, in deference to the progeny of the Deity.

"Plato was an Athenian, son of Ariston and Perictione, or Potone. His mother traced her lineage collaterally, up to Solon, through his brother Dropides, father of Critias, father of Callaischrus, father of Critias, who was one of the Thirty, and of Glaucon, father of Charmides and the Perictione, of whom and Ariston Plato was born, the sixth from Solon,—Solon, who himself claimed descent from Neleus and Poseidon

(Neptune). Ariston also was said to be a descendant of Codrus, son of Melanthus, reputed, according to Thrasylus, to be descended from Poseidon. But Speusippus, in his book entitled 'Of the funeral banquet of Plato,' and Clearchus in his Encomium of Plato, and Anaxilides, in his second book concerning Philosophers, aver that it was a tradition at Athens, that when Ariston attempted to consummate his union with the beautiful Perictione, he failed of success, and as he ceased his attempt he had a vision (ὄψις) of Apollo; in consequence he left her pure from the marriage rite until after her confinement; and so Plato was born, according to Apollodorus in his Chronicles, in the eighty-eighth Olympiad, on the seventh of the month Thargelion, the birthday, according to the Delians, of Apollo himself." (Diog. Laertius, Plato, *sub init.*)

Compare with this; Jesus of Nazareth was the son of Joseph and Mary (Matthew i. 16). Mary traced her lineage up to David the king, according to several apocryphal Gospels and Justin Martyr, though it is remarkable—it is significant—that none of the canonical writings hint at such a descent. Joseph, on the other hand, is traced by two writers, though by irreconcilable routes, up to David the king, to Abraham, Adam, and God; as Ariston up to Kodrus, Melanthus, and Poseidon. The vision of the angel of the Lord is Hebraistic equivalent for the ὄψις of Apollo; and the indulgent and hopeful self-control of the Athenian and Jewish husbands, run in parallel lines or rather upon an identical line. Later tradition, which fixed the birth of Jesus at the solstitial epoch of the 25th of December, birth-day of the Sol Invictus, has completed the agreement with Plato, reputed son of Ariston, but in reality of the Sun-god.

We cannot even rely upon the statement as to the age of Jesus at the commencement of his public career, that he was just thirty years old; this is a deduction from the date of the registry of Cyrenius, a date adopted for the birth as affording a sort of excuse, far-fetched and improbable enough, for transferring Mary for the nonce from Nazareth to Bethlehem, the city of David, and so getting a fulfilment of a reputed prophecy.

The number of the women who admired and followed, ministered to him and provided for him, is a notice that may be accepted, and perfectly explains itself by all that is best and weakest in the sex.

There is great difficulty in discovering the historical truth as to the position of the Apostles relatively to Jesus, his pretensions and anticipations, during his life. Had the compilations which we call the Gospels even been put together by any of them, we should have had comparative facility in marking the track of personal motive and feeling; but neither the compilations, nor the narrative materials out of which they are built up, come direct from Apostolic hands, and for the most part could never have been touched by them at all. In their completion we receive them directly from sections of the Church that were in qualified, but still in resolute opposition to the views as well as the authority of the Apostles generally on some most important points, and then to the authority of the Apostles as distinguished from Peter.

As the case stands, the tone ascribed to Jesus, in his intercourse both with Apostles and disciples, is constantly that of superiority and reserve. He intimates only in the most oblique manner that he is the Messiah; the first suggestion does not even come from himself. He is given to seclusions and solitary prayer; to occasional activity, and then retirements which stimulate curiosity, and foster zeal and reverential acquiescence. He teaches in parables that are suggestive, though indeed most of those ascribed to him are of later date. He does not proclaim the fact or preach the doctrine that he is the Messiah; he produces the belief. When the recognition of his pretensions is made, he enjoins secrecy, till the secret becomes one known to everybody. The interpretation of all this is equivocal; the mysteriousness is probable as a fact, but also and equally as imputed in opposition to the fact. When the sect, after his death, took a development and form unknown to himself, and quite inconsistent with the anticipations he had encouraged or allowed to spring up in the Twelve, and which to a great extent they continued to retain, a motive arose to ascribe to them dulness in understanding his drift, and to assume that they never were really admitted into his confidence; Christ himself had been vindicated by the ascription to him of more or less direct predictions of the new state of things, in plain words, in indirect words, or in pregnant parables, all to become legible by the light of that grand invention,—the baptism of fire, the descent of the Holy Ghost.

With every allowance for this undoubted motive operating to modify the records, a residuum of History, I think, remains undissolved. It is compatible with many probabilities that Christ did maintain, even with his nearest followers, a certain mysterious reserve, which only heightened respect and expectation. There is after all the grand presumption that the Apostles had at least no such detailed communication of his anticipations as to render a notion so inconsistent with them as his death, resurrection, and reappearance, quite incapable of being entertained and reconciled with it. The indispensable policy of safety would enforce upon him certain caution; and thus, concurrently with injunctions to keep silence as to his Messiahship, we have evasions of jealous authorities by frequent changes of place, wanderings without where to lay the head, separations from companions, unexpected transferences from one part of the lake to another.

The announcement of the approaching kingdom and its moral conditions go on concurrently, and zeal at last can brook no longer the delay in the declaration of the expected leader.

In the first three Gospels, the merit is assigned to Peter of breaking the ice, and being the first to announce the manifest Saviour. In the enumerations of the Apostles also, Peter comes first, and in Matthew he is designated πρῶτος. The fourth Gospel carefully derogates from this as from several other points of superiority of Peter. It even gives the first recognition of Jesus as Christ to the Baptist, and again to Peter only through an intermediate channel.

After the appointment of the twelve, the great overt act of Jesus was what I have no doubt is historical, his entry into Jerusalem, in such guise, and so attended, as constituted an open claim to the fulfilment in person of an admitted and reverenced Messianic prophecy.

Popular enthusiasm seems to have arisen, and for a

time to have surrounded and sustained the prophet; an historical fact may lie hid in that record of a tumult about the Temple, and the violence to profaning dealers and money-changers. There is confused hint of mystical reference to a crisis on a third day, to the destruction of the Herodian temple and its half-heathen magnificence and adornments, and to a restoration, no doubt according to more primitive and purer ideal,—the central notion of that restoration of all things and renovation of Israel, that the Rabbins connect with the coming of the Messiah, and that prophecy could be cited to support. "The Lord whom ye seek shall suddenly come to his temple, even the messenger of the covenant, whom ye delight in; behold, he shall come, saith the Lord of Hosts." (Malachi iii. 1.) "For thus saith the Lord of Hosts; Yet once, it is a little while, and I will shake the heavens, and the earth, and the sea, and the dry land; and I will shake all nations, and the desire of all nations shall come: and I will fill this house with glory, saith the Lord of hosts. The silver is mine, and the gold is mine, saith the Lord of hosts. The glory of this latter house shall be greater than of the former, saith the Lord of hosts; and in this place will I give peace, saith the Lord of hosts." (Haggai ii. 6–9.)

I do not doubt that Jesus expected, and led the people to expect, a divine interposition, credited as easily, and on much the same grounds, as the passage of the Jordan promised by Theudas; the cleaving of the Mount of Olives by the Egyptian; the rescue of leaguered Jerusalem, anticipated by the descendants of the Gaulonite. "A false prophet," says Josephus, "was the occasion of these people's destruction, who had made a public proclamation in the city that very day, that God commanded them to get up upon the Temple, and that there they should receive miraculous signs of their deliverance. Now, there were then a great number of false prophets suborned by the tyrants to impose upon the people, who announced this to them, that they should wait for deliverance from God; and this was in order to keep them from deserting, and that they might by such hopes be carried above fear and care." (Josephus, Bell. Jud., vi. 5, 2.)

The charge on which it is related that Jesus was condemned, was the having asserted his power to rebuild the Temple, after its destruction, in three days. This reads like a very probable perversion of words having reference to the anticipated intervention of God; that they were intimations of the resurrection of his own body is, of course, a posterior gloss. I think it quite possible, indeed, that the anticipation of his third-day resurrection may even have been due to this expression or prophecy; his declaration having failed in its obvious and simple sense, his devoted followers were likely enough to cast about for some other sense more pliable, and they who seek under such influences fail not to find.

At Jerusalem, again, we have the same traces as before of prudential evasion of the easily jealous and unscrupulous authorities; then retirement from the city at night to the Mount of Olives or to Bethany, and the discovery of his person and his retreat at last, only by the betrayal of an associate, one of the selected twelve.

When the appointed critical time—hour or day—had passed, had failed, popular excitement sank, sank perhaps but to revive in indignation; and the self-reliance of the prophet himself had to abide the direst of all trials. I find it difficult to believe that the depression which comes before us so affectingly in the scenes of the supper and the garden agony, that declares itself in the seeming dulness or sullenness before accusers, and in the very indifference to favourable interference from Pilate, is not true general representation of the bowed spirit that finds its true faith effectless, and plunges back into its recollections to seek in vain, not the source of its error, but the explanation of its disappointment. The feeling of confidence in a promise accepted as divine makes head to the last, but at the last gives up with that bitterest cry of undeceived despair that ever was uttered, "My God! my God! why hast thou forsaken me!"

III. THE APOSTLES AFTER THE CRUCIFIXION.

The great turning-point in the revival of Christian enthusiasm after the death of Jesus was the origin of the belief in his resurrection, a belief which chiefly fostered the expectation of his reappearance at any moment, and the revelation of his kingdom.

The important complicity of Peter on this occasion is presumable from the report of Paul, that "he was first seen of Cephas, and then of the twelve." The Gospels, however, are unanimous in ascribing the first hint or information of the resurrection, though but from hearsay, to the women, especially to Mary Magdalen, out of whom Christ had cast seven devils; and (1) and (4) assign to Mary Magdalen the distinction of the first interview with Christ risen, while the pre-eminence of Peter is restricted to his having been the first to entertain the possibility of such an event. In the fourth Gospel he has to divide even this merit with John. Only in (3) is there a possibility that the appearance of Jesus to Peter may have been anterior to that at Emmaus to Kleophas.

It is not at all impossible that a disposition to reduce the merit of Peter may have caused the introduction of Mary Magdalen into the story. But otherwise there is much verisimilitude in the origination of belief in vision of the risen Master, having commenced among his grateful, devoted, enthusiastic feminine followers, Mary Magdalen, James's Mary (or 'the other Mary,' Matt.), and Salome, and Johanna, wife of Chuza Herod's deputy, and Susanna (Luke viii.), and the rest of the women who came with him out of Galilee, "who ministered to him of their substance" (Luke viii. 3). We may even say that the probability is assisted by his mother Mary not being enumerated among those who were witnesses of his reappearance.

What morsels of truth there may be in the stories relative to the entombment, it is now impossible to say. There can be none in the tale of the guard set to watch it at the solicitation of the Jews, lest a report of a resurrection should get abroad. The sealed and guarded chamber reminds of the circumstances of custody of the holy vestments of the Temple, as told by Josephus (Antiq., xviii. 5). Much more congruous would be the appointment of a guard to watch the corpse upon the cross, an authenticated and reasonable precaution. Tradition was quite competent to transform disappearance of the body from the cross into disappearance from a rock sepulchre, if a seeming fulfilment of prophecy were advantaged by the change.

Historic detail, however, as I have said, is not recoverable; the community may probably enough have been dispersed in the horror and affright of the unexpected catastrophe,—may have retreated forthwith to Galilee again, of which there is much appearance,—or some at least may have lingered or lurked in Jerusalem long enough to receive from the women the report of their affectionate attempts to render the last offices to their Master; and to entertain, more or less confidingly, their averments of vision and reappearance. It is quite in the spirit of enduring feminine faith in a spiritual pastor and promiser, to resort to any alternative whatever, and however strange, unnatural, supernatural,—rather than give up a cherished faith in honesty and truth.

There is some interest, however, in collating the traditions as we have them, and in tracing back some of the stages of their corruption and change, albeit that at last we may but come to a fundamental tradition as taproot, that was itself no more than a prime figment of error, deception, or self-deception.

The narratives in the Gospels have such exact verbal agreements in the midst of their divarications, that we can only treat them as the same record, varied by omissions, additions, and substitutions; and this applies even to some consecutive narratives in the same Gospel.

(4.) "On the first day of the week, while it was yet dark, cometh Mary Magdalen to the tomb, and sees that the stone was taken away from the tomb;" she runs therefore and tells Simon Peter and John that they have taken the Lord from the sepulchre, "and we know not where they have laid him."

So John; in Matthew, the Magdalen has with her the other Mary; in Mark, Mary and Salome; in Luke, the women generally and certain with them. All these three Gospels then pursue the story in tolerably parallel lines,—

(2.) A young man in white garment;—

(3.) Two men in shining garments;—

(1.) An angel of lightning aspect, in garment white as snow, rolls away the stone and sits on it, frightens guards into a trance (1 and 2), bids the women not be afraid, and (1, 2, 3) announces that Christ has risen, and bids them refer the disciples (1, 2) and Peter (2) to appointment in Galilee, whither he has gone before.

Luke (3), instead of the latter clause, refers the women to their memory that while yet in Galilee Jesus had announced his death and resurrection,—a very obvious gloss for the writer of the Acts of the Apostles, who notes specially that the disciples continued at Jerusalem; he rejects, therefore, the adjournment to Galilee, and substitutes a notice of Galilean reference more in harmony with his system and scheme. He does not, however, quite throw away the other version, but finds a place for it in the first chapter of Acts, where, after Jesus has ascended into the sky, two men in white garments address the Apostles: "Ye men of Galilee, why stand ye staring up," etc.

The women deliver the message (1, 3), or are frightened, and tell no one (2),—a notice which looks like an honest attempt to satisfy some who were of their associates at the time, and might well be surprised at having never heard a word of such great incidents.

(3.) The disciples disbelieved, but, according to some

manuscripts, Peter ran to the sepulchre and looked in, saw the clothes left, and retired,—not to rejoin the doubting disciples, but to himself or his own resort, marvelling at the event. (4.) John, as well as Peter, makes the quest, and, like him, retires home.

The first actual reappearance of Jesus related in (3), is to two journeyers to Emmaus, who have much appearance of being the originals of the "two young men" or the two angels in shining white garments who recur in other narratives.

Then we have a notice (2) which commences abruptly, as if the previous incident were unknown to the writer, as indeed the narrative only occurs in certain manuscripts. "Having arisen early on the first day of the week, he appeared first to Mary Magdalen, out of whom he had cast seven demons." This is not given by (3), but in (1) and (4) we have further details; (4), the Magdalen makes a second visit to the tomb, when she brings Peter and John, and it is after they retire that she sees the vision of two angels in white sitting in the tomb,—a trajection of the earlier incident given by (1), (2), and (3). They ask her why she weeps; she repeats her loss, and before receiving an answer turns and sees, as she supposes, the gardener; is asked the same question again, and gives the same reply. Jesus announces himself, declines the attempt of Mary to touch him, and sends a message to "his brethren" of his approaching ascension. Then we find this first positive reappearance of Jesus ascribed to the occasion of the visit of Mary Magdalen and the other Mary (1), who, passing from the interview with the angels with fear and great joy, are greeted by him, and they actually embrace his feet, and he sends by them to his brethren the very same message they have just received from the angels, to proceed to rendezvous in Galilee. Here, therefore, as in (4), we find that what is given in one form as an interview with angels is repeated in another as an interview with Jesus; just as previously the interview with informants, who are bluntly a young man or two men, takes form as an interview with angels.

There is no impossibility in the nature of things that the first belief in the resurrection may have taken the most distinct and detailed embellishments at once; but if we arrange the contradictory tales in order of simplicity, we have this sequence.

The women first report the disappearance of the body; then this becomes a hearsay from a youth that Christ has risen from the dead; and then, by easy transition, a revelation to the same effect from angels; then a vision, not of angels, but of Jesus himself, though still not tangible; then a manifestation of Jesus, not only visible and audible, but embraced; and lastly, he appears to disciples themselves, suggesting and submitting to the philosophical test of handling, of eating and drinking, and that certified aliments. Earthquake, lightning, etc., the prostrate guard, the amazed authorities,—all these heightening effects complete the tableau with a strange intermixture of the artistic invention that supplies and bodies forth the form of things unknown, and the lame ingenuity of an attorney priming very incompetent witnesses in order to stop holes, as they declare themselves, in a case that no ingenuity or hard or easy swearing will cause to hold together.

That it was after Christianity had made much Gentile

progress that the Gospel materials took their present form, might be securely inferred from the characteristics of the story of the resurrection and its incidents, which, as they tell it, is under far heavier obligations to the stock details of heathen disappearances and reappearances than to anything we find in the fund of Jewish associations. In proof of this, I might transcribe Plutarch on the aphanism and deification of Romulus, with its parallels and precedents. He refers to more examples than he thinks it necessary to relate,—such is the general resemblance of the growth,—and finishes with some remarks on deification, so pointed, that while their immediate application is to the worship of the Roman emperors or Antinous, it seems strange if they were not also intended to glance at the rapidly spreading superstition of a new sect of religionists.

The founder of Rome was said to have vanished from earth in the midst of splendours and convulsions as lavishly expended as we find them in Matthew,—the darkened sun, horrible thunders, boisterous winds, and flashing lightning. To the senators is assigned the part of calming and dismissing the anxiously searching people, with the injunction to worship their king thereafter, as snatched up by the gods. Minds, however, were still unsettled, till a witness of approved honesty and dignity supplied detailed evidence of the fact, and a verbal message. Julius Proculus, like the travellers to Emmaus, met Romulus on the way, glorified in person, and in white and shining armour, in fact transfigured; and between the credit of the man and some celestial motion or divine inspiration, the tale was then believed.

In like manner the Greeks had a story, how Aristeas died, and how his body disappeared, and how some who came from the country related that they had met him since, pursuing his way to Crotona. The body of Cleomedes, styled, by the Pythia, last of the demigods, vanished as marvellously; on which and on the like resurrections of the body and ascensions, Plutarch has some remarkable enunciations.

The disciples, assembled, it is said, by appointment on a mountain in Galilee, received from the risen Jesus this declaration and commission: "Behold, supreme power is given to me in heaven and on earth; go, then, and inform all nations, baptizing them in the name of the Father, the Son, and the Holy Spirit, teaching to observe all things whatsoever I have enjoined to you; and behold, I will be with you to the conclusion of the age (epoch); Amen." (Matt. xxviii. 16, 20.)

Such was the reputed charter of the Church that struck for control of general humanity; it is strangely parallel in purport, and even in terms, to that which Roman legend, as we find it in Livy and Plutarch, professed to rest upon for title to universal dominion. "It hath seemed good to the Gods that we should be away from them and sojourn a certain time among men, and then, having founded a city destined for the greatest sway and glory, to dwell again in heaven. But be of good cheer, and tell the Romans, that by exercise of sobriety of mind, along with valour, they will attain the greatest pitch of human power; as to me, I will be to you the gracious divinity Quirinus."

Whatever may be the relative dates at which the two records were written down, I have no doubt that they are interdependent by common relation to common sources. The reflections of Plutarch are not without pertinence to both. "On no account, therefore, does it become us to dispatch the mortal bodies of good men along with themselves up to heaven, but to consider that their virtues and their souls, by course of nature and divine justice, proceed from men to heroes, from heroes to demigods (δαίμονες), and then from demigods, in virtue of a certain sacramental refinement and sanctification, and escape from mortality and its affections, become associated with the Gods, not by civil enactment, but in verity and of consistent reason, as attaining to the most excellent and happiest perfection."

There is a fine poetic irony in the Roman legend, whoever may have been the inventor; it is told with circumstance sufficient to captivate the "brute folk," the gaping multitude, and at the same time suggests a political and naturalistic explanation for the men of the world, who would reject a miracle. So Homer sings how Jove sent Sleep and Death to carry the body of Sarpedon to Lycia,—the body which, he has already hinted, had become unrecognizable, disfigured by the turmoil of the fight for its possession, and about which therefore a marvellous tale might be told, without fear of contradiction.

The belief in the apparition and then in the actual bodily resurrection of Jesus commenced, according to the narrative, with the women of his society, but among the Apostles and disciples was first accepted and insisted on by Peter. Peter it is who divines the compatibility of all that was essential in the mission of Jesus with the fact of his violent death, and he is presented to us as coming forward to reinforce the movement, to propound a theory of its significance in the new aspect, well backed up with harmonizing prophecy, and to reorganize administration by electing an Apostle to succeed the traitor. In the first instance, strict Judaism and close attendance at the Temple are in accordance with the instant hope for the re-establishment of the kingdom of Israel by the descendant of David; but larger ideas are present, at least in germ,—the grand morals overruling the asceticism of John; a spirit of genial self-sacrifice vivifying the Ebionitish professional poverty in community of goods or no goods; enthusiasm, contagious enthusiasm, evincing itself mentally, in sudden capacity of emancipation from cramping prejudice; and in such astounding bodily manifestations as it were too much to expect should not be mistaken for miracles.

There was a lull of harmony in the company at the first revival; but the ruling mind of Jesus being withdrawn, the idiosyncrasies of the members of the alliance, and their very prepossessions anterior to his influence, soon began to assert themselves.

In this place it is enough to epitomize the sequel. The expanding sect broke through its Jewish limitations, and struggled to shuffle off the shackles of ceremonialism. James and the Church at Jerusalem, in opposition to the tendencies of Peter, strove to retain or re-fasten them. Peter, obeying his own instincts, is zealously progressive when alone with the Gentile Church at Antioch; he is cowed, and vacillates, on arrival of rigorists from James; recovers himself, and breaks boldly with tradition in the Council at Jerusalem. But the mischief was done; even in the Gentile

Church there was a section glad to have Apostolic sanction to quote in favour of authority and ceremony; and so it has been from that day to this, that Peter, the one Apostle who spoke out boldly and without qualification for the emancipation of the mind, has been seized on as the representative of all that confines and crushes it, and finds himself the elected patron saint and protector of the most corrupting and deadening ceremonialism.

CHAPTER III.

THE MIRACLE AT THE BEAUTIFUL GATE.

I. JERUSALEM AND THE TEMPLE.—II. THE CARTOON OF THE MIRACLE AT THE BEAUTIFUL GATE.—III. THE FIRST EXPANSION OF THE GOSPEL IDEA.

I. JERUSALEM AND THE TEMPLE.

THERE is considerable difficulty in reconciling all the notices given by Josephus of the dimensions and relative positions of the boundaries of the Temple and its dependencies. The examination of the site, as it exists at present, has removed some uncertainties, but has introduced, at least, as many more; and a far completer survey and study must be waited for before the historian can be fully and accurately interpreted. Still, much of the difficulty applies to mere matters of detail; and a description, confined to general terms that may be relied on, need not, after all, be too indefinite to have its use and interest.

The Jerusalem of the time of Jesus Christ, together with its suburbs and the Temple, occupied four hills, which differed in size, height, and form, and were separated by valleys of various declivity and depth. The entire group formed a sort of hilly promontory, between a pair of converging valleys and divided by a third intermediate, which all trended southward. On the east, south, and western sides, the site had such deep escarpment as to render fortification easy and effectual. The valley of Gihon lay between the city and eminences westward, and turned in an easterly direction, as the valley Hinnom, till it joined the valley Kedron, which bounded the city to the east and running north and south, separated the mount and platform of the Temple and Mount Bezetha, together with the newer northern city, from the Mount of Olives. High table-ground to the north-east, Scopus, afforded a view clear over the city to the country beyond and the sea on the horizon.

The original site of the city of David, called by Josephus the upper city, or upper agora, was on the hill to the south-west of the group, the highest and steepest of all, and most fitted for the stronghold of an early community. This, no doubt, was Mount Zion, though Josephus never applies, indeed, never even uses the name. Its northern boundary was a straight line of declivity, running east and west above the valley that separated it from the lower city—the Acra of the Asmonæan princes. The same valley branched southwards, into a depression dividing Mount Zion from the mount and platform of the Temple, Mount Moriah, to the east.

In the time of Jesus Christ, the walls of the mount of the Temple formed part of the exterior fortified circuit of the city to the north as well as eastward. An artificial trench, or cutting, separated the north line of wall of Moriah from the district or suburb of the city beyond; this was Bezetha, which received its proper loop of fortification, some fourteen years later, from King Agrippa.

The hill on which the Temple was built was originally a rocky steep, with a gradual rise from the eastern part of the city towards the crown or summit, but, at first, scarcely affording area sufficient for the holy house and altar. Josephus ascribes to Solomon very important commencements of substructures and embankments to extend the platform, especially towards the east; on this side, he says, he founded a single portico, while on the other sides the holy house stood free; this was the Solomon's porch of the New Testament.

The Asmonæan princes reduced the height of Acra, and, at the same time, filled up much of the valley, in order to unite the Temple with the city, to improve the access. But, apart from intermediate advances, it was Herod the Great who made the most extensive changes. Besides giving addition to the height of, at least, a portion of the platform, he extended the peribolus northwards, and doubled the enclosed area. He rebuilt the Temple, completed its quadrangle of enclosing porticos on most magnificent scale, and connected all with his system of fortifications. Still there was something left to be done by Herod Agrippa in the time of Nero; what, does not very clearly appear, except that it was based upon reparation of Solomon's eastern portico.

It was in the eighteenth year of his reign that Herod the Great had taken measures for rebuilding the Temple on a scheme of general magnificence, as well as of enhanced area and elevation. In deference to popular jealousies and apprehensions, he prepared the materials for the new structure entirely before meddling with the old, and provided a great store of priestly garb for the large proportion of labourers, who of necessity must be

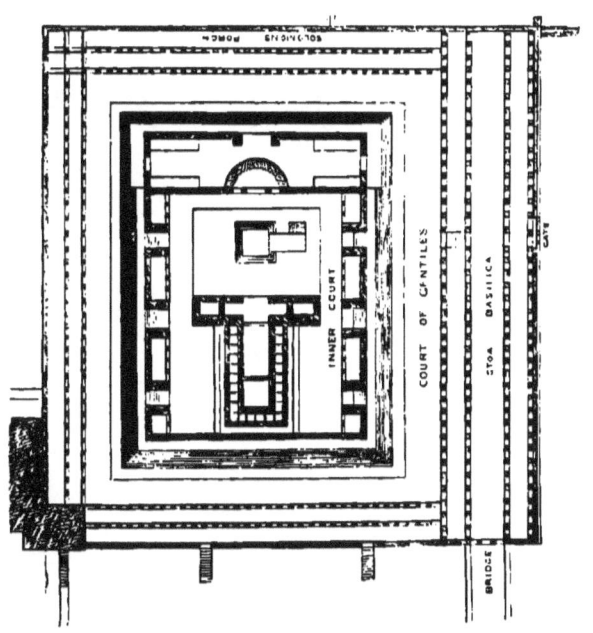

PLAN OF THE TEMPLE AT JERUSALEM AS REBUILT BY HEROD.

From Fergusson's 'Modern Architecture.'

priests, and who were instructed for the occasion in the various requisite handicrafts. The naos was completed in eighteen months, and within eight years the chief part of the porticos and the peribolus.

The width of the platform, east and west at the southern extremity, "from declivity to declivity," was a stadium; the other measurements that are given complete an area of a double stadium of six stadia circuit, which is much less than is shown by the existing site. There is some error or ambiguity in the description or its interpretation, which, however, it is not worth our present while to delay by investigating. The Temple proper, with its courts, which Josephus calls the hypæthral temple, and the surrounding porticos, was a stadium square. It may have had various exterior dependencies; and at the north-west angle of the platform stood the great fortification of the tower Antonia, so named by Herod after his benefactor, the triumvir. This was an extension of an Asmonæan work, originated, no doubt, as it was continued, as a political security over the head-quarters of religious and sacerdotal agitation. In general form it was a square tower, with secondary towers at the angles. It was raised upon a precipitous rock, revetted carefully at the base, to render ascent or descent equally impossible. The heights given by Josephus are manifestly exaggerated, and not worth quoting. It was, of course, in military communication with the walls and with the palace on Zion, in what exact way we need not stay to inquire; and, besides full accommodation for a garrison, it contained, says Josephus, all the appliances of luxurious life,—in multifariousness a city, in magnificence a palace.

The garrison had direct access from Antonia to the northern and western porticos of the Temple.

Besides this access, the grand peribolus of the Temple had five proper entrances—one in the middle of the south side, and four on the west. Of these one led to the king's palace, across the contracted *pharanx*, or ravine,—this was probably the most southerly; two to the suburb, *proasteion*; and the last to "the other city" (query Acra?), by a descent of many steps, with corresponding ascent opposite.

The southern portico of the Temple—the stoa basilica—was especially magnificent; and it is presumable that this was in direct connection with the western gate that led to the palace. With every deduction made for the extravagance of the describer, it must have been a sumptuous, and may easily have been a noble work—" a work," as he calls it, "among the most memorable of all beneath the sun."

It consisted of three avenues, formed by four rows of columns, of which one was engaged in the wall, doubtless the southern external peribolus wall that skirted the edge of the precipice. One hundred and sixty-two Corinthian columns, twenty-seven feet high, were so disposed that the side avenues were thirty feet wide, and the central nave forty-five feet, or as wide again. This middle avenue, or nave, was also of superior loftiness, enhanced, as I read the description, by a frontal wall surmounting the epistylia and having engaged columns.

The ceilings were formed by systems of lacunaria, exquisitely elaborated with cedar beams.

The agreement with the early Christian basilica, that we are familiar with at Ravenna and Rome, is salient on inspection. In fact, the title 'stoa basilica,' or Portico of the King, does not in itself imply any reference to the regality of Herod, or to communication with the palace. It is a generic title, derived from the celebrated stoa of the Archon Basileus at Athens; and was transferred again, at a later date, to the grand structures of Trajan and Maxentius; and thence it has been continued to the Christian churches, which acquired like form and design by inheritance or imitation.

It is rather strange that Josephus omits particular mention of this stoa in his description of the Temple, in his 'Jewish War,' but expatiates upon it in his later work, the 'Jewish Antiquities.'

The east, west, and north sides of the quadrangle had also their porticos, with double rows of columns; that on the east, opposite to the chief entrance to the Temple, being Solomon's Porch, as we have seen.

The dimensions, the heights especially, that Josephus gave of a structure that was utterly in ruins when he wrote, were intended by him to be wondered at, not to be criticized.

Within the square enclosure, which was thus entered by one door through the stoa basilica, and by four from the western side, was another very strong enclosure; the interval between the two was the Lower Temple, and still more specifically, the Court of the Gentiles, with its double porticos of white marble columns, ceiled with lacunaria of cedar, and having its hypæthral portion paved with various-coloured marbles. The enrichments of paintings and statuary were alone wanting, out of deference to religious objections.

The circuit of these porticos, then, is given as " six

stadia, Antonia being included;" make of this statement what we may. Into this court both Greek and Roman were admissible; but on the understanding, I apprehend, that they were σεβομένοι—"the devout men" of Acts, the class of whom we find such numerous traces,—the converts,—proselytes made by the zealous proselytizing Jews, who are a wonder and a by-word with Horace, and whom we find in Josephus eagerly snatching a proselyte, especially the rich or powerful, as worth having, even though remaining uncircumcised; while others, less indulgent, urge or insist on the obnoxious rite. To this court, thus far, the Gentile proselyte was admitted as a worshipper, after what purifications, professions, or sacrifices, or contributions, who shall say? for, doubtless, admission here as well as elsewhere had its limitations. "Devout women" were probably also admitted, as this class, undebarred by the rite, were numerous and important.

The second ἱερὸν within this court, was surrounded by a marble enclosure of three cubits high, elegantly wrought. Here columns equally spaced displayed in Greek and Latin the law of purity (ἁγνεία), forbidding any alien in race to present himself in the Holy place, or sanctuary (ἅγιον), for so the second *hieron* was styled.

The ascent to it from the first *hieron* was by fourteen steps (apparently within the enclosure just mentioned); it was four-square above, and surrounded by its proper wall, and by a terrace of ten cubits breadth between the wall and the edge of the steps.

The steps, and probably the terrace also, only embraced the north, east, and south sides, not the western, on which the wall of the sanctuary had no portals.

This we learn from a notice, that in an attack on the sanctuary, engines could be advanced towards the west wall, because there were there no steps.

The expression just quoted, that the sanctuary was four-square (τετράγωνον) *above*, may therefore indicate the distinction that, measured along its proper wall, it was a true square, not merely quadrangular; while below, whether about the marble enclosure or the lowest step, it was, from omission of the steps and terrace westward, somewhat shorter from east to west than from north to south (2 cubits = 3 feet).

I assume that the area of the second *hieron* was a true square, answering to the general circuit exterior to the porticos. Upon this area the platform of the sanctuary may naturally be moved westward, to the extent of the joint breadth of the omitted steps and terrace; and this will agree with other notices that the Temple lay towards the west side of the area, and will give importance to the grand eastern entrance, by allowing a wider court in front of it.

The external height of the wall, including the steps, so I read my author, was forty cubits; but the internal, only twenty-five. The difference of fifteen cubits is left to be made out by the fourteen steps already mentioned, and then by five more steps which led up from the platform, or terrace, to the entrances. Even so, the full difference is not accounted for; and the suspicion is awakened, has Josephus substituted cubits for feet in the heights throughout?

The wall of the sanctuary, which had no entrance on the west, had four portals on the north and four on the south. A single grand portal on the east gave admission first into the court of the women, which was also entered by the north-east and south-east doors; this court was formed by a wall of division parallel to the east front, and pierced with a central portal, which, however, was not accessible to the women.

Nine of the gates, their folding-doors, jambs, and imposts, were sheeted with gold and silver. Within, beyond the entrance, there were single porticos, as splendid as those of the outer court, though smaller. The portals are given as thirty cubits in height by fifteen. Within, the space widened out, and, between the gates pairs of columns, if not more properly piers of twelve cubits circumference, supported tower-like chambers more than forty cubits high. These appear to have been above the exhedræ of the porticos; they remind of the pylons of an Egyptian temple; and it was against one of these structures, between two of the northern portals, that we read of Titus directing his engines when he assaulted the sanctuary.

The inner eastern portal, directly opposite the naos, was much larger than those of north and south, being, we are told, fifty cubits high, with doors of forty cubits, and was much more lavishly enriched with silver and gold.

Fifteen steps, says Josephus, led from the wall of partition of the women to the greater gate, being much smaller—less steep, I apprehend, as well as probably narrower in tread—than the five steps at the other entrances. The form of expression used seems to imply that these also were within the line of the dividing wall.

The outer eastern portal was of Corinthian brass, but

far exceeding in dignity the gold and silver enrichments of all the others. As the fifteen steps just adverted to are indicated as ranging with the five steps of the flank portals, it follows that the area of the women's court, from which they started, was on a level with the terrace or platform around the hagion. Fergusson makes it lower—with what authority?

The court of the women, says Josephus, was open for the worship of women, as well those who were natives of Judæa as those from without, being of Jewish race. The mention that both classes were equally participant in the privilege, indicates that there was such a claim of superiority on the part of the native Jewess, that it might not be taken for granted. Even so, their admission was contingent upon being free from ceremonial impurity; and the admission of the Jew also, whether priest or lay, into the inner αὐλή, was upon the same condition. I think this inner "aulé" must be held to comprise the entire *hagion*, including the women's court; and it is improbable that any Jew, ceremonially unclean, was admitted through the great eastern portal into the court assigned to the duly purified females. As to the afflicted with leprosy and fluxes, they were excluded, not only from the Temple, but from the city itself. This is the testimony of Josephus. How is it to be reconciled with the averment of the Rabbins respecting places for the leprous within this court?

In the contest of the factions anterior to the siege, the zealots holding the Temple are driven from the outer court by Ananias and the multitude; but the high-priest hesitates to attempt to force the sacred portals of the inner court from other considerations, besides the advantage of the defenders from above. In fact, he held it unlawful, even should he have the better of the conflict, to introduce the multitude, which had not been previously purified. (Bell. Jud., iv. 312.)

In this gate, which, from its material, Josephus calls the Corinthian gate of the Temple, we must recognize the Beautiful Gate of the Acts of the Apostles. It faced the porch of Solomon; it is the brazen gate of the inner *hieron*, fronting the rising sun, before which the men of power of Jerusalem, and most distinguished Pharisees, in concert with the high-priests, convoked the people, and endeavoured, by arguments, precedents, and warnings, to divert them from that last tightening of restrictive exclusiveness that committed them to revolt, to ruin. This was on the occasion when, after King Agrippa had soothed popular agitation for a time, it again broke loose, and on the persuasion of Eleazar, son of Ananias, the high-priest, a very bold youth, it was determined to reject thereafter both gifts and sacrifices offered on the part of aliens. The resolution was especially aimed against the sacrifice which was accustomed to be made on the part of the Roman emperor, and for the safety of the empire. "This," says Josephus, "was the true beginning of our war against the Romans, for it was a rejection of the sacrifice of Cæsar in their favour." Vain it was to urge, by appeal to surrounding monuments (Ant. xv. 11, 3), that from all time it had been admitted to accept gifts for the Temple, and adorn it with dedications from aliens; and vain to denounce, on principles of common humanity, the anti-social resolution, that with the Jews alone among all people, a foreigner should not be admissible on any terms whatever to contribute to sacrifice, or participate in worship. Such exclusion, it was urged, would be revolting inhumanity, if directed against an individual; what must be the consequence of the insult to the Roman people and the Roman emperor?

Thus it was that the crisis of Jewish history and polity was declared on the steps of the beautiful Corinthian entrance of the inner temple, at the verge of the partition-wall of the Court of Israel, and the Court of the Gentiles. The fatal victory for the time remained with the bigots. Here they repudiated with brave self-consistency the last slender admission of the common relation of aliens from Jewish blood to a common God; inaccessible to sympathy, it is true, but at the same time superior to death and danger. Unallured by bait of peace and profitableness, they turned away fanatically enough, but with more dignity than their race has always been equal to, from the proffered price of religious privilege, the authorized spoil of the Egyptian.

Josephus presents us with three well-defined forms of the relation of Judaism to the devotional sympathies of the alien, in the eager proselytizer, who, still strictly Jewish, will relax his rigour for the sake of a convert, though not for his own sake; the zealot, who also will compass sea and land to gain a convert, if he may only subject him to a common ceremonial slavery; the fanatic, who repudiates the alien on any terms. The virulence of the fanatic was largely due to fear and jealousy of the expansive tendency of the proselytizers, feelings in themselves well founded enough The world was ripe for a revulsion in its forms of religious belief, and that, moreover, in the direction of unity. The spirit

H

which, in our own day, we have seen operative politically, to combine and knit and centralize scattered national kinships, was then abroad in the religious, and even the superstitious conditions of the Roman world. There were many causes that rendered Judaism the most promising stock for the new graft, but Judaic egotism might well be alarmed at the very spread of its influence; the exclusive religion had mistrust of being overwhelmed and lost in its own conquests; and the proffered empire, repudiated by the central stock of the great monotheistic race, was snatched by an aspirant sect, the heir of a majestic enthusiasm, which had the vigour, though not without painful struggle, to disengage itself from its original attachments, appropriated from Judaism every element conducive to universal influence, and hesitated at no modification of its details in order to secure for common humanity a basis of common worship.

Of one important epoch in this history we shall find a typical expression in the subject of the Cartoon of the Beautiful Gate of the Temple, when in good time, as we hope to do, we arrive at its consideration.

For the Jewish recusants,—there on the very spot where the risk was accepted, the forfeiture was demanded and paid; there, where the retribution was challenged, it fell, and alien legionaries were lighted through the holy precinct to a tumult of slaughter, by the flames of the sanctuary.

But to resume. Other ceremonial restrictions await us as we proceed. The Temple itself (ὁ ναὸς—τὸ ἅγιον ἱερόν) lay in the middle (Bell. Jud. v. 5, 4) of the Court of Israel, with an ascent to it of twelve steps.

The naos and the altar in front of it were encompassed by a partition, about a cubit in height, of fine and elegantly-worked marble, to separate the priests from the general people. I should infer that this fence (γείσιον) was external to the steps, just as we have seen that the fence ran round the inner hieron externally to the steps that led up from the level of the Court of the Gentiles.

Priests who were ceremonially unclean were excluded, no less than the lay in like condition, from the inner αὐλή, which I understand to include the Court of the Women. All, however, of the stock of the priests were, if clean, admissible within the priests' partition; but those who were disqualified for the ministry by a defect of body, lameness, deformity, mutilation, could only enter dressed in private clothes. The priests without personal blemish alone officiated at the altar, and wore the sacred costume of fine linen.

The high-priest officiated only on Sabbaths, new moons, and festivals, and arrayed in splendid and special garb. A still more gorgeous sacred costume was assumed by him on one day once a year, a general fast-day of the nation, when he entered the very apartment of the God of Israel,—the Holy of Holies.

The altar in front of the Temple was fifteen cubits high, upon a square plan of fifty cubits by fifty, and was formed and fashioned with no aid from iron, and untouched by iron tool at any time. At the upper angles it had hornlike projections, and the ascent to it was by a gentle inclined plane from the south; in effect, therefore, it was a large elevated platform rather than an altar such as the term usually implies.

How far it was placed in advance of the Temple is not stated. The Temple itself was, on its frontispiece (πρόσωπον), one hundred cubits high and broad, an erect square, for anything that appears to the contrary,—the question being open whether the height given may not measure merely up to the central apex of a pediment, besides the general reservation as to the trustworthiness of the heights.

At the back of this frontispiece, which was twenty cubits in depth, the Temple was narrower by forty cubits, the joint width of the shoulderlike projections of the front. The width of the temple behind was thus contracted to sixty cubits.

The first entrance was twenty-five cubits wide and seventy high, and had no valves; the whole front was resplendent with gold; and through this grand portal the entire first chamber, or division, of the interior was visible, with all the enrichments of the second portal— the proper doorway of the inner temple.

Josephus proceeds to say, that while the inner temple had a double story, this "first *œcus*" was carried up the full height of ninety cubits, which would leave ten cubits for the roof: it was fifty cubits wide and twenty deep. The expressions employed would rather favour transposing the two last dimensions, but the dimension of twenty cubits would not admit the door which is afterwards described. To the right and left of this porch therefore there remain twenty-five cubits to make up the full one hundred of the width, and leaving ample space for apartments after deduction for the thicknesses of exterior and interior walls. In 'Antiquities' (xv. 11, 3) he states that the Temple was built of blocks of white marble twenty-five cubits long, twelve broad, eight high; but it may be doubted whether he is not here referring, in rather a general way, to the largest stones employed in any part whatever, of the temple or the substructions. In Bell. Jud. v. 5, 6, he gives for some of the stones, 45 : 5 : 6 cubits.

The second portal was sixteen cubits wide and fifty-five high. It was covered with gold, as was also the entire face of the wall; about it and above it, under the cornice or coping (Antiq. xv. 11, 3), was extended a golden vine, with grapes depending in bunches the size of a man. (Bell. Jud., v. 4.)

I can only refer here to my essay on the Moses of Michael Angelo for illustration of the symbolical connection which, from ages long anterior to Tacitus, and down at least as late as the great Florentine, was recognized between the lawgiver of the Jews, and Bacchus, the victor of Asia.

In the Old Testament, Israel is typified by the poetic fervour of the prophets, as a vine; and in the New, we trace the metaphorical associations of both the vine and the door, in the parables and tropes of the discourses of Jesus.

It appears to be implied that this door had valves ($\theta\acute{\upsilon}\rho\alpha\varsigma$), but there was also extended before them a rich Babylonian curtain, wrought with various colours and materials, in which Josephus is fain to detect a symbolical reference to earth, air, fire, and water. More definite is his notice in the 'Antiquities' that the embroidery represented flowers and columns, and in the 'War,' that it set forth the general theory of the heavens, but without introducing the zodiac,—an offence from its representation of animals.

On passing through the door, "the ground-floor portion of the naos" was arrived at,—an expression to be noted, as in accordance with the previous reference to an upper story, which Josephus fails to describe specifically.

The height of this portion is given as sixty cubits, the length the same, and the breadth twenty.

The joint projection of the "shoulders" of the frontispiece is forty cubits, and this, added to twenty, the breadth of the naos behind, leaves a breadth of twenty cubits intermediate on either side to be accounted for, —in what manner we shall see.

The length of sixty cubits was, however, divided unequally between two apartments,—the first of forty cubits, and the second, the most remote from the entrance, the very adytum, the Holy of Holies,—twenty cubits.

The proportions of the first apartment (20 : 40 : 60) would thus be 1 : 2 : 3, and those of the Holy of Holies, of which the absolute height for anything that appears was the same, would be a triple cube,—a pile of three cubes.

Within the first apartment were the world-renowned candelabrum, the table, and the altar of incense: the candelabrum, with its seven lights, answering to the planets; the table, with the twelve loaves, for the zodiacal division of the year; the altar, for those thirteen kinds of incense derived from sea and land, the habitable and desert, which signified on warranty of Josephus, that all things are of God, and for God.

The last division was again divided off by a curtain; whether by doors also, as in the other case, is not said.

Within it, according to our present authority, there was nothing; nothing is heard either of Ark of the Covenant or copy of the law; it was inaccessible, not to be violated, not to be looked on—the Holy of Holies (ἅγιον ἁγίου).

Something is said by the Rabbins of a low stone base within (Winer, p. 585, note 5)—something of their wonderful tales respecting it. The notice at least affords another chance for theorizing respecting the place of the rock in the Mosque of Omar.

The description proceeds:—" About the flanks of the lower naos were numerous œci of three stories, and on either side there were entrances to them from the gate (no doubt from the grand porch of the front); but the upper-story part of the naos (ὑπερῷον), had not a continuation of these œci, and in so far was more contracted. It was loftier, to the extent of forty cubits, and narrower than the part below; and this height, added to the sixty cubits of the ground-floor portion, makes up the full height, one hundred cubits."

It was by the addition of these *œci* to the flanks of the naos that the projection of the "shoulders" of the porch was reduced as we have seen. The doors into them from the porch must, it would seem, have been on the right and left of the grand doorway with the golden vine; there was space to the right and left of this of fifteen cubits, whereas their plan only overlaps the end divisions of the porch by five cubits.

The statement that these constructions were applied to the flanks of the naos, appears to preclude the continuation of them round the back of the Temple, and yet it seems improbable that the wall of the Holy of Holies was made an outer wall. Taking the description, however, as it stands, it will be found that the plan of the sanctuary and the œci, excluding the porch, forms a square; and as their height is equal, and equal to the side of this square, they together form a cube.

This excludes also the upper story of the naos, to which Josephus gives a height of forty feet, by breadth twenty, and length sixty,—exactly the same proportions and dimensions as the first division of the naos, only that the dimensions of the length there is here assigned to height.

In the porch, ten cubits are given to the roof; if we assume the same for these upper chambers we have a remainder of fifteen cubits; but here Josephus gives us no help.

He also omits to say anything of the purpose of the side-rooms. Conjecture is free, and I ask a bold question.

Can it be possible that all Jews except the priests were always excluded from a near view of the interior of the Temple, with its golden furniture and splendid hangings? It would be little enough that they could see of them from their proper court, twelve steps below the level of the naos platform, and with the huge altar interposing between the most direct point of view. Judas, no priest, is spoken of as casting down the thirty pieces of silver in the porch of the Temple. Are we not to understand the entrance-porch of the naos, not one of the external porticos?

Is it possible, therefore, that at certain times at least, and under some conditions, the porch was more generally accessible, and that Jews other than the priests

might then pass through the side-doors, and, proceeding to the several stories of the attached structures, look into the naos from internal openings of the upper rooms?

There is, however, a probability that these chambers were used, to some extent at least, as treasuries,—the γαζοφυλάκια mentioned Bell. Jud. v. 5, 2; vi. 5, 2,—in the same manner as we find treasuries established at Delos, Delphi, and wherever wealth could count on the protection of religious awe. Solomon's temple had such a system of enveloping chambers, and certainly not affording inlook to the interior of it.

Rabbinical authority is cited (Winer, 585) for the continuation of chambers at the back of the Temple. Here we are afloat upon conjecture, and I am almost inclined to guess that the axis of the Temple, east and west, was made up to 100 cubits, equal to the breadth of the front—a point assumed by Winer, but for which I do not find the authority—by prolonging the plan and elevation of the nave, so to speak, to the extent of twenty cubits westward. Apart from this, however, the full 100 cubits might be easily made up by taking some of the dimensions as truly internal, and exclusive, not only of exterior walls, but even of walls of partition. The thickness of all these was certainly—thus much is indicated by the dimensions of the stones that are given —to be measured in cubits.

The Temple of Jerusalem, with its surrounding courts and quadrangular belt of porticos, has much resemblance to the design of the mosques of the Mahometans, their kindred in blood and religion. So, again, the square frontispiece of the Temple, with its mighty open porch flanked by lateral apartments, seems not unrelated to the façades of later Eastern architecture.

"Now the outward aspect of the Temple in front wanted nothing that was likely to surprise either men's minds or their eyes, for it was covered all over with plates of gold of great weight, and at the first rising of the sun reflected back a very fiery splendour, and caused those who made an effort to look upon it to turn away their eyes, just as they would have done at the sun's own rays. To strangers, when they were at a distance, this Temple appeared like a mountain covered with snow; for as to those parts of it that were not gilt, they were exceedingly white. On its top it had spikes with sharp points, to prevent any pollution from birds settling on it." (Bell. Jud., v. 5, 6.)

In the final conflagration of the Temple, some of the priests, who had mounted on the roof, plucked up these spikes with their lead setting, and hurled them on the Roman soldiers below. It availed little; the fire gained upon them, and they retreated to the top of the wall, which was eight cubits broad: which wall? what wall? we ask in vain. Here, however, wherever it might be, they were safe for a time, till famine obliged them to surrender, and they were passed on to death.

To Josephus I refer for the vivid picture of the storming of the Temple, the slaughter of its defenders, and the destruction, by fire and sword, of the multitude of all ages, sexes, and conditions, who to the last believed and expected that the God of Israel, whose peculiar dwelling was in the holy house, would at last interpose supernaturally for the deliverance of his temple and his people.

How few words suffice for the conclusion!

"And now the Romans, upon the flight of the seditious into the city, and upon the burning of the holy house itself, and of all the buildings round about it, brought their ensigns to the Temple, and set them over against its eastern gate, and there did they offer sacrifices to them, and there did they make Titus, Imperator, with the greatest acclamations of joy."

Of the two Jewish leaders, Simon, who had held the city, was slaughtered like Pontius or Vercingetorix, as part of the show of the triumph of his victor,—brutal remainder of the era of human sacrifices. John, the leader of the zealots, the especially fanatical party, had his life spared, and was kept in perpetual imprisonment. I recognize here again the tradition of policy from the earlier age of Rome, when, on the suppression of the Bacchanalia, so many votaries were so eagerly dispatched, but the chief of the sect was retained a prisoner for life, with even peculiar care for the preservation of his life. This policy was probably inspired by the conviction that to destroy an admitted religious chief who was in their power, would be but to make the dangerous distinction vacant for a free successor.

II. THE MIRACLE AT THE BEAUTIFUL GATE OF THE TEMPLE.

The narrative in Acts, which supplies the subject of the third Cartoon, is in these terms:—" Now Peter and John went up together to the Temple at the hour of prayer, the ninth hour (3 P.M.). And a certain man, lame from his mother's womb, was being carried along, whom they placed daily at the gate of the Temple called

'The Beautiful,' to ask alms of those entering into the Temple; who seeing Peter and John, as they were about to go into the Temple, asked to receive alms. And Peter, looking at him fixedly, together with John, said, 'Look on us.' And he gave heed to them, expecting to receive somewhat from them. And Peter said, 'Silver and gold have I none; but what I have that give I unto thee: In the name of Jesus Christ the Nazarite get up and walk.' And, taking him by the right hand, he raised him up; and immediately his feet and ankles were strengthened, and, springing up, he stood and walked and entered with them into the Temple, walking, and leaping, and praising God. And all the people saw him, and they recognized him as the man that used to sit for alms at the Beautiful Gate of the Temple; and they were filled with wonder and amazement at what had happened to him. And as the lame man that was healed detained Peter and John, all the people ran together unto them at the porch called Solomon's, greatly wondering."

We have no difficulty in identifying the Beautiful Gate as that bronze portal on the east of the Temple, and facing the portico of Solomon, which led from the Court of the Gentiles, through the Court of the Women, to the Upper Temple, the Court of Israel,—the entrance-gate which Josephus describes, as we have seen, as far exceeding in embellishment even those others which were overlaid with the precious metals.

There are manifest indications that Rafael did not design the architecture of his composition without reference, directly or indirectly, to the recorded plan and details of the place. We easily recognize the suggestions of the historic notices, though with no intrusive affectation of archæological precision. In the ranges of columns four deep, we have a detail adapted from the stoa basilica; and the subjects of vintage with which these columns are encircled are very fairly derived from the admission of a symbolical golden vine, branching around the golden portal of the very sanctuary itself. The variegated marble of the pavement is to the same purpose, and from the same source. For the rest, the architecture is treated with freedom enough. It is in parallel perspective, and the plinths of the bases of the nearest columns are close up to the base line of the picture. The painter has taken two of these columns in such a way as to frame in his principal and central group, and to give a vista directly down the four pairs of columns to a doorway indicated at the back, where a lamp burning the daylight, indicates a sacred precinct. To the right is another parallel range of columns in the same direction, and by all architectural analogy the lateral spacing of these should be the same. Regularity here, however, would have carried the nearest just beyond the limit of the picture; this evidently was thought undesirable, and nothing remained but either to modify the regular spacing, by bringing the central columns nearer together, which would have contracted the space for the chief group, or to take a liberty, and leave the responsibility to be divided between the architecture and the perspective, and this was the course adopted.

The most natural interpretation of the architecture is, that Peter and John are standing between the two columns, by the angle of a tetrastyle portico, of which each front column was the first of a rank of four. This inference presents itself from the appearance to the left of rows of fourfold columns, at right angles to the plane of the picture, and most naturally appearing as the counterpart of the front. But, besides the anomaly of the widely-spaced intercolumn, the doorway and lamp seem to imply a central vista, in which case we miss a row of columns that should have stood on the left. An old engraver introduces a base in position here, but Rafael had good reason for leaving them out. The pictorial result is most happy. The chief group is in an architectural frame, which aptly expresses the scene at the decorated entrance to the Temple. The columnar magnificence of Herod's porticos is expressed in the files of columns in perspective, with fanciful capitals and enriched shafts. The termination of the colonnade to the left gives an openness, that relieves the scene from oppressive confinement; while a fresh breeze seems to blow in from the landscape-glimpse of the Mount of Olives in the distance. On the right hand, the more contracted columniation, by whatever licence it is obtained, enhances the importance of that in the centre, and the getting one more front column into sight helps to carry the colonnade easily out of the picture.

The historian, for reasons we may hereafter appreciate, is careful to mark John as contributing to the miracle "by looking fixedly" on the subject of it as well as Peter (ἀτενίσας—a word that occurs elsewhere in connection with these quasi magico-mesmerical operations). The Cartoon does not neglect the point, and compensates John for the more immediate activity of Peter by presenting his front face, and pointing his expressive hand to the cripple's head.

There is something in the gesture and mien of John that has the slightest possible indication of the tenderness that might lapse, by undexterous handling, into the sentimental. The boundary between the highest refinement of grace and affectation is the most delicate and perilous of all, in morals as in art. The saving distinction lies in the latest finishing touches, and if these are lost or degraded, the creation of angelic purity is on the brink of caricature that instant. Not even a Madonna, an infant Christ, or a boy John of Rafael himself, can be ensured against the lowest disgrace of all in expression, if the restorer is to repaint, or the repairer to clean off, these last ethereal high lights. The danger is much the same when the design has to pass from the original surface to the burin of the engraver, through all accidents of mind and hand and operation. No apology is here designed for the expression of John in the Cartoon, but much explanation how it is that engravings may resemble it so nearly, yet so utterly falsify expression. To those who are inclined, I leave the prosecution of the inquiry how far Correggio can be placed on the same line with Rafael, or how many steps below him in respect of harmonization of the expressions, of which the sentiment so easily, but so fatally, may become self-contemplative.

"What I have, give I unto thee," finds its expression in the expansive gesture of the hand of John, and the fully-extended arm, of which the outward turn involves, for perfect ease, the turn of the head to relieve the muscles of the shoulder, and thence derives the virtue of its expression. In another point, adherence to the text is equally conspicuous; the Apostle with his left hand grasps the right of the beggar,—he grasps him, and at the same time seems to be, as in the text, lifting him up; and thus, as regards expression, the action of Peter embodies the energetic order, Arise and walk, as definitely as that of John bespeaks the spirit of spontaneous and ungrudging endowment. The costume of this beggar does not exhibit the squalor that appears in the beggar to the left. Nothing is seen either of tatters or rags, and he wears a linen under-garment, fresh and clean. He grasps a crutch on the ground with his right hand, reaching for it instinctively when told to rise, though the movement of his leg shows, no less than a gleam of joy, mingled with astonishment in his face, that he already feels the accession of sudden vigour that is to make him independent of crutches for ever. I am disposed to think that to him belongs also the crutch on which the figure just behind him leans clasped hands and bearded chin. In the steadfast gaze of this figure I discern an expectant gratitude to the strangers who are interested in his friend. The lame man had those who cared for him, and carried him daily to the Temple gate; and here I conjecture that we have one who has just completed that service. That he himself is not lame, or in want of a crutch, is, I think, shown by the impatience of the stalwart boy, drawing him away for departure and companionship, and his ample drapery excludes the supposition that he is another mendicant.

To the same party probably belongs the eager figure just behind, who is rushing forward with an expression at least prepared for joy.

The feet of all the figures that are seen are naked,— their shoes put off for standing upon holy ground. The cripple himself has his lower garments drawn up above the knee, to expose in true beggar fashion the miserable deformity of his extremities, to verify his plea, and excite compassion.

The marks of congenital deformity are seen not more decisively in the malformed legs and distorted foot, than in that exaggerated and peculiar conformation of the jaw that so constantly accompanies such defects, sympathetic consequences doubtless of some common cause. In the other beggar such marks do not appear; neither trace of deformity, nor positive proof indeed even of disablement. His face and sprinkled hairs, and the habit of his skin, convey the impression of only that deformity that ensues not from birth, but from customary manner of life—the true mendicant self-habituation to bodily idleness, and intentness of stunted mind on the lowest bodily requirements in their meanest forms. He leans forward, as if to attract a share of whatever benefaction may be designed for his companion or competitor; but in his bunched and protruding under lip, there is visible as much contempt of the wild promise of bodily regeneration, as some awe, seen in his eyes, at the impressive presence of the Apostles, will allow him to display.

The narrative, it is to be observed, in no way ascribes faith or any other form of moral desert to the healed cripple antecedently. The cure is described as if effected by a specific, and in a way to illustrate most exclusively the independent force and magical agency of the name of Jesus, when applied by those who had faith in its power.

Afterwards, however, unaffected gratitude is ascribed

to the recipient of the benefit, and though this is only by implication, from his accompanying the Apostles into the Temple with lively demonstrations of his new endowments, and from his detaining them so long that the crowd had time to come together, still the feelings accept the vindication of the Apostles' insight in directing their bounty where it was not only appreciated but deserved.

The genius of the miracle, the sudden gift of energy and flexibility to the cramped and helpless lamiter, seems to be symbolized in the conjoint expression of the Apostolic figures, the firm, erect, preceptive Peter, and the graceful outpour of consent and sympathy of John.

The historical localization of the incident at the entrance of the women's court, gave opportunity for the introduction of the graceful beauty of young mothers entering or returning from the Temple, on the occasion of the redemption of their firstborn by sacrifice of a lamb, or pairs of doves and pigeons.

Such a mother we see in the lovely female on the left of the picture, returning with her infant, that may be but the month old, the prescribed term for the sacrifice. Her head is one of the most exquisitely beautiful in art; she looks with interest at the marvel that is being wrought, but not with the entire diversion of attention that appears in the face of her attendant. The infant, in lady's phrase, is not very interesting; I noticed the distinct indication, in the tapestry at Milan (1861), that a certain stiffness about it arises from its being represented swaddled; the tapestry of this subject at Mantua is very beautiful. With the true absorption of motherhood, she moves on with homeward step unchecked, and her hand lies still tranquilly attentive to the even ebbings of the sleeping breath of her nursling. The feeling of this arrangement is made more apparent by the proximity of the expressive hand of the extreme male figure to the right, which is expanded, and thrilling with emotion.

The formality of the dress of this figure indicates attachment to the service of the Temple; the expression of the face is refined and candid, and it is here that Rafael shows regard to the highly significant record in a text not very far off (Acts vi. 7), "and a great crowd of the priests obeyed the faith."

The healthful beauty of this youthful matron does not suffer, but rather the reverse, from a certain festal yet simple *munditia*, in carefully tressed hair, and bandlet and ear-drop, and the settled adjustment, by gathered knot over her right shoulder, of the plain purity of her robe. Station may even be intimated by the glimpse of a female attendant behind.

In front of, and in full pictorial relief upon the white robe of this type of all social orderliness and health, is projected the broad, bold profile, in face and figure, of the secondary beggar already described. There is sufficient interval to save from repulsive contiguity. The attention of both is directed to the same incident; and even, we may say, in both cases with certain restriction. But the beggar grasps his stick with unrelaxing hands, and purses his mouth from the contracting sentiment of self; the young mother has her sympathies controlled by the inextricable ties of offspring. The priest is by some degrees more unembarrassed; but even in him we see that the free movement of admiration is, at this moment, a surface ripple at most, as he is moving on with step undiverted to his daily function of ceremony and service. A single line in the waft of his robe is sufficient to indicate this. So, doubtless, Rafael had seen many an ecclesiastic of high original endowments subdued to the daily tenor of ceremonial routine, equal still to afford a sympathetic cheer, to feel a momentary glow for the noble, but disabled for more,—disabled ever for co-operating with a stroke of the world's work, that for anything that can be discerned, he ought to have been capable even to originate. A philosopher, true; but, alack, incompetent or neglectful to disengage himself from the pin that limits the tether of the contemplative!

There is a scowling face looks from beyond the next column, whose dealings will have to be countervailed by philosophers other than contemplative.

In the more open space on the right-hand side of the picture we have groups in freer action. Another graceful female, in livelier movement, bears on her head a basket with vine-leaves, and a pair of birds; and a lovely active boy of eight years old runs on beside her with another pair hanging by a string from a rod over his shoulders. The pairs of birds indicate that here too we have allusion to a presentation and redemption of a firstborn; and it was by a liberty of the painter, doubtless not exceeding the liberty with which the law of Moses was habitually modified in practice and ceremonial, that the little fellow has deferred his appearance beyond the canonical age.

Still beyond these figures we see a pair—a woman

and bearded man, standing dignified, but somewhat formally,—side by side, with an appearance as if they were witnessing a religious celebration; and so the movement and agitation of the porch of the Temple is toned off to the tranquillity of stately function, suggestive of the Temple itself.

But it was not in the order of the art of Rafael that he should pitch down upon an excuse of simple consistency with place and time, for the mere sake of obtaining for his picture nothing more than a picturesque detail or two, and the variety of feminine and infantine forms; it could not be but that beyond this he must have discerned an opportunity for heightening the moral expression and significance of the essential subject. Had these incidents been inevitable, his genius would have found the means to compel them to such subservience; inasmuch as their introduction was optional, no doubt he aimed therein at giving point and brilliancy to his proper theme.

How this may have been I find shadowed forth in a note I made, and dated 12th June, 1856, and I do not know that I can now improve on the conception or the exposition of it.

"Cripples at the Beautiful Gate; the failure of Nature supplicating aid in the midst of the successes of Art; cripples asking alms of Apostles, seeking the goods of life from those who could forego all in order to purvey for others the blessings of the spiritual. Apostles affording remedy and release to limbs that never had been strong, never had been straight, never complete; the interpreters of moral truth stooping to avouch the unity of the source of all health, the common fount of both moral truth and material,—natural good, by giving force to the energies that right mere physical distortion, and continue the work that in ordinary course is completed anterior to birth, and never should have to look for furtherance after, still less rectification!

"The ministers of truth and benevolence stand amidst the crowd of passers in and goers out, by the side of those who, to their grief and against their will, can neither come nor go. Reaching helping hands, and saying kindly and forceful words, they are heeded not only by the objects they befriend, but some of the jostling crowd are detained by wonder and regard; some of the farers by the world's common way of ceremoniousness are drawn towards the attractive centres of sympathetic helpfulness, and a new direction, if perhaps only a counter-deviation, is given to the current of the worldly stream.

"Women are passing in and out with the appropriate offerings of thankfulness, for happy rewards of earliest pangs. Strong boys, active children, and healthy infants, move through the columns in tending of affection and protecting kinship, or rest on tender bosoms in the security that is secure because it does not know of danger, and if it approached would but defy and crow before it; and in the midst is the group round the man who has grown up distorted from the cradle where he was a sorrow and a shame to his mother, and has lived to come at last, and unexpectedly, to a later and more happy birth."

Taken broadly, the subject avouches the command of the moral over the vital powers, especially under the stimulus of healthy enthusiasm,—the reaction sympathetically, and even by simple contiguity, of mental health and force upon physical.

Make of it what we please, there is the mixed fact of physiology and psychology, that in times of great mental exaltation, marvels akin to our miracle are ever rife; and if the fanaticisms of revivals, and the like, display more abundantly an influence of disturbance, the instances are not less significant to the philosopher as intimations of the direction to which he must point inquiry. This will lead at last to recognition of the principle that the controlling tone that must be looked to, to combine in harmony all the energies of the complex human constitution, is tone of moral sense.

Vigour and promptitude and justness of perception, sentiment, and act, at every crisis where appreciation of man's relations to his fellows is in question, or his relation to that superior order which is beyond his ken, constitute moral health. This is the true vital seat of our superior nature,—spasmodic disturbances of superstition alternating with the cold callousness that responds to no stimulus of awful admiration at wonders we cannot fathom, or of self-forgetting enthusiasm in noble enterprise, are its diseases. All the evils of the world are insignificant to those that have been promoted by religiousness; all the evils of religiousness might be welcomed back as relief, if the heart must otherwise close to susceptibility of sympathy with external nature, with man, with art that is the reflex of man in nature, with a sentiment of fellowship between one's own identity and some spirit of life with which all existence is impregnate,—which we might declare was alone existence, but that here we are at the boundary of our faculties.

For we arrive at last at the ultimate principles of belief; justly we may, and in prudence we are bound to test and scrutinize what are set before us as such, since busy motives would thrust in the simply traditional, the merest figments, the narrowest class-authorizations; but reduce the list acutely and conscientiously, and with as successful shrewdness as we may, the first principles will ever remain transcending demonstration. These are the primary axioms, to challenge which is simply to throw down the entire fabric of human consciousness, not to say knowledge, which rests on nothing else; to endeavour to analyse which, is simply to struggle with an all-powerful wrestler, who foils without effort, and can maim at will; it is blindly to harness ourselves to the dizzying mill-horse round of interchanging equivalent propositions, or to rise, time after time, only to stumble again over hopeless paradoxes, whichever way we turn. Infinity is a dominant conviction,—and by its nature it defies definition. Space without a limit is inconceivable,—and with a limit no less so; and it is the same with Time: effect without a cause is inconceivable,—and no less so a cause that is not an effect. We would not, and assuredly we cannot, divest ourselves of conviction of free choice in action, yet briefest consideration reduces the pretension to an absurdity. The justice and benevolence of the order of the world are ideas that are repugnant to all the observation of any man who has observed, or felt, or reflected;—and yet, independently of early impressed associations, there is not a man who does not instinctively and infallibly recur to the assumption, and, roused to indignation at the spectacle of an ill-assorted universe, find himself unawares appealing to a reliance on an ulterior, on an ultimate, correction, in virtue of the necessary supremacy of Truth and Right, of Sympathy and Love.

A grand condition of moral health is such a degree of attainable enlightenment as will disabuse the world of beliefs and systems that have been falsely foisted upon it as substitutes for, or superior to proof.

Supernaturalism has always been a liability of the childish world; always an instrument of the designing priest; always willingly favoured by the politician who, interested in restraining fierce populations in awe, could not afford to neglect a ready influence that would serve his momentary need, if not last his time, even when he knew it was a bad or a dangerous one.

To the root of supernaturalism, the axe must be laid by the reformers from whom the world has any hope. Nay, the very fibres of its roots must be followed up, and drawn out and demonstrated, like the attachments of a cancer. In this work there are two main divisions. Most difficult is the task to elucidate the natural curiosities of the border-lands of mental and vital phenomena in the individual, or, as reacting between several; nay, as between humanity, and brute and vegetable and even unorganized nature—the physics of sympathy. The indications and records of mesmerism and of religious revivals have already helped to much; the unexplored, at least the unexplained, beyond, is still farspreading, deep. The other requirement is the more properly historical, and consists in such analysis as here from time to time, and more or less thoroughly I seek to give example of,—the elucidation of the real circumstances that were the foundation of a story that has come to be unadvisedly accepted as literal history, and the demonstration of the varied influences and their mutual reactions, which perverted the record, and gave the form and impress to the false coinage too long current at a fictitious value.

As every generation continues by contagion, as much as by descent, the mistakes of generations preceding, knowledge of history is an essential element of self-knowledge; and so it becomes necessary, above all things, that men should be aware, not only which of their opinions are false, but how the falsehood originated, and how it was communicated to them.

But to return to and to conclude with the Cartoon.

The bounding and elastic boy in front is the very embodiment of youthful health and strength, and capability of happy and harmonious development; a child still in all his contours, but we discern foreshadowed within them the promised outlines of the fully grown and knit Herculean man.

He is, in fact, set here as the very symbol of the strength which failed to the infancy of the cripple, but is now on the point of being infused into his maturity by a compensating miracle. He presents to us unsuspectingly, but not therefore with less effect, an image of glad exultation in strength, which the moment of the representation forbids to be exhibited in the distorted mendicant, though the spectator familiar with the story may see him already, in imagination, walking, leaping, and praising God.

It will be observed how happily the height of the

standing boy-figure ranges with that of the kneeling beggar in corresponding position on the right. The broadly illuminated line of his arms and shoulders helps the symmetrical opposition, and his grandeur of proportion, besides other appropriateness, makes him competent to sustain the balance.

But the happy invention and placing of his significant action is, above all things, to be admired. In his position, as from his age, he is inattentive to, or out of sight of the miracle, and pulls at the girdle of the man who, resting his hands and chin on the crutch-head, as already described, is fixed immoveable in reverential gaze on the wonder-working Apostle. The action of appeal, the energetic endeavour to rouse the otherwise engrossed, is a variation upon the motive of Peter's lifted hand, and lifting grasp, and encouraging command, "Get up and walk."

The value of such a reflecting episode in giving distinctness to the chief incident is extraordinary; and yet for this result it is not necessary that the relation should be thus definitely recognized; nay, it is not of necessity that it should even have been so by the painter himself.

The pulling arm of the boy; the drawn arm of the cripple, the freely extended arm of John, consent in most harmonious composition. In two faces only, salient enough, no doubt, but still in the background, is found the expression of hostility that accounts for the sequel of the anecdote. The most vindictive face is that to the right, seen between the nursing mother and the Levite; of the other only half is discernible, cut off by the left-hand column, on the inner side of which we see a half-face, expressive of startled astonishment.

Other faces, interfered with by the architecture in the same way, give scattered distribution to the crowd, and thus is evaded an appearance of the groups fitting into their spaces with unnatural neatness. Certain accidents of seeming awkwardness are admitted, in order to permit contrived combinations to have the air of happy accidents. It pertains to this artifice that here, as in the group of Apostles in the charge to Peter, we have an indication of one considerable figure, which fills out the mass of a group, but of which the face is hidden altogether.

There is more art in the apposition of the illuminated and shadowed portions of the several figures than I am competent fully to expound. On the right we have that sharply-cut relief of the edges of a limb in shadow on a brightly illuminated background, that Rafael always treats with such mastery, and with a force that he is still careful to keep subordinated. On the right we have as broad a contrast, but there it is the illuminated front figure that has its bright edges outlined upon obscurity in the background. In the intermediate group, in the centre, such oppositions are superseded by the blending of shadows into shadows, the graduation of lights into lights.

Colouring.—I copy the following memoranda from hasty notes.

Peter wears yellow robe over blue tunic; John wears green robe over red tunic; both as in the Charge to Peter, excepting that here we have no reddish reflections in shadow on Peter's mantle.

Peter's head is relieved upon the green shoulder of

John,—just escaping the less desirable background of the red robe. Coloured stripes are seen along the bottom selvage of John's tunic.

The beggar has a blue jacket bound broadly with red; the edge of his linen, both at neck and legs, is neatly crimped. His face is happily relieved against his own blue sleeve, and the shadow of that of John. The more ignoble and less afflicted beggar is simply in sordid sackcloth, with no linen visible. His bottle hangs by a leather strap.

The female behind has green tunic, a light blue robe; very fair hair. The "Levite" has red sleeve, passed through brownish-yellow tunic—so to call his sleeveless jerkin—and blue cap.

The man leaning on head of staff has a brown dress, and the next a leather brown tunic, with dark-blue robe. The boy tugs at the blue girdle of the first, and his very red flesh-tones are boldly relieved upon a mass of dull, dark draperies.

The woman with the basket on her head has a shot blue and pink tunic; her robe is red, but seems to be lined with white, and, being reversed at the lower part, expresses her movement, and gives a relieving background for the flesh-tones of her boy,—a light background here, as a dark in the other instance.

III. THE FIRST EXPANSION OF THE GOSPEL-IDEA.

Let us now turn to the historical point of view, and consider what was most probably the foundation in matter of fact of the apologue thus developed, or, at least, what were the historical conditions that led to the composition of such a fable on no proper historical base whatever.

The qualification is important, for indications are decisive that the compiler of Acts and Luke had not only the purpose to digest his materials into orderly sequence in time and space, but that he also had lively recognition of the successive manifestation in the history, of new germs of development. This insight, which would simply sharpen observation in dealing with authentic materials, might seriously mislead in building up materials that had proved themselves so plastic to influences of prejudice, party, or simple imagination before they came to his hand.

According to Acts, the Apostles remain at Jerusalem after the crucifixion at the Passover, and it is on the day of Pentecost ensuing that leading incidents of lively revival and conversions occur; but when we find no more mention of Pilate, and that all the political circumstances seem changed, as in a dream, we are guided to a different inference; it seems more consistent to rely on the tradition which reports a temporary retirement of the Apostles from public attention, whether to Galilee or elsewhere, and to infer that their activity at the metropolis was probably not renewed till that interval after the recall of Pilate when the Jews were, for a time, treated with mildness, and even flattered and indulged.

It is likely enough that they came up to a succeeding Passover—an occasion of such indulgence; and though we may suspect, with Strauss, that the fact that the day of Pentecost was the anniversary of the giving of the old law, and also the day of first-fruits, may have suggested the date for the declaration of the new law, and the first great influx of conversions, this very significance was, in truth, a fact quite as likely to cause an actual outburst of enthusiasm on that day preferentially, as to originate the tale of one that never happened.

At Jerusalem, in any case, we find the Apostles in unbroken association, expecting the present reappearance of Jesus as heir of David, to establish the kingdom of Israel; and by natural consistency, Mary and the brethren of Jesus are mentioned as of leading importance in the company.

That the Apostles should still be looking forward to a kingdom of David at a time when they were the well-memoried depositaries of the parables and preachings so highly and so lucidly spiritualized, recorded in the Gospels, might seem extraordinary enough. We may elicit however very self-consistent history when we are convinced that the spiritualization of the kingdom was a later ascription to Jesus.

We have here without doubt, what was regarded by the compiler of Acts, not to say the still earlier author, as a consistent sketch of the opinions that were probably or might very possibly have been held by the Apostles at this epoch. It gives a certain account of the revival and the sudden extension of the society, connecting it with the inclusion of Hellenistic converts, who reappear so importantly in the history; and with the origin of that notorious phenomenon of the Christian sect, the speaking with tongues. It shows the Church persecuted in its origin by Sadducees, protected by Pharisees, and supported by a crowd of believing priests,—a situation which quite agrees with the Pharisaic assertion of the resurrection; the emphasis on "the fixed counsel and foreknowledge of God;" the theory of the Holy Spirit; the assiduous frequenting of the Temple, and above all, with the instant expectation of a Messianic kingdom under a descendant of David.

True, that this sympathy is very inconsistent with the invidious position assigned to the typical Pharisee of the Gospels; but again we may accept it as in all essentials very probable history, when we find the Apostolic section of the Church largely leavened with "brethren of the sect of Pharisees;" and it is thus we obtain positive proof that much is assigned to the mouth of Jesus in denunciation of Pharisees, that originated in discussions with a section of the Church opposed to them, upon questions it never even occurred to Jesus to entertain. Here we clutch the most important clue to New Testament interpretation; and it becomes certain that a favourite instrument of controversy, between restrictive Pharisaic Christian and expansive opponent, on the part of the latter at least, was the free ascription to Jesus of enunciations and parables that glanced in the direction of their controversial argument.

Then in rather surprising association with the Pharisaic elements in these chapters of the revival, we have frequent references to the rite of the Baptist, claims to authority and miraculous power by a sacred name, and mingled enthusiastic and ascetic communism.

The belief in the miraculous power of the Apostles, and even the actual production of some therapeutic effects unaccountable enough to philosophy, are borne out by the testimony of St. Paul as to his own pretensions and powers; and the history of many a century after may teach us that of all anecdotes and incidents that gained credence without foundation, or with equivocal foundation, the miraculous were the most easy, the most natural, the most unquestioned.

The rite of baptism and the urging to repentance under terrorism of the last day,—a terrible day,—carry us back to what is most venerable in the ministry of John the Baptist, and forward to the long abuse of a demoralizing superstition. Salvation, the getting off scot-free, dodging destruction by the veriest leaping of a gate and turning a nook, by the engaged help of a cunning man who has got hold of a secret, a way of purifying, or the knowledge of a mystical name:—these are notions that we find up and down antiquity, as we find them up and down superstitious countries in all ages. This is very different from the Baptist's symbolical rite and condition of moral requirement, and not on John must be visited the mischievous interpretations and mysticisms that have perverted both. It is indeed disagreeable to find ascribed to Peter, probably a disciple of John, the preconisation of the name of Jesus as a mystical charm, a magical conjuration of the very vulgarest type. In the story of the lame man healed, it is true, we have in one phrase, "His name, and the faith which is by him, have given this man soundness;" but in all other occurrences we have "the name" alone insisted on:—iii. 6, "In the name of Jesus," etc.; iv. 7, "By what power or by what name have ye done this?" iv. 10, "By the name of Jesus Christ;" iv. 12, "There is no other name under heaven given among men whereby we may be saved," etc.; iv. 30, "Signs and wonders through the name," etc.

We are not justified in charging all this vulgarity upon Peter, nor in dividing it between him and the compiler of Acts. The story of the lame man healed by the Apostles, as we now have it, is probably the result of numerous traditions, of repeatings and recopyings that each did something to corrupt or else to compensate; the medley of result is before us, and the analysis is the more perplexing as in the study of the Acts of the Apostles we are, for the most part, without the aid that is so abundant in the case of the Gospels,—varied versions of the same incident.

In the instance before us, however, there is a certain variety of version discernible not very far off, and significant enough to merit some examination.

The variety is of much the same character as the duplications and reduplications that we have followed out in the accounts of the resurrection.

The narrative of the healing of the lame man at the Beautiful Gate of the Temple, introduces incidents and notices that have a parallelism in the sections referring to the day of Pentecost and to the sequel of the death of Ananias.

At the day of Pentecost, as here, we have a marvel, an excited assemblage, an address of Peter, a multitude of conversions (ii. 41 and iv. 4),—the numbers being kept carefully progressive, 120 in i. 16, then 3000 added in one day, then 5000; and a concluding description of the unity that reigned in the society, the undisputed authority of the Apostles, and—most important, the establishment of community of goods and prevalence of material comfort; all points which we easily see are emphasized because in contrast to the later state of affairs.

Compare ii. 42–44, and iv. 32–37.

" And they continued steadfastly in the Apostles' doctrine and fellowship, and in breaking of bread and in prayers. And fear came upon every one; and many wonders and signs were done by the Apostles. And all who believed were together, and had all things common; and sold their possessions and goods, and parted them among all, as every one had need. And they continued daily with one accord in the temple, and breaking bread from house to house, did eat their food with gladness and singleness of heart, praising God, and having favour with all the people." (Acts ii. 41–46.)

"And the multitude of those who believed were of one heart and one soul; neither said any of them that aught of the things which he possessed was his own, but they had all things common. And with great power the Apostles gave testimony concerning the resurrection of the Lord Jesus; and great grace was upon them all. Neither was there any among them who lacked; for as many as were possessors of lands or houses sold them, and brought the prices of the things that are sold, and laid them at the Apostles' feet; and distribution was made unto every man, according as he had need." (Acts iv. 32–35.)

In the second narrative appears what may easily have been the germ of the more extended account inserted earlier, of the descent of the Holy Spirit; "And when they had prayed, the place was shaken where they were assembled together; and they were all filled with the Holy Spirit, and spake the word of God with boldness" (iv. 31). Traces of modification are abundant in the earlier account (ii. 42), at least as salient. What speaking with tongues really meant,—a nervous unintelligible jabber it is described by Paul, and was so reproduced by Irving,—could scarcely, one would suppose, have been unknown to a companion of Paul; it is not the less evident that as the tale stands, apparently by tampering or interpolation, the marvel is coolly asserted to amount to supernatural talking of foreign languages by the uninstructed in them, if not to the still more wonderful transmutation of a single language spoken, into distinct languages in the ears of various-languaged auditors.

But the excitement respecting the lame man led to a collision, so runs the story, with the Sadducaic authorities, and this is the point of comparison with the narrative that succeeds.

Peter and John in one case are apprehended, in the other the Apostles generally. In both cases Peter boldly reasserts his doctrine before the Council; then the accused are taken out of the Court; then ensues a private discussion; the accused are then brought in again, to be warned in one case, beaten and warned in the other, and so they are dismissed. And in both narratives a protecting influence is ascribed to the favour they enjoy with the people.

In the second narrative the popular Pharisaic teacher Gamaliel, protects them with a success that owes nothing to historical accuracy or logic. He urges that in this instance, as in former, the disappearance of the sect will follow on the death of the leader, but cites a Theudas in time and terms at variance with reliable record in Josephus, and treats the influence of Judas the Galilean as defunct,—prematurely indeed. The title of both to Pharisaic protection, we have already explained.

Now in these narratives there are two texts especially of which it would be interesting to know, I do not say the authenticity, which respecting records in such a case is of very qualified nature, but the source and origin. Were they the introductions of the compiler, were they of the original writer of the anecdote, or whence intermediately?

In both the addresses of Peter it is just at the end,—it is just when the influence of his words has fairly secured their effect, that advantage seems to be taken to insinuate a corollary that might have offended earlier, and even at last is but touched faintly and covered dexterously by connection with a favourite dogma or a revered text.

On the day of Pentecost Peter assures his new penitents—" For the promise is to you and to your children and to all that are afar, as many as the Lord our God shall call."

The reference here is distinctly to a conversion of Gentiles; though the words as spoken will carry the gloss that their prophesied conversion would be through reception of full Judaism; and in any case there is the condition of a divine election and predestination. Nevertheless, this is early days for urging such a point, —the sudden and immediate manifestation of the kingdom of David being still in question. It can scarcely be accepted as a genuine historical date; but it bears the impress of being an expression, by a writer who lived pretty close to the Apostolic community, of what tendencies were early at work in favour of expansion, and of his opinion that Peter had it at heart to further them, though he could move, however perseveringly, still only cautiously.

Cautiousness and reticences and vacillations notwithstanding, I have confidence that I shall show in due time that Peter's feelings, in favour of a comparatively liberal Gentile inclusion, were original with him and heartfelt. It is the value I attach to other evidence that induces me to see more authenticity in these early hints than is allowed by those who regard them as traits, introduced by the compiler, to keep up consistency with the later positions in which he intended to exhibit Peter; and who regard all liberalism as transferred and plagiarized from Paul, and falsely ascribed to the earlier Apostle, in order to effect conciliation of parties. But we shall see.

In the meantime the parallel hint or intimation, at the very close of the second speech, is this,—" Ye are the sons of the prophets, and of the covenant which God made with our fathers, saying unto Abraham, And in thy seed shall *all families of the earth* be blessed. *Unto you first*, God, having raised up his servant, sent him to bless you, in turning away each of you from his iniquities."

There is much of the spirit of John the Baptist in this; much that reads like the regermination of earlier thoughts, in reaction from the temporary check received by interference of the exciting ministry and enterprise of Christ. It is quite within the probabilities that there were revivals of other impressions among the other Apostles, carrying them into special divergences.

At any rate, then, the record of these incidents and speeches, real or ascribed, passed through the hands of writers who were cognizant of the later discussions as to the extension of the Christian sect, so as to include

Gentiles and Samaritans, whatever may have been the stipulated terms. Indeed, I am disposed to think that it was only in virtue of later accounts of his concern in some of these that John got mentioned here,—John, who is no doubt invaluable in the Cartoon, but who takes the part of so mere a supernumerary in the narrative of the protagonism of Peter. He was associated with Peter, as we read, in giving seal and sanction to the reception of Samaritans; and he is mentioned by Paul (Galatians ii. 9), along with James and Peter, as consenting to his scheme of a Gospel for the uncircumcision, at a time when the notion would have shocked the general Church at least, and probably most of the other Apostles.

Taking all into account, I am now further disposed to declare a symbolical reference to the same class of ideas in the details with which the miracle is furnished forth. I am disposed to think, that when the original writer described a miracle as wrought upon a man who had lingered without the ἅγιον, the Court of the Israelites, miserably begging alms, in consequence of a disability from birth, and as then enabled, in virtue of the name of Jesus, to enter the Temple along with the Apostles, walking, leaping, and praising God, he embodied a designed type of the Gentile rescued from the disabilities of his descent, and made a worshipper of a common God, among a common family. It seems to me that the only other alternative is to recognize the type as that of a section of Jewish people, under ban from mixed blood; but of this hereafter.

No doubt the parallelism will fail,—it is the nature of such, if pressed into detail; and no doubt the sum of implied liberality, after all, assumes reception into formal Judaism: but the symbolical intimation is, because illusory, the more in harmony with the oblique, if not equivocal, verbal intimations in the speeches already commented on.

Jewish bigotry was so sensitive on the subject of Gentile inclusion, that no tenderness in touching it would lull suspicion; there was offence in even touching upon it at all, in however guarded terms, in however strict observance of limitations laid down by bigotry itself. Much was to be done before Jewish privilege could listen with tranquillity to reduction to mere precedence. "Unto you first," would only provoke the reclamation, "unto us exclusively." We are therefore bound to interpret the word, plain or figurative, of those who were bold enough to moot the subject at all, as carrying force and point much in excess of the cold import of terms.

An analysis of the designedly symbolical details of some of the miracles, as well as non-miraculous incidents of the Gospels, will be further justification and proof hereafter. At present, I pursue the line of illustration obtainable from Josephus.

Josephus has miracles to relate, prefiguring and preceding the desecration of the Temple, quite as wonderful as those that fill the first chapters of Acts, and, rogue as he was, I think it probable enough that he reported them in good faith, and with full belief. A sword-like comet hovered above the city for a year; at the feast of Passover, in midst of night, a wondrous light illuminated altar and naos for the space of half an hour, as if it had been day. More wonderful still, a cow, brought by the

high-priest to sacrifice, gave birth to a lamb, in the very midst of the Temple. (Bell. Jud., vi. 5, 3.)

But our present interest is claimed chiefly for the following wonder, in which the opening of the Beautiful Gate of the Temple by supernatural influence is interpreted as premonitory of the end of the theocracy, or at least of the exclusive religious privileges of the Jew; a parallel to the moral of the passage of that very gate by the healed cripple.

It is followed up by another marvel of the same purport on the day of Pentecost; and I do not entertain the slightest doubt that in these two anecdotes of Josephus we have narratives, derived from common root at least, with those in the Acts of the Apostles. Whether this common root were earlier and independent; whether the symbolical marvels originated with the Christian community, and were metamorphosed from moral to political significance, and so arrived at Josephus; or whether the Christians were the remodellers of stories half developed to their hands, who shall say? It is quite enough to recognize the common relationship, and to lay to heart the instructive hint, how freely such a metamorphosing *vis naturæ* was at work at the time.

"The Eastern Gate also of the inner *hieron*, which was of brass, and very stiff (στιβαρωτάτη), and closed about eventide with difficulty by twenty men, and bearing upon iron bars, with very deep pivots let into a threshold of a single stone, was discovered about the sixth hour of the night standing open of its own accord. The watch of the Temple ran to inform the military commander, who came down, and with difficulty was able to close it. This, again, seemed to the vulgar a marvel of the happiest import, as if God were setting open for them the gate of good things. But the instructed understood the immunity of the Temple as spontaneously determined, and the gate to be freely opened to the enemy, and amongst themselves they interpreted the sign as significant of desolation. . . . And at the time of the feast of Pentecost, when the priests entered the inner hieron, as was their custom for their service, they said that they were first sensible of an agitation and a noise, and, succeeding these, of a number of voices, crying, ' Let us depart hence.' "

CHAPTER IV.

THE DEATH OF ANANIAS.

I. THE CARTOON OF THE DEATH OF ANANIAS.—II. THE CONTINGENCIES OF COMMUNISM IN THE CHURCH.

I. THE CARTOON OF THE DEATH OF ANANIAS.

THE subject of the death of Ananias is the proper pendant of the miracle at the Beautiful Gate, and completes the emphatic sanction of the authority of the chief Apostle. A miracle of severity follows up one of benignity, and symbolizes the possession of the power to bind no less than to loose, to condemn than to absolve,—the prerogative of the second key.

The story which is depicted, and which provisionally we accept under conditions that admit of full sympathy, runs in these terms, and on this wise:—

Acts ii. 42. "And they gave themselves continually to the teaching of the Apostles, and to the distributing and to the breaking of bread, and to prayers. And fear came upon every soul; and many wonders and signs were done through the Apostles.

"And all that believed were together, and had all things common; and sold their possessions and goods, and parted them to all, as any one had need."

Acts iv. 32. "And of the multitude of believers there

was one heart and one soul; neither said any one that any of the things that he possessed were his own; but they had all things common.

"And with great power the Apostles gave witness of the resurrection of the Lord Jesus; and there was great favour toward them all; for no one among them was in want, for as many as were possessed of lands or houses sold them, and brought the prices of them when sold and laid them at the Apostles' feet.

"And Joses, who by the Apostles was surnamed Barnabas (which is, when interpreted, a son of consolation), a Levite, a Cyprian by birth, having land, sold it, and brought the money and laid it at the Apostles' feet.

"But a certain man, named Ananias, with Sapphira, his wife, sold a possession, and kept back part of the price, his wife also knowing of it, and brought a certain part and laid it at the Apostles' feet.

"And Peter said, 'Ananias, why hath Satan filled thine heart, for thee to cheat the Holy Spirit, and to keep back part of the price of the land? Whiles it remained, was it not thine own? and when sold, was it not in thine own power? why hast thou laid this deed in thy heart? thou hast not lied to man, but to God.'

"And Ananias hearing these words fell down and breathed his last, and great fear came on all that heard these things. And the young men arose and wound him up, and carried him out and buried him.

"And it was about the space of three hours, when his wife, not knowing what was done, came in. And Peter answered her, 'Tell me whether ye sold the land for so much?' And she said, 'Yea, for so much.'

"And Peter said unto her, 'How is it that ye agreed

together to try the Spirit of the Lord? behold, the feet of them that have buried thy husband are at the door and will carry thee out.' And she fell straightway at his feet and breathed her last; and the young men coming in found her dead, and carrying her out buried her with her husband.

" And great fear came upon all the Church and upon all that heard these things." (Acts v. 11, Sharpe's translation.)

The picture commits Rafael to a point of view from which the incident appeared to him to embody a merited punishment inflicted by a legitimate and wise authority.

Painters, no less than poets, may be mistaken, and set forth faults as virtues, affectations as sincerities, errors as heroisms. But the greatest of both sorts approach so nearly to the infallible in appreciation of the most delicate moral gradations, that we are usually more prudent when we cast about rather for the explanation of their decisions, than for apologies.

Otherwise, from the commonplace, which under ordinary conditions would also be the common-sense point of view, Ananias is punished capitally for a lapse which was induced in no slight degree by the Apostles themselves, when they sanctioned, if they did not originate, a system of communism that ought never to have been established, and that exposed all concerned to an unfair and unreasonable temptation. The system itself, in fact, according to the history, speedily breaks down, from suspicions at least of malversation, not to say of embezzlement, in other quarters; and when the Apostles found that murmurers did not spare imputations even on themselves, the thought arises that they might have seen cause to revise their indignation at the fault of Ananias.

The narrative, however, assumes very different conditions; and as these, if liberally accepted, are in themselves consistent, the painter was quite at liberty to adopt them, being careful always to provide them with distinct expression.

Again, there is apt to be a painful jar on the feelings at an example of summary judicial destruction dealt by the spiritual leader on his own responsibility; and the incident seems perniciously contrived to authorize all the abuses and miseries that have flowed from the interference of ecclesiastics in government, from the power of churchmen in the cabinet and on the judgment-seat.

But on the other hand, if we are to appreciate and enjoy the truth that is in the picture, we must admit the conditions it essentially postulates, and take its own word for its own meaning. The historical Ananias,—if such there were,—must for the time be left aside, and his representative be charged with whatever unqualified wickedness the painter imputes. For this we have not far to go: the crime that is punished before us is embezzlement of the earnings of the laborious, of the alms contributed by the benevolent, the right of the widow and the needy; it is committed under a mask of religious zeal; hypocrisy is covered by conspiracy and a lie; and so the most virulent of moral poisons are poured into the stream of charity and sincerity at the very source,—at that new source from which they were just set on flow to regenerate the world.

In all this, assuredly, there is no apology for Papacy

or Prelacy in any form that either have ever subsisted: quite the reverse; for the moral of the tapestry bites with the edge of satire into both. The representative of the ruling genius of the court of the Clements and the Innocents, is not St. Peter, and does not stand on the dais along with him, but lies denounced and stricken in Ananias.

The story was not likely, it may be, to be so read in the Sistine Chapel; but it was something at least that there it should be written up in universal language.

For the nonce, therefore, we recognize in the St. Peter of the picture the conscientious, the stern, the just, and in truth, benevolent judge, who cuts off from the healthy system of regenerated society the false growth that now attaches only to its surface, but neglected or indulged would penetrate to and prey upon its vitals. The history of the common Christian movement that gave the promise and did much towards the performance of recovering society on the basis of charity and truth, from a condition not so unimproving and hopeless as usually represented, but certainly bad enough, is signalized at its very commencement by an act of uncompromising rigour, the indispensable complement of such a scheme.

Charity, tenderness, and philanthropy are qualities that only subsist in their highest, purest, and most operative forms when they are capable of animating energy as well as relaxing violence. The meekness of the dove does not more absolutely require the wisdom of the serpent for safeguard than for usefulness; and both are compatible with, both in fact are helpless or mischievous unless associated on occasion with, the prompt, unsparing courage of the lion.

Rafael, with the happiest invention and unfailing command of expression, has succeeded in presenting pictorially the living image of every motive and characteristic involved in this description.

The scene is a large apartment, into which open daylight is admitted with satisfactory freedom, and which is marked by free ingress and inlook as the semi-public hall and haunt of the new community. The pre-eminence and rule of the Apostles are indicated by their occupation exclusively of a dais, raised by two steps above the level of the floor. It forms three sides of an octagon; the front side, which has formal correspondence with the paved or parquetted divisions of the floor, is open; the sides retiring on the right and left are enclosed by a rail. All is executed in simple chapel-like carpentry, and the expression of combined formality and plainness is completed by the curtain or tapestry of plain unfigured drapery that covers the wall behind, and forms a set background for the group of Apostles. Their relative elevation above the congregation corresponds with the repeated expression of offerings being laid at their feet.

The leading part and position ascribed to Peter are asserted by his position exactly in the centre and well in front of the apostolic group. He stands with an expression as much of collected solemnity as severity. His air is that of a judge who declares a sentence, and who indicates its fulfilment with a clear sense of its justice, and its necessity no less. His extended right arm and down-pointed finger make the gesture that accompanies the last and fatal word *death*, and give to the fall of Ananias the effect of astonishing suddenness.

The text of the narrative does not in the first incident ascribe words of deadly denouncement to Peter, but they are supplied in definite terms in the case of Sapphira, and are fairly, are inevitably, imputed to intention in the first case. The gesture, therefore, of Peter implies deliberate and definite condemnation; the appeal to the sanction of the judgment, "Thou hast not lied unto men, but unto God," is assigned to the Apostle beside him, who seems by symmetrical position a special assessor, and points to heaven.

In Dorigny's engravings the figures are fortunately or designedly reversed, so that they correspond with the tapestries as executed and intended to be executed. The expression in the case before us would have been qualified most importantly had the denouncing and demonstrative arms of the two condemning Apostles been the left arms.

Let us remark also the sympathy with which the index finger of the left hand in each case starts out in agreement with that of the more active hand.

The prostration of the large frame of Ananias is sudden and absolute; he is in his first position from the fall; the next will leave him lifeless on his back. The first instinct of a man consciously falling is to spread the hands to save himself: the bent right arm and doubled-back hand of Ananias seem sufficiently to indicate the merest awakening of the instinctive impulse arrested and frustrated by the too-speedy doom. I am not sure whether it is over-refinement to think that in the closed left hand remains clutched the unhallowed gain that tempted to destruction.

The eyes are distorted, but the mouth does not gasp,

and the muscles of the face are rather constricted than convulsed.

Of the two figures that are immediately behind Ananias, the more remote stoops eagerly forward, and, not seeing that all is absolutely over for the wretch, and that he is no longer sensible, points to the Apostles, as if to direct his attention and reinforce their words. In this figure I am disposed to recognize Barnabas. A nearer figure, with turban-like hat, leans forward more timidly, or rather cautiously, towards the fallen figure, and scrutinizes the dying features with astonishment, displayed in his extended hands and arms, but which yet does not quite overpower curiosity.

On the other hand, the two opposite figures in full view of the catastrophe start away from it in horror and affright,—with horror and affright in both instances, though the alarm is naturally displayed most distinctly by the female figure in countenance and gesture.

She looks back, and has indeed her eyes riveted upon the dying man, while her movement is in the opposite direction, and her hands are extended also outwards. This is the natural impulse of extending the hands to feel that the way is clear for retreat in one direction, while the eyes are fixed upon the object of dread in the other.

This impulse is less decided with the young man: his open mouth shows how his breath is taken away by his horror and surprise, and nature, for the instant, is paralysed; but still his gesture is recoil, and not, like that of the woman, retreat. The exact extent to which there is an admixture of apprehension in this figure is made out most effectively by the immediate contrast with the woman, and then by the comparison of his hands with those of the man behind Ananias. The hands of this standing and stooping man are stretched and rigid in unchecked wonder; those of the kneeling youth have that degree of contractility that may be retained by one whose energies are suspended, but not unnerved. Between abandonment to the sentiment of surprise or awe, and abandonment to the impulse to retreat, there is the impulse to retire with the reservation of force for employment on a vantage ground. The difference is between the impulse to retreat in dismay and to retreat upon guard.

The half-kneeling position of these figures is explained by that of the group beyond them, in whose act of bodily submission to apostolic authority, no doubt, they were a moment ago participants.

I only count eleven Apostles on the platform. According to the sequence of the incidents in Acts, the full number had been already completed by the appointment of Matthias to the place left vacant by Judas. I am inclined to think, however, that Rafael deliberately antedated the incident; and I find it rather agreeable to believe that he thought the authority for such an act would not bear to be weakened by participation of any others than the immediate delegates of Christ.

I know not whether reasons of any value could be reckoned on for naming the Apostle with whom Peter is here conspicuously associated, James.

We are less liable to error in recognizing John in the Apostle in graceful light drapery, who is occupied in the distribution on the left of the picture, the right of the tapestry. The hair and features are those assigned to him elsewhere, and the painter has willingly withdrawn him from the immediate scene of severity to functions more congenial to his traditional character. To his companion in the work of charity and just administration, I shall return.

Seven Apostles are grouped behind Peter and James (or Andrew, Peter's brother). The six immediately behind Peter give effect to his judicial dignity by varied indications of excitement. One joins his hands, and looks up to heaven; others look down upon the criminal with as much compassion as may not palliate a heinous fault, and two others interchange an observation in the background. The general effect of the group is to convey the impression that all are cognizant of, and assenting to, the judgment announced by the leaders in front. But the independence of the leaders, *primi inter pares*, is intimated by the feet of the Apostles behind being all turned towards the left of the picture, equivalent to an indication that they leave the conclusion to Peter. This joint movement is also very valuable as connecting them with the work already proceeding in the hands of John; they are moving on to proceed with the due guidance of those very functions of benevolence which it was the sin of Ananias that he did his best to vitiate.

But there is another Apostle on the platform yet unmentioned, at the extreme left. He gives me the impression of a certain isolation or retirement; he does not partake of the movement observed in the others, and I am half disposed to believe that here again, as in the charge to Peter, we have Thomas, the undecided, on the point of sympathizing, but not sympathizing without a pause, and on this occasion a pause of awe that is almost horror. On the left-hand side of the picture—in all cases I refer to the redressed design—are two figures laden with bales, contributions to the common stock. One of them seems just aware that something is going on; the other, who always suggests to me the idea that he is but employed in his work as a porter, is absolutely unconscious of an excitement.

Still, beyond them, and only in part within the picture, a female of rather engaging appearance enters. She is counting money from one hand into the other, and no doubt is Sapphira. The remoteness of time and space are shortened up pictorially; and that she is not an object of attention to any other person in the picture is quite sufficient to carry her away as the representative of an arrival "three hours after." The act of counting intimates the intent of reservation: wherefore reckon, when all was to be given up unconditionally? Her face has a very marked expression of painful regret, which is easily construed as grudging unwillingness. As usual with Rafael, the single face is not left to enforce its sentiment without assistance from comparison. There is another female head just behind her, of which the erect neck and free aspect mark the cordial and the unembarrassed.

The position of Ananias corresponds with his entrance having been from the same side, and with his having been confronted on his arrival.

At the opposite end of the picture, we have the completion of the story as I have extracted it, and an indication of an important development a little further on in the history.

The Apostle associated with John reminds me, by his rather wild than luxuriant growth of hair, of that Apostle in the Cartoon of the Charge to Peter, that, from the spirit of his movement, and his clasping a book, I have called James, the son of Alpheus, or of Cleopas, for the names are probably the same. He holds here the purse from which St. John is making distribution; two members of the community are submissively on their knees, and apparently are waiting for their turn; the third, however, is a man who stands and holds out both hands, while he looks up at least with a craving, if not with an expostulatory air. St. John lifts his hand, and divides his fingers with a movement of enumeration, as if correcting a demand, and on the faces of two females beyond there is a shade of discontent,— the more probably as the hand of one is extended,—in what sense, unless prematurely, close to those of the craving applicant. Their head-dress seems to be expressive of widowhood—conventional weeds.

In this applicant, therefore, we have another phase of the same money-grasping temper that is signalized in the catastrophe that is the subject of the Cartoon. It was thus, indeed, that Rafael set forth in painting the purport of the text: " In those days, when the disciples were increasing, there arose a murmur of the Hellenists against the Hebrews that their widows were overlooked in the daily service. And the twelve called the multitude of the disciples, and said, ' It is not pleasing for us to leave the word of God and serve tables; wherefore, brethren,' " etc. (Acts vi. 1, 2.)

A feeble and aged man is seen ascending a flight of steps above this group, attended by a youthful female, emblem of the better charities of the association.

II. THE CONTINGENCIES OF COMMUNISM IN THE CHURCH.

Did any such incident, we ask, really happen at all?

That supernaturalism is assumed in the narrative as it stands is self-evident, though here, as elsewhere, commentators have been so bold, or so weak, or so insincere, as to deny it. The first denouncement might be equivocal by itself, but not when illustrated by the terms of the second; "the young men" are at hand to remove a corpse as promptly in one case as the other, and the implication is unavoidable.

When this superstitious or ignorant element permeates a narrative, we are at once justified in assuming the possibility of any degree of departure from literal truth in twenty different directions. Who shall say in which? As regards Ananias, the words of the denouncement bind us to no more than a possibility that the agitation of detection was too much for a rogue of a hypocrite, who possibly had a heart-complaint. Nay, the mere sudden death of a very worthy fellow might easily get distorted into such a form after a transmission or two. Then, the gossip Report varies from her word, and tells that the catastrophe was of a woman, not of a man; then, the double versions are accepted as severally true; and then, by natural sequence, the pair of victims might easily become man and wife; and twenty other processes of transformation, equally plausible, equally possible, might be contrived.

How easily such tales arise among sects disposed to magnify the office of their preachers, may be seen at large in the anecdotes of precisely parallel judgments, which Mr. Buckle has collected from the memoirs of the Scottish divines. The divines themselves accept or claim the importance to be derived from such hideous catastrophes as complacently as their followers were forward to ascribe it. No doubt the form and the facility of belief in such tales arose from prepossessions as to the true Apostolic type, and they might never have been told as they were, or told at all, but for the model that was furnished to imagination by the incident in the Acts of the Apostles. But this is precisely the significance of the whole matter, and illustrates to the nines the mental process by which the Apostles were credited with authority, to be exercised as fiercely as by their predecessor of old—the punisher of Gehazi with leprosy to the last generation.

But let fiction be answerable for as much of the tale as it might, or even for all, the result, as expressing certain assumptions of likelihood, is an historical fact of the highest interest—a monument of plastic moral influences, beliefs, and invitations to belief.

That the Apostles acted so or so, may be simply fabulous; but it is a fact of high significance that zealous adherents, more or less near to them in time, thought it quite consistent that they should so act, with such powers, to such purpose.

We have a sketch of golden days of Apostolic supremacy, general and unquestioned, with headship of Peter.

We have a sect organized upon the basis of community of goods,—a plan rejoiced in as diffusing comfort through a society, otherwise acquainted with the hardships, if not the squalor of poverty.

We have this sect striking, in fact, for imperial power, and asserting civil and criminal independence; virtually in insurrection, they commit themselves to the enterprise by unhesitating exercise of the power of life and death in protection of the principle of their association.

These ascriptions admit for the most part of more than presumptive authenticity. It is rather a different question to what extent they belong to the original scheme or teaching of Christ. Much that was compatible with his career and triumph, as he foreshadowed it, would have to give way, or take another form, when his anticipations were with violence falsified; and, at the same time, the specialities of his followers acquired freedom to come into play, and it were strange if all tended in one direction.

We have it on the authority of St. Paul, that even among the converts made by himself, accomplished as he was, the wealthy and the instructed were rare exceptions; how much more so in the following of other teachers? St. Paul himself is no inculcator of the proper merit of poverty,—rather of energetic and well-directed industry; but even in his writings we trace the influences that in an access of sympathetic enthusiasm would relax the springs of exertion.

It is when he is writing to the Corinthians a reply to their inquiry respecting marriage; he makes tender, though rather reluctant, concession to the weakness of humanity, but, "after all, he is disposed to argue, wherefore marry?"—the Lord is at hand; it is but a question of a very short time; and self-denial in the interim will not be without merit. The world has seen in later days how these motives may gain strength, and when instant anticipation of the end of the world has been rife, the thankless labour of provision for a future that was never to arrive has been given up.

A vein of tradition is distributed through the Gospels, sometimes incongruously enough, which preserves the enforcement, in terms most uncompromising, of unconditional abstinence from industrious forethought. Here, we may reasonably suspect, are preserved original dogmas of the early Church, whether derived from Christ's own lips or not. To take no care for the morrow, to let the morrow care for itself, to lay up no treasures, to look for support offering itself as spontaneously as that which feeds and fosters the beauty of the lilies of the field, to be content with a daily bread that is dependent on heavenly response to prayer from day to day; —these were maxims that at some epochs might seem marvellously justified by inflowing and unforeseen contributions, but the ultimate upshot could only be a state of chronic, sordid, and dependent, if not importunate, poverty.

In the parable of Dives we find mendicancy and rags transformed into virtues that merit heaven with no specified moral conditions; and the epistle of James expounds a theory of desert that is not much more dignified. Here we have the commencement of Christian monkery,—the dependence of a horde of watching and praying devotees, for all the wants left to them by fasting and celibacy, on the contributions of a world bound theoretically to the same system, but, fortunately for all, too perverse and reprobate to give up the industry that for both alike is indispensable.

The exaltation of the lowly was certainly pushed to an extreme, but the abuse is not chargeable on the instructions of Jesus, as probably conceived, for the occasion for them would not have arisen had his career actually fulfilled the course which it seems clear that he looked forward to.

It is quite consistent, then, with the tradition of the golden age of the Apostolic Church, that we find it afterwards exposed to the sufferings and the shifts of poverty. To what else could the system come? In fact, Paul seems to speak of the Church at Jerusalem as "the poor," as if that were its understood and current designation. The passage, which we shall hear more of, occurs in Galatians, where he relates the solicitations or suggestions of the Apostles that he should be instrumental in turning the Gentile converts to account as contributors to the necessities of the Jerusalem Church.

In all this there is a trace of the asceticism of the Essenes mixed up with somewhat of the habitudes of the professional hierophants.

The illustration of the assertion of sovereignty takes a parallel course. Certainly we do not find again in the New Testament an overt act so pronounced as the deaths of Ananias and Sapphira, but the motive looks out in all directions. Cavil as we may at the historical title of the early speeches of Peter in Acts, they express the narrator's belief at least; and no assertion can be stronger than their claim for Christ reappearing to exercise and to delegate authority equivalent to that of the Roman Imperial seat. There is nothing hard of belief here; for no phenomenon is more frequent in history than such pretensions on the part of exalted religionists. Nothing is put into the mouth of Peter that is not quite as distinctly implied in St. Paul's Epistles to the Thessalonians, illustrated as they are by the notice in Acts that at their probable date his doctrine was being challenged and checked as treasonable towards Cæsar.

The principle is asserted in his rebuke of the Corinthian Christians, for carrying their causes before the heathen tribunals. "Know ye not that the saints shall judge the world?" In the Gospels we find preserved the sketch of judicial procedure to be adopted by the brethren, and which may be considered as the first peeping point of that germ that grew and spread web-like over the world as the Canon Law.

CHAPTER V.

THE STONING OF STEPHEN.

I. THE TAPESTRY OF THE STONING OF STEPHEN.—II. THE GOSPEL AS ACCEPTED BY HELLENISTIC JEWS.—III. THE SCATTERED CHURCH; THE RESIDENT APOSTLES.

I. THE STONING OF STEPHEN.

THE Cartoon for the Stoning of Stephen, the next subject of the series of tapestries, does not exist.

An outline of the design, derived from the tapestry, will be found in Kugler's 'Handbook,' translated by Eastlake; and this and my notes of the tapestry at Mantua supply the foundation of the few remarks I have to make on the composition.

The incident illustrated is thus introduced in Acts vi. 1:—"And in those days, when the number of the Apostles had multiplied, there arose a murmuring of the Hellenists against the Hebrews, that their widows were neglected in the daily distribution ($\dot{\epsilon}\nu$ $\tau\hat{\eta}$ $\delta\iota\alpha\kappa o\nu\iota\dot{q}$). Then the Twelve called together the body ($\pi\lambda\hat{\eta}\theta o s$) of the disciples, and said, It is not satisfactory for us to leave the word of God, and serve tables; wherefore, brethren, look ye out among you seven men well attested, full of the Holy Spirit and of wisdom, whom we will appoint to this business; but we will give ourselves constantly to prayer, and to the service of the word. And the saying was agreeable to the whole multitude. And they chose Stephen, a man full of faith and the Holy Spirit, and Philip, and Prochorus, and Nicanor, and Timon, and Parmenas, and Nicolaus of Antioch, a proselyte: whom they set before the Apostles, and having prayed, they laid their hands upon them.

" . . . . And Stephen, full of faith and power, did great wonders and miracles among the people. And there arose certain of the synagogue called that of the Libertines, and of the Cyrenians and Alexandrians, and of those from Cilicia and Asia, disputing with Stephen, and they were not able to resist the wisdom and the Spirit with which he spoke."

Beaten in argument, they resort to riot and to prosecution, and the catastrophe is thus described:—"But he, being full of the Holy Spirit, looked up steadfastly into the heavens, and saw the glory of God and Jesus standing on the right hand of God, and said, Behold, I see heaven opened, and the Son of Man standing on the right hand of God. Then they cried with a loud voice and stopped their ears, and ran at him with one accord, and cast him out of the city and stoned him. And the witnesses laid down their clothes at the feet of a young man named Saul. *And they stoned Stephen while he prayed, saying, Lord Jesus, receive my spirit.* And kneeling down, he called out with a loud voice, Lord, lay not this sin to their charge. And saying this, he fell asleep. And Saul was consenting to his death."

This narrative bears marks of extension by the accretion of several versions. The narrative is complete where

THE STONING OF ST STEPHEN; a tapestry of the Sistine series, in the Vatican

the italics commence. The notice immediately preceding recurs in the concluding phrase, and the prayer is interposed, and repeated with a variation.

The treatment of the incident by the painter will not occupy us long.

At the right-hand corner of the picture Christ and the Father, attended by angels, are seen above in the opening heavens. To these the countenance of the martyr is directed; he has fallen on his knees, as if impelled by the storm of blows from behind, but with no attempt to shield himself, with no regard to the impending fragment of rock that will evidently be fatal; he spreads his arms before the crowd of his murderers with an expression of shielding them, and the air of supplication in their favour, according to his last words, "Lord, lay not this sin to their charge." The extended arms mark the attitude used by the early Christians at the words, "Let us pray;" but Rafael combines the feeling of intercession.

A man behind him, rising on the foot, has raised a huge stone with both hands to the full height of his reach, and is about to dash it down directly upon his head. The man on the left of the foreground stoops down, and, while he keeps his eye on his victim, in his impatience seizes a stone with each hand. A persecutor behind seems aiming for a cast at once, without waiting to get near; and another, also with uplifted stone, is crowding forward for an opportunity. The crowd passes out of the picture; stones on the ground tell of violence already delivered.

On the right-hand corner of the foreground Saul, yet beardless, is seated on the garments of the witnesses, one of whom is the stooper in the foreground, with bare shoulders, and he encourages them with rancorous gestures. In the tapestry at Mantua I noticed the neck and part of a bottle on his seat behind. The scene is fixed, agreeably to the text, without the city.

Stephen wears a dress with sleeves, and with a certain set, make, and finish, that suggest the established ecclesiastical costume of a deacon.

It will be observed that the vision of the glory of God, and the Son of Man standing at his right hand, is transferred by Rafael, with his usual happy and concentrating boldness, from the scene before the Sanhedrim, to the execution.

II. THE GOSPEL AS ACCEPTED BY HELLENISTIC JEWS.

Let us now endeavour to appreciate the true historical basis that supports the narrative of the career of Stephen. The view I shall propound is, I believe, new; for I do not find it set forth by either Zeller or Baur. In one sense, for me, it is old enough, for I shall have little to say that I do not find already recorded in my note-books of some twenty years' standing; and have only to transcribe conclusions that I find I set my hand to under the date 24th January, 1842.

How perfectly in order and of necessity it was that money jealousies should arise in a society framed on a system of communism, has already been remarked. It is to be noticed further, that the administration complained of was that of the Apostles themselves, and that they were more peculiarly identified with the Hebrew section of the community; it may even be suggested that the aspect of the case bears out a suspicion that the imputed partiality had existed. By the tenor of the narrative the Apostles found a handsome excuse for resigning an invidious office that they could no longer administer in their own way; at least, the community, when they had provided satisfactory successors, seem to have disregarded their representation of the incompatibility of the two ministrations, the economical and the spiritual; for three at least of the deacons, Stephen especially, and Philip by name, and Nicolaus inferentially, as eponym of the Nicolaitans, come before us as active preachers.

The names of all the newly-elected deacons are Greek, which justifies the inference that the Hellenist division of the Church already very considerably outnumbered the Hebrew. The enthusiasm that had extended the society with such rapidity had evidently spread in some directions more rapidly than others; the Church had incorporated faster than it could assimilate, and the result was a serious disturbance of balance among the classes composing it.

The depth and breadth of the distinction between Hellenistic and "Hebrew Jew," in its most pronounced form, must be carefully appreciated. It touches the very commencement of the most important of all the schisms of the Church,—that by which the original and self-consistent portion of the sect became separated from the progressive party that had gathered to it, lost the lead, and at last all but died out as an obscure and secondary sect,—heretics in the eyes of Christians still more than of Jews, while its intrusive successor advanced to the conquest of the world.

The motive emergency is spoken of as a matter of 'the daily ministration;' and it seems probable, therefore, that seven deacons were appointed, that they might take duty successively through the seven days of the week.

While the Apostles were so assiduously in attendance at the Temple,—and it will be long after this that we shall hear from Apostles themselves, that "the thousands of brethren at Jerusalem who believe,—who compose the Jerusalem,—the Hebrew Church, are still all zealous for the law,"—we need not be surprised at the regulation of the sect by the order of the Jewish week. With the Hellenistic Church, however, an important change, in this respect, became ultimately established; when exactly, we know not; the seven-day division, which was in truth as much Pagan, Egyptian especially, as Jewish, was retained, but the chief day, the se'nnightly festival, was moved from the Jewish Sabbath to the day succeeding; a variation of the greatest significance.

The ascription of the several days of the recurring seven to the presidency of the several planets, had long been established among the heathen,—how much beyond all power of alteration is seen by the idolatrous titles having continued down to the present time, both in Latin and Teutonic form. Even the Jew might be traditionally reconciled to designating his Sabbath day the day of Saturn—of Cronos, for while his religious antipathies were committed most distinctly against the worshippers of the heavenly host, of the celestial array of angels of the planets, of sun and stars, the hints of history of his own religion and worship, indicate an original astral departure. The analogies of the worship of Moloch are constantly intruding themselves as we follow the phases and developments of the worship of Jehovah; and Moloch is equivalent of Saturn and Cronos.

(For completer illustration of the point, refer to Mr. Mackay's 'Progress of the Intellect,' vol. i. p. 122, etc.)

In Greece the brighter Olympic divinities superseded the sombre and cruel rites of Cronos; and in that diversified mythology the Sun became the symbol, at least, of every predominant godhead in turn. The recurrence of festivals, and the measurement of periods, were dependent on marked epochs of sun and moon; and thus Greece, and the nations it influenced, however superior to the fetichism of star worship, had a direct point of contact with the sun-worshipping East.

The result appears to have been that, the Jews apart, most of the nations that were affected by the spread of Christianity had been accustomed, from all time, to regard the sun as the grand type, as well as index, of times of festival, quadriennially, annually, even weekly. On the succession of the new religion, it was as natural to put Christ into the place of the superseded Sun-god, as it would be repugnant to all feeling to associate the Saviour with the surroundings of Saturn. Accordingly, the great yearly festivals of Christianity were adapted to the ancient occasions that marked, and of necessity still mark, the vicissitudes of the sun; or rather, they fell into them by heritage from the worn-out creeds; the birth of the Saviour, substituted for Mithra, designates the winter solstice, his death and resurrection the revival of spring at the vernal equinox, and the birth of John the Baptist, as the last prophet of the Old Covenant, was assigned to the summer solstice,—the epoch of transition of the year to shortening days. And so the motive that appropriated the distribution of the Christian year operated, I do not doubt, with still greater force in determining the weekly festival to the day of the Sun. We shall presently understand how strong a repugnance between the Jewish section of Christ's Church, and those less rigidly or purely Jewish, promoted a preference for that day as a festival, which marked sympathy with the increasing party of converts, and favoured alienation from Judaism.

All this however comes hereafter; at present we have to trace the special relation of the Hellenistic Jews to the Hebrew Jews in the infant Church. General characteristics of Hellenist and Hebrew we may find elsewhere; but for the peculiar form of Hellenistic Judaism at present in question, we have to rely almost entirely on the history of the deacons, and especially on the implications in the defence of Stephen.

The prolonged domination of Greek powers in Western Asia and Syria had caused a considerable infusion of Greek language and manners even among the Jews of Palestine. Still more extensively and importantly was this the case with those who were scattered in such numbers about the rest of the world. Tenacious of nationality and cult as the Jew might be, the modifying force of contingencies through successive generations was irresistible; the original dialect was lost, if the customs were retained, and the customs became relaxed or even relinquished though the recollection of them might be cherished to the verge of bigotry. The periodical attendances at the Temple, so strictly insisted upon in the Law, were of necessity given up.

All these were points upon which it was in the nature of the Jew, that the native of Judæa and still more of Jerusalem should plume himself, as titles of superiority in holiness, as compared with the Hellenist. The suspicion of mixed race, of impure descent,—a decline from Judaism more repugnant than all other, would always attach, and with sufficient confirmations, to the Hellenists. The Jews of various countries had, doubtless, then as now, their traits of subnationalities; and children of Jewish mothers and Heathen fathers, like Timothy, were of course numerous.

Paul, it is true, asserts himself as a Hebrew of the Hebrews, though he was born at Tarsus; his education was at Jerusalem, and his command of the Hebrew tongue was accepted as presumptive proof of Hebraism, and he is first introduced to us also with a Jewish name, Saul; but an enemy might have interpreted his claims less indulgently.

These disputes and pretensions were as prevalent at the date of the return from captivity as at any subsequent period. The resolute religious enthusiasts who came back to restore Jerusalem, looked with contempt at those of their brethren who shunned the risk and were content to abide in the settlements they had gained in a new country; and they were quite as prompt to repudiate fellowship with the kindred tribes who, like the Samaritans, had remained in Palestine, and were open to more than suspicion of mixed race as well as of idolatrous concessions.

In Egypt, Jewish communities existed from all time, and in the days of Jeremiah they were swelled by a large emigration under the pressure of encroaching As-syrian power. Here sprang up difficulties and compromises together, as to observance of the law.

"Latterly the law had required every Jew to present himself in the Temple at Jerusalem at each of the great feasts; but this was a burden too heavy for those that dwelt at a distance. Once a year, however, at the feast of Tabernacles, this religious journey was still called for; 'and if the family of Egypt,' says the prophet Zechariah (xiv. 18), 'go not forth and come not up, they shall have no rain, they shall have the plague wherewith the Lord will smite the tribes that come not up to keep the feast of Tabernacles.' " (Sharpe's 'Egypt,' i. p. 103.)

At a later date, the formation of a numerous Jewish community with its wealthy and learned classes in the heart of the commercial and cultivated city of Alexandria, led to still more decided and important results. Here Jewish literature became deeply tinged with Greek characteristics, became highly Hellenized, and produced a form of literature and philosophy highly remarkable, to say the least, from the combination of a stock still truly Jewish with the refinements of Platonism, and even with traces of notions merely Egyptian.

This literature is represented by the Septuagint, and then very specifically by the writings of Philo of Alexandria, a contemporary of Josephus and St. Paul. Some of the most peculiar notions and phraseologies of Philo are found in the writings of St. Paul, genuine and ascribed; an abundant crop of them in the Epistle to the Hebrews, an epistle which by correlation to its title, and no less by its contents, we may regard as by a Hellenist,—and again in the speech of Stephen, which we shall have to consider presently.

I believe it is pretty clear that to the bigoted Hebrew, the Samaritans and the Hellenistic Jews of the dispersion were much upon a par, and both little better than Gentiles. Something like this is implied in the text in the fourth Gospel: "Then they said, Will he go to the dispersed among the Gentiles, and teach the Gentiles? God forbid." The Epistle of Peter is addressed unequivocally to "the sojourners of the dispersion in Pontus," etc., yet alludes to their condition previous to conversion, as heathenism.

The Talmud again is fair traditional evidence of the relation of the two divisions of the nation. "The Rabbins express without disguise their hatred of the language of the Greek Jews, and still more of the Septuagint translation, which formed in fact an ecclesiastical partition between the two parties." (Gfrörer.)

However the Hellenists were regarded by the Hebrews, they might of course be as bigoted as they pleased on their own account notwithstanding. The writings of Philo, as well as the incidents of the mission he undertook to Rome, indicate attachment to Moses and the Temple of Jerusalem of the strictest kind. There was certainly no lack of bigotry among the synagogues that Paul found in his widely-extended journeys, and it is in the Hellenistic synagogues at Jerusalem that both Paul and Stephen encounter rancorous and deadly opposition when their preachings verge in the direction of liberality.

Still, it was amongst the Hellenists and Hellenistic deacons that liberalism arose, and asserted not only even ground of privilege for Hellenist and Hebrew, but such a conception of Christianity, of religious merit and devotion, as opened doors of sympathy and equality for the Samaritan also, and in very short time for that outer Gentile world that completed the circuit of humanity. They had suffered persecution, and had learnt mercy; they had been the victims of fratricidal rivalry, and lived to invite all mankind to make common cause. Apollos, a cultivated and accomplished Jew of Alexandria, who had embraced enthusiastically the pure theory of the preaching of John the Baptist, may be taken as a fair type of the class of Hellenists from which had previously issued the comprehensive charity of Stephen.

A spark alone was wanting in those years to fuse provincialisms into nationality, and nationalities into largest humanity. Men's minds had grown accustomed to the mighty ideal of the whole civilized world in theory, administered in unity, on the model of a peaceful family; however the practice might seem to halt for and invite the furtherance of a renewed and helping impulse from the hand of God. But the following anecdote may be an illustration at an earlier date—and bigotry is independent of chronology, of what the nature and the spirit of the rivalries had been, that were destined to combine, volatilize, disperse, in a moment, in minds warmed and irradiated by the fire of an exalted sympathy.

The incident I quote is dated in the reign of Ptolemy Philometor, some 160 years before Christ.

"A dispute arose at Alexandria between the Jews there and the Samaritans who reverenced the temple built at Gerizim about the time of Alexander, and the contention respecting the rival temples was carried before Ptolemy himself. The Jews averred that it was

the temple at Jerusalem that was built agreeably to the laws of Moses, while the Samaritans made the same claim for that at Gerizim. They begged the King to sit with his friends as assessors, and hear the arguments on this subject, and to inflict death on whichever party should be adjudged to be worsted.

"Sabbæus and Theodosius undertook the argument on the part of the Samaritans, and Andronicus, son of Messalamus, was for those of Jerusalem and the Jews. They took an oath by God and the King to conduct their proofs in accordance with the law, and engaged Ptolemy to put to death whichever of them should be found falsifying his oath.

"The King accordingly associated many of his friends as a council, and took his seat to give audience to the speakers. The greatest excitement prevailed among the Jews who were in Alexandria, respecting the peril of their ancient fane. By the concession of Sabbæus and Theodosius, Andronicus commenced the pleadings, and proceeded with his proofs from the law and from the successions of the high-priests from father to son, and from the honour shown to the Temple by kings of Asia, in dedications and splendid gifts, while of that on Gerizim none took notice or made account more than if it had not existed. By these arguments and many more to the same effect, Andronicus persuaded the King to give judgment that the Temple had been built at Jerusalem in accordance with the laws of Moses, and to put Sabbæus and Theodosius to death." (Josephus, Antiq. xiii. 3, 4.)

As to the Samaritans in Judæa, Josephus more than once characterizes them as always prepared to renounce kindred with the Jews whenever the latter were in trouble; but as soon as they prospered, equally forward to declare themselves Hebrews, and to vindicate their descent from Ephraim and Manasseh, the sons of Joseph. He calls them a colony of apostates from the Jewish nation, and their city of Shechem, about Mount Gerizim, the common refuge of all who had made themselves chargeable at Jerusalem with the crimes of eating profane food, violated Sabbath, and the like.

The story of Stephen proceeds. His opponents in the Hellenistic synagogues of Jerusalem were unable to contend with him—" were not able to resist the wisdom and spirit with which he spoke." Among these synagogues is mentioned that of Cilicia, and it is probable that Paul, as a witness, if not a party to these disputations, was unconsciously receiving some of the seeds of doctrine that germinated so vigorously a little later.

" Then they suborned men, who said, We have heard him speak blasphemous words against Moses and against God. And they stirred up the people, and the elders, and the scribes, and came upon him and seized him, and brought him to the council, and set up false witnesses, who said, This man ceaseth not to speak blasphemous words against this holy place and the law; for we have heard him say that this Jesus of Nazareth shall destroy this place, and shall change the customs that Moses delivered us. And all who sat in the council, looking steadfastly on him, saw his face as if it had been the face of an angel."

The gist of the accusation is so far borne out by the very reply put into the mouth of Stephen, that we can only consider the historian to call the witnesses false witnesses in virtue of an idiom that stigmatizes a charge as false which, substantially true, is pressed for an unfair, unjust, and malignant end. It is quite conceivable that all witnesses who bring innocence to grief should be called false witnesses, whether they compass their end by charge of crimes never committed, or of acts committed indeed, but not in reality crimes.

It is not necessary to discuss the probability of the long speech ascribed to Stephen before the council, having been really delivered by him. The importance of it will be scarcely less should it prove only to embody the characteristic topics and modes of treatment in favour with a new party in the Church. Thus much, I think, can be made out very coherently and consistently with other notices of the new movement that are not wanting. In such case it matters not much whether the heads of the defence were brought away by an eyewitness of the trial, or whether they were made up by one who lived sufficiently near the time, or was in possession of such materials as enabled him to construct a condensed justification of the principles of Stephanic Christianity.

The speech, in fact, becomes more intelligible if we take this broad view,—accept it on its own statements, and put almost out of mind the terms of the charge to which it purports to be a more specific reply than is really the case.

The grand point of the speech is the averment, that in Christ is fulfilled the prophecy of Moses: "A prophet shall the Lord your God raise up unto you of your brethren like unto me: him shall ye hear."

The parallelism of Christ and Moses runs upon the correspondence of their relation to their brethren enslaved and scattered; of their services to them as deliverers, and givers of sacred laws; of their treatment by them,—scorned, rejected, or slain.

But the prophecy, or what is taken as such, speaks of a contrast, or intimates one, as well as a parallel; and Moses predicts a successor who, like him in other respects, will be more fortunate in gaining the hearing,—failing which, it was that he himself was reduced to a compromise, to substitution of ceremonial law for lively oracles.

So special, however, on the part of Hellenistic Jews was the view of the relation of prophet to people, that it was not enough to illustrate this in the position of Moses alone. The relation was traced from a still higher point; and the historical introduction required to define the position of Moses was taken advantage of, to set forth two other authoritative parallels in the histories of Abraham and of Joseph.

The appositeness of this long historical introduction becomes at once apparent, when we observe that it is so guided as to discredit, by the authority of the most revered names, the ceremonial prejudice of the restriction of divine favour to a particular locality; in fact, to Jerusalem or Judæa.

Not exclusively, it is set forth, had the God of the Hebrews been manifested in this city and this holy land; in fact, his favour, and the haunt and attachments of his most favoured servants, had been associated with localities now regarded—surely, therefore, inconsiderately—with aversion and hatred.

Abraham was of Mesopotamia, and it was there the God of Glory appeared to him; after his call, there was an intermediate migration and residence at Haran before he came into Judæa; and in Palestine, at last, he had no inheritance, not so much as to set his foot on, but only the promise of reversion for his posterity. Abraham himself, therefore, was in much the same degree of domiciliary remoteness from Jerusalem as his descendants, who still were sojourners in Babylonia and the East.

The posterity of Abraham, still and ever the objects of divine care, were conducted by God to Egypt, and in Egypt they became a numerous, a wealthy, and dignified community,—an anticipation of the contemporary communities so flourishing at Alexandria, at Heliopolis, at Cyrene, and so forth. Jacob himself, the very eponym of the race, settled in Egypt, and there died; and if his bones were not left there, where were they transported to? Was it not to Sychem, to the now so-shunned and abominated region of the Samaritans,—a region that had, moreover, been sanctified and accepted, not to say adopted, by Abraham?

It was in Egypt, like any modern Hellenist, that Moses was born; he was brought up in the very palace, the seat in Egypt of all idolatrous abominations; he was even accomplished in all the learning and language of the Egyptians—acquirements still more alien than the learning and language of the Greeks. He took refuge in Midian, and was more than a wanderer there, for there he begat two sons.

It was in the wilderness of Sinai that Moses received his commission as a prophet and deliverer; and there was given the command to put off his shoes from his feet, because the place whereon he stood was holy ground: the same observance for the same regard obtained then, in the Arabian wilderness as in the worship of every Jew in the proud and exclusive temple on Mount Moriah.

So much for the ascription of especial merit and holiness to birth, or residence, or periodical visitation, or worshipping in one restricted locality, or within one limit of consecrated ground; so much for the consistency of putting under ban the very localities—Chaldæa, Samaria, Midian, Egypt—that had been hallowed and accepted by the manifestations and miracles of God, and the homes and actions of his most favoured servants.

The history of Moses is then pursued through the account of his difficulties with the Israelites his brethren, whom he came to liberate and to enlighten. He had to allay political rejection, parallel to that of Jesus, and the disappointment of a religious apostasy, of which the result was to condemn the nation to a debased material worship instead of a spiritual: it was by this catastrophe that the great work of religious enlightenment was left over for a future generation and prophet, —for Jesus the Christ.

The slavery of the Israelites in Egypt is a manifest parallel to the condition of the Jews under the Romans, and the allusion would infallibly be so understood. It is as certain that the speech, by whomsoever composed, has for its purport to compare the rejection of Jesus in person with that of Moses, who, only concerned to heal the dissensions of his brethren, and to exercise his power of protecting them from oppression, is ungratefully and spitefully entreated, and forced to fly for his life.

As regards the religious aspect of the question, a theory is then propounded of the origin and character of the ceremonial law, and of the Temple especially. This was the true key of bigoted Judaism. The Jew, who renounced idolatry in its more palpable forms with unfeigned antipathy, clung to the symbolical Temple with all the more blindness and tenacity, till his reverence for it became, in fact, equivalent to idolatry; much as the Protestants have filled up the void made by secession of Catholic images and relics and hagiology, by unreasoning and stupefied veneration for the Bible and the Book of Common Prayer.

There is a certain incoherency in the current of the speech, but I feel confidence in the interpretation that Stephen represents the Israelites as having, by their worship of the Golden Calf, forfeited the first and nobler revelations of which Moses was the messenger,—the "lively oracles," the words of life, the spiritual dispensation. God, in consequence, gave them over to a worship that was essentially astral; they were consigned to the penal infliction, self-sought, of a heavy and degrading ceremonialism of sacrifices and offerings, to symbols that were little better than heathenish in origin and effect, the star of Moloch, the sacred tent of Remphan migrating from region to region within the promised land, and without. Such, in very origin, was the venerated Temple—the holy place, and such the law; and even this,—of secondary origin, and delivered through intermediate agency of angels, had not been observed, and all claim of merit through it was forfeit and futile.

In the Epistle of Barnabas, the Jews are represented as having forfeited the covenant of God when Moses, through their apostasy, broke the tables of the law. (Compare Justin's Dialogue with Tryphon, pp. 66 and 68 ed. Otto, and other authorities cited in the notes.)

It is true that on turning to Exodus we find the instructions for making the tabernacle given to Moses previous to his breaking the tables, and before the transgression with the Golden Calf. But it is not less true, and, in connection with Stephen's speech, most important and remarkable, that the entire section containing these instructions,—Exodus xxv. 1, to xxxi. 17,—is by one hand, pertains to the record Elohim, and stands in its present place as an interpolation. (De Wette's Lehrbuch d. Alt. Test., p. 197.)

The tabernacle of Moloch, as referred to by Stephen, seems related to the ἱερὰ σκήνη, or sacred tent, mentioned by Diodorus Siculus (xx. 25) in the camp of the Carthaginians. Stephen, following Amos, evidently regards the tabernacle and its services from the same point of view as Hezekiah regarded the brazen serpent. This, as we are told in Numbers xxi. 7, was made by the the express directions of God to Moses; yet, nevertheless, Hezekiah recognized it as the idolatrous symbol it really was,—relative of the Agathodæmon of Phœnicia and the serpent-symbol of Cos, where we even find a festival of the ἀνάληψις ῥαβδοῦ,—and broke it to pieces unsparingly.

Of all the customs which Stephen was charged with design to change, circumcision was the most important, and the most obstructive to expansive views like those of his party. There was, I do not doubt, a controversial purpose in his reference to its origin with Abraham, before the time of Moses. The point is mentioned in John vii. 19-23, in the course of an argument for liberal observation of the Sabbath.

The charge recorded against Stephen included the speaking blasphemous words against God as well as Moses. We have here an intimation of the doctrines which gave the imputation colour. Long before, Hellenized, and even Orientalized Jews had been shocked at the coarsely anthropomorphical expressions applied to Deity in the Old Testament,—relics of the archaic conception of Jehovah as a family or national god. In perplexing passages they substituted the agency of the "angel of the Lord;" with the more inflexible logicians, the God of the Old Testament came to be regarded as an inferior spirituality.

Even Josephus (Archæol. xv. 5, 3) and the Rabbins, as well as Philo (de Decalogo), the author of the Epistle to the Hebrews (ii. 2), and Paul (Gal. iii. 19), agree that it was not the Lord, but the angel of the Lord, who spoke to Moses on Sinai. Josephus interrupts his narrative to plead, with an awkward air of embarrassment, "Every one is at liberty, of course, to hold his own opinion as to what I now relate; but I am bound, and merely undertake to set forth what I find in our sacred books, as I find it."

The Jewish-Alexandrian philosophies were the great source of these hesitations and evasions (Dähne xi. 62), and the phrases of the speech before us betray their influence in every line.

It was not God simply, but the God of Glory, who was seen by Abraham. In Philo (De Monarchia, i. 6),

Moses, assured that God is invisible, solicits to see at least the glory around him; and proceeds, "but thy glory I conceive to be the powers attendant on thee as guards." The reply again is, that these also are invisible, intellectual, objects not of sense but of intelligence, if any intelligence were capable of more than apprehending the mere adumbrations even of these. It was not the Lord, simple and unqualified, but the "angel of the Lord," who appeared to Moses in the burning-bush, and declared himself the God of Abraham, of Isaac, and of Jacob. Moses was in the desert with "the angel" who spoke to him on Mount Sinai. The Jews received the law (which, however, they failed to observe) "by the disposition of angels." "He who spake to Moses" furnished the model of the tabernacle which remained with Israel until the days of David, who desired to find a tabernacle for "the God of Jacob;" and for whom Solomon built a house.

"Howbeit," he turns off, "the Most Highest (as distinguished from the angels) dwelleth not in what is made with hands; as the prophet says, Heaven is my throne, and earth the footstool of my feet; what house will ye build for me, saith the Lord, or what is the place of my rest? Has not my hand made all these things?"

The text here cited from Isaiah has many parallels in denunciation of ceremonialism among the old prophets; history is never discontinuous, and recorded or not,—whether expressions of such feelings left their traces in literature, or art, or not, they descended no less by the infallible channels of tradition, and there is no wildness in the belief that the spiritual view of worship, to which Stephen was giving utterance, came down to him like the dialect in which he spoke, like the physiognomy that marked his race, from antecessors and progenitors, who had looked with repugnance at the original tabernacle itself, had even suffered, like Stephen, for the unpopularity or imprudence of their denunciations.

In most worships a Temple has either commenced or ended by being accepted as a symbol of the cosmos, —the *mundus*, the universe. The principle is seen distinctly in the Roman or Etruscan precepts for setting out a consecrated precinct, whether a camp or a sanctuary, as a *templum*. Philo Judæus, in his second book, 'De Monarchia,' has an interesting parallel of the cosmical temple of the divinity, and the Temple at Jerusalem, its earthly symbol; and accepts the correlation without repugnance. Thus we may seem to gain but little by renouncing a symbolism, harmless enough, and at any rate ornamental. But the denouncement of local consecration, the equivalent of desecration of all without the limit, had more value. It cut through the very heart and root of the bitter uncharitableness of the unsociable Jew; and it was doing good service to denounce as mischievous a system which degraded the universal into the national, the local, the sectarian,—almost into the private and particular.

Thus Stephen has declared the equality of man before God, and the nullity of the ceremonial law; and finally, fatally for himself,—so at least runs the record, taken for what it may be worth,—he hurries on to declare his anticipation of the development and destinies of the Christian movement and its founder.

"But he, being full of the Holy Ghost, looked up steadfastly into heaven, and saw the glory of God, and Jesus standing on the right hand of God, and said, Behold, I see the heavens opened, and the Son of Man standing on the right hand of God.

"Then they cried with a loud voice, and stopped their ears, and ran upon him," etc. etc. (Acts vii. 55.)

By the reference in the exclamation of Stephen, to the prophecy of Daniel, he designates Jesus as the Son of Man, whose manifestation is there foretold; and in the expected form of this manifestation we are presented with the modified aspect in which the Kingdom of Jesus now presented itself to at least a considerable section of the Church.

The section of Daniel referred to, is in reality a history in quasi-prophetical or allegorical guise, after the fact, of the establishment of the Macedonian, the fourth great monarchy,—the secondary Syrian Empire that grew out of it, and the troubles and persecutions of the Jews by Antiochus Epiphanes. The fifth monarchy, a divine revelation, is to conclude all; of this the Son of Man is to be the leader, and his saints the ministers and inheritors.

Daniel vii. 9, "I beheld till the thrones were cast down, and the Ancient of days did sit, whose garment was white as snow, and the hair of his head as pure wool: his throne was like the fiery flame, and his wheels as burning fire. A fiery stream issued and came forth from before him; thousand thousands ministered unto him, and ten thousand times ten thousand stood before him: the judgment was set, and the books were opened. . . . (Ver. 13,) I saw in the night visions, and, behold, one like the Son of Man came with the clouds of heaven, and came to the Ancient of days, and they brought him near before him. And there was given unto him dominion, and glory, and a kingdom, that all people, nations, and languages should serve him: his dominion is an everlasting dominion, which shall not pass away. . . . (Ver. 27,) And the kingdom and dominion, and the greatness of the kingdom under the whole heaven, shall be given to the people of the saints of the most High, whose kingdom is an everlasting kingdom, and all dominions shall serve and obey him."

Here, again, we have an anticipation by Stephen of another Pauline conception, namely, that of the second coming, as delivered in the Epistle to the Thessalonians. Daniel's prophecy is as evidently the model for this, as it was for that of Stephen, or the inditer of the speech assigned to him, whoever he may have been.

Stephen's last words carry the imputation, "who have received the law by the disposition of angels, and have not kept it." This charge against the zealots, of themselves not keeping the law, for which they were such sticklers, comes up elsewhere. John vii. 19, Jesus says, "Did not Moses give you the law, and yet none of you keepeth the law? why go ye about to kill me?"

From the nature of the law, and the circumstances of the time, it was of course impossible that the law should be fully observed, even by the most scrupulous; and where was an authority competent to set any part of it aside? The zealot was therefore in a dilemma, which made him inconsistent enough, between arbitrary neglect and rigid exaction of observances. Bigotry, however, is not repelled by an incongruity; the zealot relaxed no little of his requirements, but his more liberal-minded opponents did not fail to press him with his inconsistency. This I believe to have been the gist of St. Paul's argument, as well as of those just cited, when he urged upon Pharisaic Jews at Antioch that even they, zealous and Jews as they were, in many respects habitually violated the law, "lived as did the Gentiles;" what, then, was their authority for fixing on Gentiles the law of the Jews that was so loosely worn by themselves?

The citations of Scripture in the speech correspond with the Septuagint version, but are made and applied with extraordinary irregularity and inaccuracy.

The command of God to Abraham, quoted as given in Mesopotamia, was given, according to Genesis xi. 31, and xii. 1, after his departure to Haran, and is therefore confounded with the command to quit Ur of the Chaldees. (Gen. xv. 7; Neh. ix. 7.)

Ver. 4. The departure of Abraham after the death of his father is not reconcileable with the dates given. Abram, we read, was born in his father's seventieth year (Gen. xi. 26), and quitted Haran when he himself was seventy-five, and therefore when his father was 145 (Gen. xii. 4); his father, however, as we are told, lived to be 205.

Ver. 5. That Abraham did not possess a foot of the promised land is at variance with the strict letter of the narrative of his purchase, Gen. xxiii.

Ver. 14. The number of the family of Jacob invited to Egypt by Joseph is also at variance.

Ver. 16. Here are two errors, or at least divarications: first, that all the sons of Jacob were buried in Palestine;

second, that he himself was buried in Sychem, not in the Cave of Machpelah by Hebron. (Gen. xlix. 30.)

Again, we read that it was Jacob who bought a field of the sons of Hamor (Gen. xxxiii. 19), and Abraham who bought the cave of Machpelah.

Ver. 22. The eloquence of Moses does not agree with Gen. iv. 10.

Ver. 43. The text of Amos has Damascus, not Babylon.

Some of these discrepancies have the air of being due to independent traditions and controversial glosses, rather than to simple lapse in quotation. There appears, for instance, to have been a popular view that Abram's father was dead when he migrated, adopted probably from tenderness to his piety. (Cf. Philo Judæus, Migrat. Abr., Op. i. p. 464.)

III. THE SCATTERED CHURCH: THE RESIDENT APOSTLES.

The account of the death of Stephen is followed up by a most remarkable, and in itself surprising notice. "And in that day there was a great persecution against the church which was in Jerusalem, and all were scattered abroad in the countries of Judæa and Samaria, except the Apostles."

Some qualification is manifestly requisite here; either the scattering of the community was much less general than stated, or there is a mistake as to the Apostles being able to stand their ground. How is it, we may ask ourselves, that the incongruity did not appear to the writer or compiler of Acts? Was it that he was aware that the course of the narrative would bring him back to find the Apostles at Jerusalem? But then it was open to him to assume that they had found their way back. Was it that he felt repugnance to represent them as fugitives, while others were martyrs? If he were persuaded that, incongruous as it might appear, the fact was as he states it, he may easily have fallen back, and have rested assured that his readers would fall back, upon the general impression that things of the greatest improbability are often true notwithstanding, and that this was one of them. After all, the claim of the Apostles to supernatural protection was in reserve in the background.

I believe, however, that a very simple qualification of the terms of the narrative will make all clear, and this qualification is abundantly supported by incidental confirmations. It seems to me certain that the persecution which was first provoked by Stephen only attacked the portion of the Church which was actively participant in his views,—views highly contrasted with those that we find now and afterwards entertained by the Apostles, and therefore by their adherents. We are here, in fact, at the very point of divergence of a great party in the Church,—a divergence that we shall find quite serious enough to account for such differences of fortune as that the Diaconal section should be hunted down and dispersed, while the Apostolic remains at home and enjoys immunity.

Persecution is now for the first time spoken of as coming from the Pharisees. The earlier notices of the troubles of the Apostles ascribe them to that Sadducaic faction of which the sympathies, as characterized by Josephus, would be not more opposed to their doctrine of resurrection than to their action upon the religious excitability of the lower orders, and the stimulus lent to Messianic agitation,—the eager hope of the speedy kingdom of God, if not restoration of the line of David.

A large fund of precepts in the Gospels is directed against Pharisaism, as developed in ostentatious piety and almsgiving, exclusive regard to preceptive morality, and reliance on minute, burdensome, irrational ceremonialism. Opposition to these corruptions of true devotion was the very strength of the preaching of the Baptist, and I do not doubt struck deep root through the ministrations of Jesus, and gave effect to much of the teaching of the Apostles; only on this supposition of communicated force from personal character can we account for the full vigour and vitality of the Church, and the general tone of its records after his death. But after his death, other influences gained in countervailing power; the exciting anticipation of his return in power was predominant; it attracted adherents in large numbers, who were still imbued with attachment to the law of Moses with the greatest bigotry, and the colour that was thus given to the Church at large, threw, I suspect, more influence than was well, into the hands of those of the Apostles who had least realized the true extent of the antithesis, between the spirituality of Jesus and the Baptist, and the paltriness of ceremonialism.

This is the explanation of the startling account that we read late in Acts, of the condition of the Jerusalem Church. "You see, brother, how many thousands of Jews there are who believe, who are all zealots for the law." Apostles, it is clear, accepted them as believers on what would well seem to Stephen or to Paul very easy terms; and by the same rule, the populace of Jerusalem and their Pharisaic leaders would not readily appreciate a difference with Stephen as a ground of quarrel with the Apostles.

It is open to those who please to take the view that the contrariety between Stephen and the Apostles was a transference to an earlier date of this later difficulty of Paul; for myself, I see in the parallelism a recurrence of similar effects from permanent conditions, and take one incident as confirming, not as superseding the other.

Perfectly in accordance with these inferences, is the complication introduced into the affairs of the Church by the interference and influence at Antioch of brethren of the sect of Pharisees, who came from James at Jerusalem. The tendency, at least, of all the notices is concordant, and we cannot ascribe too much historical importance to the crisis before us, as affecting the course of Christianity and colouring its records.

We have before us the explanation of some of the leading incongruities presented by these records. Partly in their fragmentary condition, partly in their compiled, partly in their progress from the state of loose records to compilations, the Gospels were modified extensively by a branch of the Christian sect alienated to some extent from the Apostles, and even opposed to them, though bound at the same time to a respectful theory of their position as transmitters of the faith and the first dispensers of the Holy Ghost. The memorabilia of Jesus passed, in fact, through the hands of those who had more definite theories of his mission than personal knowledge of its facts, and every form of mythical corruption had thus free inlet. In all integrity of good faith, as well as by laxity of pious lapse, most uncritical inclusions and exclusions would have sway. But the most important result of such conditions is this, that the Gospels contain entire sections of incidents and speeches ascribed to Jesus, which he not only could never have had part in, but that most certainly were originally composed consciously as apologues, as allegories, as illustrations,—as poetic illustrations or whatever else, but certainly not as candid narrative of credited matters of fact. How these stories came first to be so accredited is a difficult question. In some cases, it may be that imagination and inspiration were confounded by the writers or inventors; who shall limit the tricks of self-delusion among the talkers and the interpreters of the unknown tongues? Howbeit, when controversy was rife—was raging within the Church, and the authority of the founder was liable to be appealed to by one side or the other, there was manifest temptation to model citations, to supply from invention instructions of the Saviour; and when these were so admirably in keeping with his spirit, so cogent in their natural truth, so naïve in irresistible illustration, acceptation of them as authentic by the zealous, credulous, and uncritical age was inevitable. The incongruities of time and sentiment were not perceived, and as to the marvels that shock a modern, they were confirmations for the contemporary.

To adduce a conspicuous example; I am of opinion that the parable of the Prodigal Son was a Hellenistic figment of this class,—the controversial import of some of the reflections on the Pharisees will find their place hereafter.

The Prodigal Son has usually been interpreted as the

type of the Gentiles admitted to the privilege of Christianity; but from some trait, I infer that, originally at least, the parable was designed to enforce the same moral as the first section of the speech of Stephen,—the admissibility of the Hellenized Jew, including in the term Jews denationalized by residence out of Palestine in any country whatever. The prodigal is open to all the grand imputations on the Hellenist; he renounces native country and the ties of blood; he transgresses by irregular and luxurious life; he defiles himself, under whatever pressing necessity, by occupations, associates, food, that are as abhorrent to the Jew as herding swine or feeding from their very refuse; and lastly, not even his race is retained in its purity, he has consorted with harlots,—the marriage of a Jew with aliens in blood or religion was held to be nothing better.

As a quasi-historical illustration we have the supper with Zacchæus, the chief publican, or tax-farmer or gatherer, and the acceptation of his service on the ground, "he also is a child of Abraham."

We have seen what were the feelings of the Pharisees and their followers on the subject of tribute, and therefore on the abomination of subserving the collection of tribute. They are reflected upon therefore in the story of Zacchæus as pointedly as in the parable of the Pharisee and Publican praying in the Temple.

Opportunities will occur hereafter of tracing in detail how these processes have affected the accounts bearing not merely on the special party of the Apostles, but on Apostles at large,—on particular Apostles and their manner of guiding themselves. Thus is solved many a problem. How the Apostles could have acted as they did after Christ had so spoken, is accounted for by his so speaking being a later ascription by their opponents. How they could so grossly misconstrue what he spoke so plainly; how, having so long misconstrued it, they could ever remember the purport of its terms so minutely, is all accounted for. Jesus is boldly cited against his own Apostles, in words which only they could have reported, if uttered, and which, if uttered, they would either have acted on or suppressed.

To resume;—

While Saul was harassing at least a section of the Church at Jerusalem, Philip, the deacon, with some independence and in the same spirit that marked the doctrine of his martyred colleague, went down to the city of Samaria, and there preached Christ. Miracles of healing and casting out devils are ascribed to him; he excited a general spirit of enthusiasm, so that not only the multitude attached themselves to him and were baptized, but even a certain Simon, who had previously enjoyed great influence there with small and great. Simon, it is told, had given himself out as "a certain great one;" his admirers looked up to him with such awe as to say, "This man is the mighty power of God." Such pretensions and such acceptations were not unfrequent in these days. In the 'Alexander' of Lucian we have a finished and, in all essential respects, an authentic portrait of the Goetic impostor. In the case of Simon, we have not quite a right to affirm that, impostor and mercenary as he might be, he had not some mixture of superstition in his nature, and was not, to some extent, a self-deluded fanatic. The words of our record are certainly good for thus much.

We then read that the Apostles, hearing the tidings, dispatch Peter and John to Samaria. Nothing is said of any repugnance on the part of the Apostles to the course taken by Philip, yet it is a clear incongruity that they should heartily sympathize with that very development of Christian doctrine, their disconnection with which had enabled them to stay tranquilly at Jerusalem. My own impression is, that some of the Apostles were more liberal than others, if most of them, in various degrees, were not more so than their immediate following, with whom they still found it necessary to keep terms; whom they hoped to lead round but despaired to lead direct, to larger-mindedness. The rulers of the sect, who had imperial aims, were already committed to many of the considerations that trammel the politician; accepted the services of more zeal than they could acknowledge, or even sympathize with; and then damaged consistency by compromises which had no excuse but the paramount interest of the strength and unity of the party. We shall find that the converted Paul could attach himself to some Apostles, while others and their general party held aloof; and some were ready to coincide with his plans and views beforehand, who found great difficulty in holding their ground in a discussion at a metropolitan assembly.

Paul mentions James, Peter, and John as not only influential, but also well disposed towards his large views; and it is quite in accordance with this that Peter and John should undertake the mission to Samaria, and should carry it out in a comprehensive spirit. It will be understood from what has gone before that it was much for them to accept the Samaritans as converts at all, when exposed to the cavil of a Church of zealots and Pharisees. They did this, however, by formally laying hands upon the baptized converts, and conferring the gift of the Holy Ghost, whatever this may have amounted to, whatever may have been the peculiar phenomena that certified the endowment. In another narrative, Peter is represented as boldly appealing to these manifestations in non-Judaic converts as direct revelations, and works the plea so as to reduce to silence the questioners of his liberality; and this may have been a leading motive on the present occasion. Already, in the comment on the Cartoon of the Beautiful Gate of the Temple, I have touched on the probability that the miracle there ascribed to James and John is, in fact, a symbolical representation of their conjoint activity in procuring admission into the sect of the half-blood Jew—the Hellenist or the Samaritan.

This is the aspect of the transaction as told from the point of view of those who held by the Apostles, and thought that every management and every concession made by them in favour of liberality, was to be received with submissive gratitude. But it is not to be denied that all was open to a more discontented interpretation: a fugitive evangelizing Hellenist might not unnaturally think it hard to be superseded after the work was done, by envoys, however dignified, from those who had had neither work nor danger. There is a certain air of assumed authority in the laying on of hands by the Apostles,—in the trumping of the simple baptism of Philip by the strong card of the Holy Ghost. The narrator does not by any means appear desirous to convey this feeling, but it arises from the circumstances, just as it arises when we read in the history of Paul how he takes possession of the disciples of Apollos at Ephesus, by playing off the same pretext or proof of being minister of a paramount dispensation.

Here is another of the parallelisms, in which some will be inclined to impugn the historical character of one incident, on the ground that it is a transference from the other. But again I hold by the probability of the reference of like effects to like and constantly subsisting causes. We find them operative again in the Epistle to the Romans. Paul expresses his anxiety to reach Rome; "for I long to see you, that I may impart unto you some spiritual gift, to the end ye may be established," that is, "confirmed;" a technical word already, apparently, from the forms of its recurrence in the Acts of the Apostles. He has no sooner written the words than he qualifies, in order to calm the jealousy of encroachment which he feels they might awaken: "That is, that I might be comforted together with you by the mutual faith both of you and me."

That the Samaritan story, as told, contains much general historical truth seems to me very probable, because I believe we may trace an adumbration of the incidents and of the feelings which, though not specified in Acts, were naturally suggested by them in quite a different quarter.

It seems to me probable enough that the motive of the parable of the Good Samaritan may be derived from the adventure of Philip, who, persecuted by Jews of Jerusalem, finds relief and refreshment in the zeal of the Samaritans; but there are more distinct indications of reference in the story of Christ and the woman by the

well of Samaria, which appears only in the fourth
Gospel. If such be the case, we must conclude that this
section, at least, of the fourth Gospel had early origin,
though it did not find admission into the other compilations; possibly because these were made at a time
when tradition was still too strong to adopt the personal
preaching of Christ in Samaria as history.

The story is complete as a typical expression of the
relation of diaconal Christianity and party feeling to
apostolic, and reflects a light here upon the motives and
processes of evangelical composition, illuminating the
pertinence of many a dark passage throughout all the
Gospels.

The scene is at the well of Jacob, hard by the place
that he gave to his son Joseph, the same significant locality that Stephen adverts to when enforcing, as I have
shown, the common sacredness even of Samaria. The
woman herself, the wife of many husbands, is fitting
type of the Samaritan population, regarded by the zealot
Jews as debased by indiscriminate alliance with alien
blood, and abhorred accordingly. Yet to her does Jesus
preach; from her hands he accepts refreshment; and
the gist of his inculcations, most fully in harmony with
the teachings of the deacons, is directed to the same
points,—the indifference of locality to acceptable worship, the supersession of ceremonialism by spirituality,
by worship in spirit and in truth.

The Disciples—whom I assume here to be equivalents
of the Apostles—witness the colloquy not without surprise; and in their conversation with their Master are
so far at cross purposes, from pure literalness of understanding, as to show that they are by no means per-

sonations of the new dispensation of spirituality. Jesus comes to their assistance with an explanation of his metaphor: "My food is to do the will of him who sent me, and I will finish his work." He then pursues his observations in what seems a very disconnected strain, but in the same general tone; and, what is most remarkable, the words ascribed to him can only be interpreted, after what has gone before, as reflecting on the relative position of Apostles and deacons in the evangelization of Samaria.

"Say not ye there are yet four months, and then cometh the harvest? Behold, I say unto you, lift up your eyes and look on the fields, for they are ripe already with harvest. And he that reapeth receiveth wages, and gathereth fruit unto life eternal; that both he that soweth and he that reapeth may rejoice together. And herein is that saying true, One soweth and another reapeth. I send you to reap that whereon ye bestowed no labour: other men laboured, and ye are entered into their labours."

Of course, the suggestion is open that this is not an independent, but a derived allusion, as being simply an embodiment, in a quasi-anecdote of Christ, of the story that had been read as we now read it in Acts. I abide, however, by the view I have taken, believing that only thus can the harmony with Stephen, as well as with Philip, be reasonably explained.

One other matter remains to be remarked upon before we quit Samaria. Simon—Simon Magus—presents a mercenary motive to the Apostles, in order to obtain the power of conferring the Holy Ghost; and Simon Magus, it must not be forgotten, was an accepted convert, a baptized member of the Church. His offer was rejected by Peter with a severe rebuke. Luther translated this, "Dass du verdammt sei mit deinem Geld," and gave it point by a marginal note, in order to apply it to the simony of the Roman Catholics; for Simon has been posted from that day to this as representative of all traffickers in the cure of souls for money; he is contrite, and escapes more easily than Ananias.

That such an offer should have been made by such a convert is quite in the order of events, and natural at that time, as in forms transformed it has continued natural ever since. The Magus was a man of the world; he held himself beaten by more artful or more gifted rivals; and powerless to contend, took the natural alternative of negotiating for collusion and partnership.

I am not sure that other circumstances may not have helped to suggest his proposition.

The condition of the Church at Jerusalem, the poor saints, rendered contributions from converts welcome, not to say indispensable; and so established a matter was it in those days for Jews all over the world to send contributions to the Temple, of which its personal establishment, of course, shared the benefit, that no forfeiture of independence might be felt by the Church of the Apostles at Jerusalem, in being helped or supported in the same way. When Paul came to his understanding with the Apostles, " they would he should remember the poor, which he also was forward to do;" and on two occasions, from Antioch first, and then from his wider journeys, he took up collections, which, in his speech to Agrippa, he calls "alms and offerings for his nation."

Did Peter and John institute such a collection at

Samaria, and thus give opening for a claim on the part of a liberal contributor, for participation in functions and dignities,—much as if a modern endower of a church should think it fair to reserve the appointment of the clergyman? However this may be, cavillers in the Church at a future time seem to have been prompt to stigmatize the money contributions brought in by Paul as no better than simoniacal corruptions, and attempts to purchase allowance of Apostleship. Such, at least, is the explanation that seems to me natural, of the pleasure taken by controversial opponents of Paul in referring to him as Simon Magus.

The departure of Philip from Samaria is related without comment; but the feeling rises inevitably, as the tale stands, apart from unrecorded qualifications, that he seems to quit rather obscurely, and that he must have been charitable indeed if he felt no discontent at being so quietly dismissed and superseded. Oddly enough, an occasion for much the same feelings is exhibited in the story of the Samaritan woman, who has to reconcile herself to being no longer an object of interest after her function of introduction was fulfilled. "And many more believed because of his own word; and said unto the woman, Now we believe, not because of thy saying: for we have heard him ourselves, and know that this is indeed the Christ, the Saviour of the world." (John iv. 41, 42.)

Philip's encounter with the Ethiopian eunuch may quite easily be a mere figment, deliberate, or of spontaneous origin; and, quite as easily, it may be a quasi-poetical expression of a series of years of activity southwards of Egypt. The story finishes with one of those indefinite turns that seem intended to gain a point by cheating the devil; a miracle is laid in the way of the reader—a supernatural transference in space, which it is for him to answer for if he assumes,—and if he does not. " The Spirit of the Lord caught away Philip, that the eunuch saw him no more; but Philip was found at Azotus, and passing through, he preached in all the cities till he came to Cæsarea."

Here, at Cæsarea, he was found long after by Paul, and his companion, the author of the personally expressed sections of the Acts of the Apostles: " And we entered into the house of Philip the Evangelist, which was one of the seven, and abode with him. And the same man had four daughters, virgins, which did prophesy." I have sometimes thought that to these fair enthusiasts we may owe some of the poetical and pathetic parables of the third Gospel. If the writer of Acts gained in this house the details of the Samaritan incidents we have been discussing, as critical acumen was not there in special request, supernatural and poetical colour would blend readily with the transmitted tale.

CHAPTER VI.

THE CONVERSION OF ST. PAUL.

I. SAUL THE PERSECUTOR.—II. THE TAPESTRY OF THE CONVERSION OF ST. PAUL.—III. THE RECEPTION OF PAUL THE DISCIPLE BY THE CHURCH.

I. SAUL THE PERSECUTOR.

SAUL was a Jew, born at Tarsus; a citizen, as he himself truly says, of no mean city. It was distinguished in a declining age for intellectual culture, and Strabo ranks its schools in his time with those of Athens and Alexandria; at an earlier date the tutors both of Augustus and Tiberius, were Stoics of Tarsus. We read in the Epistles of relatives of Paul settled in Macedonia; one of them was probably that man of Macedonia whom he saw in a dream inviting him over to Europe. In days long after, his sister's son at Jerusalem it still called a young man.

He was born to the rights of a Roman citizen, which often stood him in good stead; a Pharisee by like hereditary derivation, he was sent to Jerusalem to be taught and strengthened in his tenets at the feet of the distinguished Pharisaic teacher, Gamaliel. We can easily believe his boast of early proficiency; but much that he acquired with aptitude was certainly of such a nature that we must rather admire the vigorous health of his nature, in being capable of casting off, as an encumbrance, so much of its influence, and restoring the free use of faculties that had been so early and so falsely cramped.

Zeal for the conversion of the heathen, and hope for the kingdom of God,—the restoration of Israel,—were, as we have seen, the leading passions of the Pharisaism of the time, whatever proportion or figure may have been assigned to them in the teaching of Gamaliel; and in these ideas lay also the germ of expansive Christianity, awaiting the processes and accidents of internal and surrounding nature for their development. The fruit, as developed on Christian ground, bore natural resemblance to that of the primitive and strictly Judaic stock. When relief, as we read in Acts, came to the famine at Jerusalem from Christians at Antioch, it came from the heart of a religious society agitated, or soon to be agitated, by questions of ceremonialism,—disputes as to whether it were possible to remain uncircumcised and still to rightly serve God. Other relief arrived at the same time from Adiabene, beyond the Tigris, and this was from converts also; even from King Izates and Queen Helena, with whom we already have some acquaintance; and in the history of whose conversion, zeal and over-zeal had been manifested by teachers, Galilean like Peter, Pharisaic like Paul, but not, like them, advanced upon the ground of the new faith. Izates, like any convert of Antioch, had found himself between two instructors; the one who was willing to remit a repulsive rite, the other insisting on it as the necessary seal of acceptability, and carrying his point.

In many other important respects besides hope of the

kingdom of God, we recognize the character of Paul the Apostle as displaying characteristics of Saul the Pharisee, and the impress of his education.

To follow the narrative as it proceeds,—Saul was not only consenting to the death of Stephen, but after this event continued to harry the Church, entering into houses, and haling both men and women to prison. Still further, he made direct application to the high-priest for credentials to the synagogues at Damascus, that he might follow the dispersed members of the Church, and bring bound to Jerusalem whatever men or women of the sect, his inquisition might discover.

Here we have the same energy and activity that afterwards found occupation in a better spirit and cause; and yet, in his proceedings as an Apostle, we have not far to look for a vehemence that betrays a germ of fierceness, for a love of independent command, and a jealousy of interference and contradiction that may be under a certain control, but will ever brook control reluctantly.

"As I before said, so say l again, if any one preach to you another gospel than what ye have received from me, though he were an angel from heaven, let him be cursed." (Gal. i. 9.)

"If any one love not the Lord Jesus Christ, let him be cursed,—Maran-atha;" on this follows, with naïve unconsciousness, "the grace of the Lord Jesus Christ be with you, my love be with you all," etc. (1 Cor. fin.)

Also, it has been observed that the preacher retains a certain fondness for military metaphors,—the panoply of the Christian, the good fight,—which have a certain incongruousness with the gospel of peace and submission, equal to that we notice between Shakspeare's legal metaphors and the passion of despairing Romeo, who gives utterance to them.

The revulsion of a gifted and vehement nature from one form of religious belief to another, from one field of energy to another, as opposed, but not more opposed, than different sides in the same cause, is one of the most familiar incidents in the history of religions in their enthusiastic epochs. There is no mystery here that is not illustrated abundantly in such lives as those of Bunyan, Cromwell, Ignatius Loyola, and the rest. The occasion and incidents of the persecution necessarily brought Paul into contact and acquaintance with the opinions of Stephen, and the leading points in the story of Christ, and the persuasion of his followers. He, a Pharisee, could have no repugnance to the assertion of a resurrection in itself, nor, at least in a certain form, to the announcement of the speedy manifestation of a kingdom of God. The permanence of the law, the sacredness of the Temple, the exclusive privileges of the Jewish race,—these must have been the prejudices that were irritated by the teachings of Stephen and his followers, and that supplied the sting and venom of his persecuting spirit.

But it is quite in the order of things for young minds in the progress of their development, to hold with strong conviction two, or even more, principles, and even systems of opinions, that are perfectly irreconcileable with each other, but of which the incongruousness is hidden from them while arguing with vehemence, and even acting with violence from both.

The time comes as thoughts ripen that one or the

other thought must have the upper hand, and an older bystander may often note the first rise of a passion in a crude mind, of which he can foresee certainly that it will drive all these incongruities to an issue, bring on an absolute revulsion, and clear the mind once and for ever for the settled work of a lifetime of comparative consistency. Such a revolution in a mind, as in a State, depends far less on the introduction of new ideas than on those which, by laxity or alternation, have subsisted more or less peacefully together all along, being brought into positive contact and collision, and making their relative value decisively felt.

The result of the story shows that Paul carried within him a rising passion for a sphere of activity commensurate with the largest views, the strongest energies. Such a sphere is scarcely provided for the enthusiastic by a policy of repression, however active and however violent, and least of all when the repression declares itself ineffectual. Hopeful energy soon feels repugnance for labouring in a declining cause, and especially in the face of the spectacle of a cause that has all the characteristics of an immortal vigour.

I strongly suspect that some such conflict was already proceeding in Saul's mind when he started for Damascus; that he was already sickening at fruitless, and therefore uncongenial, exertion; perhaps had had occasion to contrast the spirit of some who were making him a tool with those whom he was making victims. There was a tale among some of the Christian Jews of the early Church who disliked him, that his defection from the Law had a certain connection with a love disappointment, and the shabby conduct of an expected father-in-law—Gamaliel, or a high-priest; and though the tale might easily be a calumny, it indicates what might very easily have been allied to a truth.

But there is a combination which advances the theory I have stated of the crisis of Saul's feelings and opinions, to something more than an unprotected conjecture.

Gamaliel, in the speech ascribed to him, enunciates the principle, that if the Christian movement is not from God it will speedily come to nought; and he is willing to commit the decision whether they who would check it are not proposing to fight against God, to the test of its vitality or speedy decay.

This is something more than a notion of an individual; it corresponds with, and expresses, the dogma of the sect of Pharisees respecting the ordering of events by a providential fatality, to which Josephus returns again and again. This was a test of which Saul, by the time he was on his way to Damascus, must have already had some discouraging experience. That the principle should have been then present to his mind is curiously in accordance with the terms of the narrative of his vision.

"And as he journeyed, he came near to Damascus: and suddenly there shone round him a light from heaven; and he fell to the earth, and heard a voice saying unto him, Saul, Saul, why persecutest thou me? And he said, Who art thou, Lord? And the Lord said, I am Jesus, whom thou persecutest; but arise, and go into the city, and it shall be told thee what thou must do. And the men that journeyed with him stood speechless, hearing the voice, but seeing no one. And

Saul arose from the earth; and when his eyes were opened, he saw no one: and they led him by the hand, and brought him into Damascus. And he was three days without sight, and neither ate nor drank."

In Paul's speech before Agrippa, the narrative runs thus:—" Whereupon as I went to Damascus with authority and commission from the high-priests, at midday I saw on the road, O king, from heaven, above the brightness of the sun, a light shining around me, and them that journeyed with me. And when we were all fallen to the earth, I heard a voice speaking unto me, and saying, in the Hebrew tongue, Saul, Saul, why persecutest thou me? it is hard for thee to kick against the pricks. And I said, Who art thou, Lord? And he said, I am Jesus, whom thou persecutest," etc.

Still a third narration occurs in Paul's speech on the steps of the tower Antonia: "And it came to pass, as I journeyed and came nigh to Damascus about noon, suddenly there shone from heaven a great light round me. And I fell to the ground, and heard a voice saying unto me, Saul, Saul, why persecutest thou me? And I answered, Who art thou, Lord? And he said unto me, I am Jesus, the Nazarite, whom thou persecutest. And they that were with me saw indeed the light, and were afraid; but they heard not the voice of him that spake unto me. . . . And when I could not see for the glory of that light, being led by the hand of them that were with me, I came to Damascus."

These extracts are for future use; at present, I have to advert to an expression in the narrative to Agrippa: " It is hard for thee to kick against the pricks." This is a proverbial expression, which occurs with general application up and down in Greek literature, but it is idiomatic for the present occasion. Not only here, but elsewhere: here, because elsewhere, it is employed to express the powerlessness of a mind that struggles, but in vain, to escape being carried away involuntarily with the flood of religious enthusiasm when it comes on in force, and carries multitudes along with it. The pricks that are resisted are the stimulant sympathies that on such occasions seem to be commanded by the preacher. These are phenomena of revivals; and preachers—Wesleys and Whitfields, like Pauls and Peters—sometimes credit themselves with a special power and the gift of a divine affluence, or the endowment of communicating the Holy Ghost. But the incident is intermittent, transitory, usually abounding at the commencement of a sect, and declining as it proceeds. The manifestations are often as much bodily as intellectual or moral. It is to such that Paul refers when he appeals to the Corinthians how independent their original conversion was of rhetoric and argument: "And my speech and my preaching was not with persuading words of wisdom, but with demonstration of spirit and power; that your faith might not be in men's wisdom, but in God's power." (1 Cor. xi. 5.)

The physiology of quasi-involuntary conversion is not more distinctly illustrated in the history of modern Methodists or Quakers, than in the primeval story of Saul amongst the prophets; and in the Greek drama, it is poetically idealized, but still most marked and recognizable, in the story of Pentheus in the Bacchæ of Euripides. In this play we find Gamaliel's idea, and his very phrase of *theomachy*, and Paul's proverb of "kicking against the pricks," and its identical application, as vain resistance to a crisis of religious belief that perforce will have its way.

We may ask beyond this, what strict historical construction can reasonably be put on the external details of the incident? We are not bound to interpret very closely. The several narratives vary from each other in certain marked details. It is quite possible, therefore, that in others where they agree they may all vary from the fact.

It is not much worth while, therefore, inquiring whether a moral crisis and disturbance may not have brought on the bodily, or a bodily trouble at least have coincided with the course of a prolonged mental excitement. The incident does not stand alone in Paul's history: his complaints of bodily weakness and trials abound; and that he regards them as hindrances of Satan, shows how little he could distinguish critically the sources of his afflictions. His trance in the Temple, and his revelations in dialogue with Christ, have many characteristics of his fit at noon on the road to Damascus. After the laxity of the statements before us—all at second-hand, to say the least—we are not bound to accept as probabilities his blindness, or his recovery under the touch of Ananias, much less that either one or the other was sudden and complete. There may easily have been matter of fact enough in both cases,— and little enough need it have been, to produce such stories as easy and natural exaggerations.

It appears pretty distinctly, from a passage in the Epistle to the Galatians, that Paul had suffered from the condition of his eyes to an extent to excite the compassion of his friends. That this weakness was constant is, perhaps, corroborated by a habit of availing himself, unless under peculiar circumstances, of the aid of an amanuensis.

"And ye know that in weakness of the flesh I preached the gospel to you at first. And my trial which was in my flesh ye despised not, nor rejected; but ye received me as a messenger of God, as Christ Jesus. What then were your benedictions! for I bear you witness that, if possible, ye would have plucked out your own eyes, and given them to me." (Gal. iv. 13.)

" For the rest, let no man give me trouble, for I bear in my body the marks of the Lord Jesus." (Gal. v. 17.)

A great light, a glory, was to the Jewish mind of the time the recognized sign and manifestation of the Divine presence; equally familiar was the idea of Divine revelations by a voice from Heaven, "the daughter of the Voice" (*bath col*).

Paul could not have heard the expostulating voice of Jesus more distinctly than the Maid of Orleans heard the voice of St. Catherine, urging her to save her country, or rebuking her timidity.

His faith in his sensations could hardly have been less firm than that of Ignatius Loyola, who beheld transubstantiation take place, and who had a vision, with waking eyes, of the Holy Trinity in Unity.

It is, however, to stand far too much on ceremony with the compilation known as the Acts of the Apostles, to concede as probable whatever supposition will save any portion of its credit for historical authenticity. It is not easy to see how such a claim can be made on behalf of any history, whatever its pretensions. It is a badge of barbarism to challenge contradiction of the king's witnesses as equivalent to perjury. So far from this, we are bound to start with the presumption that close inquiry will most probably resolve into the mythical, all stories that are in any degree, as in the present case, tinged with the supernatural,—into unaccredited narratives complicated by all the influences that distort literal truth,—from simple blunder to sinister fabrication. The detailed accounts of the incidents of the conversion of Paul are contained in Acts alone; the general statements and allusions that occur in the Epistles admit of very different trains of circumstances; but the Epistles have just so much accordance with Acts as to show how easily false inventions, or pious distortions, or involuntary misstatements, would creep into the narrative.

Paul talks with somewhat ostentatious mystification of his visions and experiences,—whether in the flesh, or out of it, he will not say, and others may think as they please; they did think as it pleased them, and some of their conclusions are before us in the story in Acts. If Barnabas, in Acts, is introduced, saying that Paul had "seen the Lord" on the road to Damascus; Paul, in his Epistle, avouches as good, and better, and makes himself on a par with any witness of the resurrection, at the same time reducing other evidence to the value of his own: he also, saw the Lord,—though it is doubtful whether he may not be referring to some other trance or vision, not to the occasion of the Damascus expedition. The Epistles also, as I have said, include an indication scarcely equivocal of some grief of Paul in ailment of the eyes, and an ascription of its origin to his religious crises; it is a mark, a scar of the Lord Jesus. Again, we cannot say with which of the several recorded, and many possible accesses of excitement this may be connected; but it was natural that fable—history if you will, should seize it, and assign it to the prime incident of the conversion, should draw inferences, and fill out the budget of narrative.

Similar tales of other celebrities were already in popular circulation, connecting loss of sight with divine visions, and both with sudden changes of belief or moral illumination. Minds were apt for analogy and eager for marvel, and whether from desire to give effect to a startling narrative, or heighten an apologue by typical embellishment, the result seems to have been equally spontaneous,—and stories ran together by inevitable fusion and confusion. Three notes are sounded accidentally together, and happen to have the relations of a perfect chord; they remain in the ear as a single sound, which the ear alone cannot resolve into its elements, and of such fulness and sweetness, that the last thing it desires is to disturb such natural congruity.

Stories were rife in many a poem, and many a tradition, of the great of old, chiefly bards,—*vates*,—ever inspired and usually prophetic, who had incurred the anger of the gods and heroes to whose services they were peculiarly devoted, by remissness, or perverseness, or over-boldness. Homer sings how Thamyris was met and blinded by the Muses: of Homer himself it was told that his blindness was due to a vision of his own hero Achilles, refulgent in arms; while Helen not only blinded the bard Stesichorus for his calumny or misconception of her true story, but through another chan-

P

nel sent him a message to recant; and it was on his making amends to the reputation and dignity of the heroine by a palinode, that he recovered his sight, like Paul, converted and repentant.

Such, and no different, I believe to be the explanation of the details of the story as it is told and retold in Acts. For the hint and the explanation my thanks, and those of others, are due to the Rev. G. Skinner, of Cambridge. We shall see hereafter how completely the probability of corruptions of history from pagan myths is borne out by the analysis of the stories of Paul's adventures at Lystra and at Philippi. When Christian biography got among Greek minds, the tale took up Greek elements as naturally as, on ground more exclusively Jewish, it filled out the tale of the deeds and sufferings of Jesus, from stores of incident found in the Old Testament. I am strongly disposed to think that Elymas, the sorcerer, had to thank the Aphrodite of his island, Cyprus, for his blinding,— Aphrodite, the mythical equivalent of Helen in some forms of tradition. It was in the Phœnician quarter of the city of Memphis, "the camp of the Tyrians," that Herodotus found in a *temenos*, which also contained a temple of Proteus, a sanctuary of "the foreign Aphrodite," whom, from certain tales, there told, he was induced to identify with Helen, daughter of Tyndarus, the wife of Menelaus. His opinion seems to have been founded upon what he heard from the priests of the temple; though there is no knowing how far he may not have given them their cue or modified their story. Helen, they said, never went to Troy at all; she was detained in Egypt,—taken from Paris along with other stolen goods by Proteus, an Egyptian potentate, and restored by him to Menelaus, after the Greeks, disbelieving the protestations of the Trojans that they had none of her, had sacked and ransacked Troy in vain.

The tale is improved upon in the Helen of Euripides; where we read, that while Helen was detained in all propriety and sanctity in Egypt, she was represented at Troy by a phantasm that served certain providential purposes, in giving Greek and Trojan a theme of bloody contention. It may seem sufficient explanation of this fiction to say, that it was manifestly suggested by a desire to vindicate Homer without impugning Herodotus, or spoiling a good Egyptian story. Or it may be supposed that the worship of Helen had become diffused in various localities before the rise of the immortal Trojan tale, and that thus an opening had been made for one of the ingenious conciliations of authority that are the delight of the harmonist. I strongly suspect, however, that Euripides had some anterior basis of tradition, which may easily have been of Egyptian origin, and, perhaps, connected with the Memphian fane. Again, several circumstances in the story are parallel to that of Iphigenia, safe in Tauris, though supposed to have been sacrificed. Artemis, it is true, substituted a hind; but it does not appear that the sacrificers were aware of the substitution, and thus the victim was, to them, an eidolon—a phantasm. On vase paintings we see the hind and the virgin so grouped that the figures cover and intermingle, as if at the very crisis of such a sleight-of-hand substitution. I suspect that a little research would bring home this same idea of phantasmal substitution to the significance of some other vase-designs, where various divinities are coupled or duplicated so markedly and interchangeably.

The cloud that interposes indulgently in the romance of Ixion is, in truth, a phantasm that saves the honour of Juno much as the Euripidean eidolon rescues the fame of Helen. The Ulysses of Homer discourses with Hercules in Hades,—his eidolon only; he himself was among the gods (Odyss. Λ. 600). I believe it was more consonant with the art of Euripides, and the spirit of his time, that he should adapt an existing, though it might be an obscure myth, rather than play off a pure invention. There was more piquancy in the course,— and piquancy was with him a leading object. I am also not a little confirmed in the view by the appearance of the notion in enthusiastic religion at a much later date. The Helen of the drama speaks of her representative at Troy as a κένη δόκησις; and an early sect of Christians obtained the title Docetics, from their dogma, which is markedly written against in the fourth Gospel, —that the suffering Christ was not the very God, or Son of God, but an eidolon—a phantasm. The source of the dogma, as Christian or heathen, I must now leave to others to trace.

I may notice as, at least, a coincidence, that this story of Herodotus follows his narrative, how the predecessor of Proteus lost his sight by impious violence against a divinity, and recovered it by human aid and intercession. He cast his spear,—a Pharaoh, into the waves of a stormy inundation, and was blind thenceforward until a feminine specific restored him to sight.

But between the epochs of Euripides and Paul, the story of Helen had become entangled with the allegorical imagery of Plato; and among his commentators we find traces of a treatment of it that may very likely have been prevalent before the composition of Acts, and may easily have helped the Stesichorean adaptation. Hermias, the commentator of the Phædrus, a contemporary of Proclus, details a scheme for allegorizing the whole tale of the Trojan war; and here the true Helen, who, when attacked and calumniated, inflicts blindness, and, when appeased by palinode and repentance, sends a messenger to restore sight,—this divine and veritable Helen is the Ideal, Beauty in the abstract, the high Philosophy, true Religion!

The Pauline Epistles contain such abundant illustrations of the prevalence of the very peculiar combinations of ideas of this same school, which we receive, insisted upon specially for the first time, in the later writer, Plotinus, that there is every reason to be satisfied that what Hermias disserts on so glibly,—as to the true and the fictitious Helens, types of obsolete and etherealized beliefs, had been freely developed and widely circulated long before.

II. THE TAPESTRY OF THE CONVERSION OF ST. PAUL.

Rafael's Cartoon of the Conversion of St. Paul is another that is unfortunately lost, destroyed some say, from the same puritanical squeamishness, at depicture of a heavenly vision, that is to account for the loss of the Stoning of Stephen. In this instance, however, there is no introduction of a figure of God the Father.

Some Mantuan memoranda and engravings from the

tapestry must therefore be our text. A small one will be found in the English translation of Kugler's 'Handbook of Painting;' a larger and much more satisfactory, in Pistolesi. The latter, like the rest of the set, was taken from the tapestry, and corresponds with it in respect of right and left sides and figures. To the left of the spectator, Paul, wearing armour, arms, and helmet, has fallen from his horse and lies on the ground, shrinking from the light of the vision, and with one hand moved instinctively to moderate it, at the same time that he looks towards the glory and the Divine speaker. His vigorous body and legs are in entire prostration, as stricken down by supernatural power. His head and arms alone express astonishment, supplication, attention.

Above, half-emergent from clouds and glory, and supported by three angels, is the figure of Jesus starting forward in a manner to express the suddenness of Paul's surprise: and with stretched right arm and raised forefinger, indicating remonstrance and command. The position of Paul is that of a man not only surprised, but already thoroughly subdued, in agreement with his first submissive question, as of subject to superior, "Who art thou, Lord?" His sword lies on the ground beside him: it seems to have become detached and shaken off in his fall, as it lies with the broken belt rolled round it. It is on the side of his right hand, but lies thus separate as if to intimate that it had fallen from his grasp as a persecutor, for ever. It is a sword of the same form which the Saint usually is represented holding as a symbol of his martyrdom; and the painter, I believe, designed the suggestion.

Some flowers and herbage are along the front line of

the picture; but the stony ground beyond, and on which Paul partly lies, indicates the beaten high-road to the great city. In the beautiful tapestry at Mantua the ground, where not covered with herbage, is yellow, as with sand. The legs of Paul, I may record, are clothed in blue.

A young man on foot, holding a spear, and with much of the appearance of a special attendant, runs towards Paul with every sign of solicitude, but with no marks of consciousness of the sudden light.

Beyond this young man are two horsemen; one of them helmeted, and both girt with swords, which appear to be uniform. Thus is conveyed an appearance of rank and file; and Paul, whose startled horse is away in advance, seems to have been riding officer-like, as his distinction in armour suggests, at the head of his company, either at its extremity to the left, or a little in front.

The seat of these two horsemen is still that of men who are riding at settled pace; and that this is not yet disturbed while their heads are turned and left arms extended in the direction of the fallen Paul, helps to express at once the suddenness of the incident, and to illustrate the particular text that they who were with him, "saw no man." It is to be observed that these immediately attendant figures are unaware of the vision; but their horses appear not insensible to an unnatural disturbance,—their hind-quarters show a check, and they turn their heads round, as shunning a light that meets their direct course. All this harmonizes with the acknowledgment by the brute creation of certain atmospheric alterations—the approach of an earthquake or volcanic eruption, and so forth, which has often gained for them from the superstitious the credit of being able to see spirits. Paul's horse has obeyed the same impulse, and is in frightened flight.

The divarications of the narratives of the incident are salient enough as I have extracted them, and the texts have furnished of old, and even down to our own times, a well-frequented tumbling-place for the literal harmonists. Scarcely elsewhere should we be able to collect, if it were worth it, so many specimens of misapplied ingenuity to illustrate how far the honest, the simple-minded—nay, the fatuous, can emulate in sophistry the hypocrites and the rogues.

In the direct history, and in the speech at Antonia, the light from heaven is spoken of as shining round Paul alone, and he alone as falling to the ground; howbeit that in the speech, his companions are alarmed at the light but do not hear the voice, whereas in the history they stand speechless at hearing the voice and seeing no one. This is one of the most natural interchanges conceivable on the part of a reporter. I suspect that the speech gives Paul's original story most accurately; he takes the dialogue upon his own responsibility, and he authenticates the great light by the averment that there were other witnesses. The historian retains the fact of the astonishment of the companions who were only witnesses of half, though a different half, of the incident, and the most wonderful part of the story,—the supernatural voice: an obvious cavil that the voice may have come from the companions, is parried by the note that they were standing speechless with amazement.

THE CONVERSION OF ST. PAUL, a tapestry of the Sacier series in the Vatican.

The speech to Agrippa has the characteristics of redundant Asiatic eloquence, which either Paul or his reporter seems to have thought appropriate to the pomp of the occasion,—that speaking before kings, which was capable of flattering the pride even of an Apostle. The wondrous dialogue is here considerably extended; the circumstances of the appearance of the light are insisted upon with marked and emphatic breaks of phraseology, and the light shines not alone around Paul, but those also who journeyed with him, and all fall to the ground together.

Rafael follows no version exclusively; he does not even arbitrate between the versions; but he introduces or avails himself of elements of confusion, which account for the origin of all. The figures nearest to the foreground we have seen, are solely attentive to the catastrophe of Paul, the alarm being confined to the animals. But beyond these we see a youth on foot, in full flight, meeting them, and looking back in the direction of the apparition. Still further, beyond the two mounted swordsmen, we see spears and horses' heads turned in the reverse way to the direction of the expedition. Some faces appear, that seem to be questioning each other; and one man lifts his hand towards his head, with a little of the expression of listening for a sound. Far in the left-hand distance, again, we seem to see a figure, who shades his eyes with both hands and elevated buckler. One young man, by the near side of Paul's frightened horse, flies almost as fast, but apparently in simple sympathy with the hubbub and confusion.

Rafael therefore shows Paul alone fallen to the ground; but while he makes some of his company and fellow-travellers cognizant only of their leader's disaster, he makes other some alarmed at the light; others perhaps astonished at the voice; and others, like the very horses, simply bewildered by instinctive or sympathetic feeling of a crisis in nature.

The engraving I am consulting does not show any hint of Damascus in the background: this is, however, displayed distinctly enough in the tapestry at Mantua.

Such was the harmony allowably elicited from these narratives by a painter; weaker mortals, who have ventured to call themselves divines, once made essay on this wise:—"All the companions of Paul fell to the ground with him (xxvi. 14), and his companions also remained standing in amazement, while he alone fell down (ix. 7); which implies, that Paul and the whole company fell down indeed at first sight together, but his associates were on their feet before him." By like process it can be shown that they both heard the voice and did not.

One biographer of Paul writes: "All fell to the ground in terror (xxvi. 14), or stood dumb with amazement (ix. 7)." Suddenly, surrounded by a light so terrible and incomprehensible, "they were afraid." "They heard not the voice of Him that spake to Paul" (xxii. 9), or, if they heard a voice, "they saw no man."

The flaws and openings of the unconformable incidents are here neatly puttied up and painted over, for the phrases would convey to the unsuspecting popular reader that some fell, some stood, that some heard the voice, and some only caught it indistinctly. All this is smooth enough; and with the certifying citations of chapter and verse and the inverted commas, what should seem more authentic?

Then, with what would be effrontery, but that it creeps into little type and a footnote, a writer will proceed: "It has been thought both more prudent and more honest to leave these well-known discrepancies exactly as they are found in the Bible."

What occasion was there for any other consideration than as to which course was the singly honest? The solution is expressed as if it were arrived at after searching for other courses that might be more prudent if less honest, or rejection of some that might have proved more honest but less prudent. Why draw a long breath for the enunciation, "Honesty is the best policy"? Why with so little real prudence intimate "I have tried both; at least, have held myself open to do so"?

But the brag of honesty is, in fact, a blind and a deception, as it is ever so apt to be; for, as we have seen above, the discrepancies are not left exactly as they are found in Acts.

There is mischief also in speaking of them as "in the Bible," not as in the particular book of the Acts of the Apostles. The vice of this paralogism merits to have justice done upon it by a Bentham. After all this affectation of candour and profession of honesty, two sophisms are set forth for those who please to choose between them, "according to their views of the inspiration of Scripture."

"Those who do not receive the doctrine of verbal inspiration will find in these discrepancies a confirmation of the general truth of the narrative."

As how? In what way does inaccuracy in reporting details certify accuracy as to the main point? and how stands the case if the discrepancies, as here, touch the very heart of the matter? if we find the miraculous dialogue expand when it is retold? if a burst of light at noonday is found reported as an appearance in the flesh of the crucified Jesus?

Is corroboration proportionate to discrepancy? or does authentication vanish by virtue of precision in report?

"Those who lay stress on this doctrine (the verbal inspiration) may fairly be permitted to suppose that the stupefied companions of Saul fell to the ground and then rose, and that they heard the voice, but did not understand it."

They may be fairly expected to suppose this, or to resort to any other stratagem, however ridiculous; but if they are permitted to do so unmolested, it will not be in fairness on the part of their opponents, but in mere despair of their common sense or common candour, out of idle negligence or sheer contempt.

III. THE RECEPTION OF PAUL THE DISCIPLE BY THE CHURCH.

It is quite impossible to reconcile the various narratives of the scene of Paul's conversion into one simple and consistent statement, though something may be done to elicit the clear facts by noting the causes and liabilities of lapse, and at last, I think enough of the truly historical remains to satisfy our interest on every point that is really of importance.

When we proceed with the story as it ensues in the Acts, we come next upon a wonderful tale of a vision of Ananias of Damascus; and this told with such strange parallelism to the vision of Peter, and the vision and conversion of Cornelius, that we feel at once that we have got into mythology. Either the scheme of the vision that dispatched messengers to the house of one Simon, a tanner, which was by the seaside at Joppa, was borrowed from that which sent Ananias to the house of Judas, in the street called Straight, at Damascus; or, what is quite as probable, both were derived from a common traditional type. Then, again, the time and the circumstances of Paul's stay at Damascus, as they are stated or distinctly implied in the Acts, are quite at variance with his own solemn asseverations in the Epistle to the Galatians. How shall we find our way through this confusion? The mere superiority in plausibility or probability of a tale is not decisive; for very often the truth lies with the least probable: strong bias, again, may seem to invalidate a strong statement that favours it, yet the bias may be justly entitled to the support of what is a strong fact, and not an invention for a purpose.

Paul writes with a decided intention to vindicate his independence of the Apostles from the beginning; the compiler of Acts is manifestly open to a bias to represent him as received cordially by the Apostles, and acting with them in sympathy; he would willingly make out a picture of Christian co-operation, but the result is a mass of inconsistencies in his history compared only with itself, and still more so as compared with Paul's Epistles. Paul himself has difficulties enough of his own, to vindicate the independence of the Gentile Christians, and yet to conserve that fellowship with the Hebrew Church that offered the only chance of reacting on his countrymen,—the matter still nearest his heart, in favour of relaxation of ceremonial bigotry.

Through such a thicket who shall penetrate? I have long made up my own mind as to the most practicable path through it; and have confidence that they who will venture with me will emerge in daylight beyond.

The next Cartoon in the series is the Sacrifice at Lystra; but before considering it, I prefer to review the record we have of Paul's life and work in the interim. His own account commences thus:—

"But when it pleased God, who separated me from my mother's womb, and called me by his grace, to reveal his Son in me, that I might preach him among the Gentiles; immediately I consulted not flesh and blood, nor went up to Jerusalem to them that were Apostles before me, but I went into Arabia, and again returned to Damascus. Then, after three years, I went up to Jerusalem to inquire for Peter, and I abode with him fifteen days. And I saw no other of the Apostles but James, the Lord's brother. Now, as to what I am writing to you, behold, before God, I lie not. Then I went into the regions of Syria and Cilicia; and was unknown by face to the churches of Judæa, which were in Christ. But they heard only, That he who once persecuted us now preacheth the faith that he once destroyed; and they glorified God in me."

The Arabia here referred to was probably not so far south as Petra, but the district known to Strabo as an Arabia, to the north-east of Palestine, and adjoining Damascus. Nothing is said of this prolonged residence of three years in the Acts; an interval—" some days," equivalent at most to "a considerable number of days," is all that is noted before Paul's return to Jerusalem.

We may safely take his own account; it could be scarcely prudent for him to return forthwith, being so changed, into the neighbourhood of the high-priest and his supporters. There was scarcely more temptation for him to seek at once an interview with the Apostles who were remaining at Jerusalem. There is the strongest proof that the sympathies of the converted Paul were towards the Hellenists in their dispersion, not towards the Hebrew Christians in their immunity. His conversion, in fact, consisted in his lively recognition of the principles of these Hellenists of the school of Stephen, and the other deacons. He might very reasonably already have some jealousy of the rigid and contracted ideas of the Apostles. Moreover, an energetic sermon or two, and a single escape from a tumult of the provincial synagogues, would scarcely be credentials sufficient to be counted on for obtaining him a hearing and a position beside the established and authoritative heads of the sect. It is quite reasonable, therefore, that Paul should have delayed his return to A.D. 40, a year when the Jewish authorities were very far from enjoying the latitude in administration allowed to them once for a brief interval by the President Vitellius.

The theme given in Acts of the preaching of Paul in the synagogues at Damascus, is the Messiahship of Jesus. After a time, the Jews, confounded in argument, resort to a plot to kill him, and, as the gates were watched,— his letter to the Corinthians says by the ethnarch of King Aretas,—the disciples let him down from the wall in a basket. Persecution, under such circumstances, recurs constantly throughout his career, and his perseverance nevertheless in addressing himself to his own people is honourable to his patriotism, as its result is no less honourable to the tenor and spirit of his teaching,—for the irritant element is ever an attempt on his part to weaken ceremonial exclusiveness.

When at last he does go to Jerusalem, it is not to meet the Apostles generally, but especially " to find out Peter." And wherefore Peter, but because he knew that with him he should find most sympathy for a liberalized Gospel,—for the movement originated by Stephen?

In Acts it is said, that when the disciples shunned and were afraid of him, "Barnabas took him and brought him to the Apostles, and related unto them how he had seen the Lord in the way, and that he spoke to him, and how he had talked boldly at Damascus in the name of the Lord,—and he was with them going in and coming out at Jerusalem."

More cordiality is implied here than can be admitted after what Paul has said,—there seems to have been certain cordiality with Peter, and some, though certainly less with James, but that was the extent of it.

Barnabas, therefore, introduced Paul as a disciple to Peter; afterwards we find a certain link between Barnabas and Peter in the fact that Barnabas at a critical moment at Antioch took Peter's course of temporizing, and had to aby along with him the rebuke of Paul. But, at the same time, the connection indicates that Peter's sympathies, however precarious, went along with Barnabas,—with Barnabas whom we shall find so active in the evangelization of Gentiles. All this corroborates the inferences already drawn from the story of the healing at the Beautiful Gate of the Temple, and from the ministry at Samaria.

The hint of uncongeniality between the converted persecutor and the Jerusalem church, is here slurred over from a bias that is intelligible enough in Acts; but it reappears even in Acts at a later occasion with reference to this very time; and Paul's own implications are thus perfectly confirmed.

His present departure from Jerusalem as related, repeats the incidents of his escape from Damascus; he reasons with and exasperates the Hellenists in the very synagogues where Stephen had given offence; they go about to slay him, and "the brethren, when they knew it, brought him down to Cæsarea and sent him forth to Tarsus." But this was probably an inferential explanation; the speech at Antonia gives quite another version of the affair, and one which is nearer to harmony with Paul's own representation in the epistle:—

"And it came to pass, that, when I was come again to Jerusalem, and was praying in the temple, I was in a trance; and saw him (Jesus) saying unto me, Make haste, and go quickly out of Jerusalem: for they will not receive thy testimony concerning me. And I said, Lord, they know that I imprisoned and beat in every synagogue them that believed on thee: and when the blood of thy witness Stephen was shed, I was even standing by and consenting, and kept the raiment of them that slew him. And he said unto me, Depart, for I will send thee far hence unto the Gentiles." (Acts xxii. 17.)

For those committed to literal harmony, the inference from comparison of this account with that of the conspiracy given earlier, must necessarily be that the murderous plotters who drove Paul from Jerusalem were certain of the Christian disciples disposed to avenge Stephen. But rejecting such a notion entirely, we can discern that Paul had in truth quite as little intercourse with the heads of the church on this occasion as he asserts to the Galatians, but that this was not, as he would imply, altogether due to his own holding off. Whether he at this time held the recognition of his claims to Apostleship by the Apostles, as cheaply as he afterwards did, may be a little doubtful; but in any case, however prepared he may have been to disclaim their confirmation of his commission, it is clear—so highly probable as to be clear to me, that he was mortified and depressed at his equivocal reception; and hence, I doubt not, the nervous crisis,—helped as usual by whatever course of fasting and prayer, of mental and bodily exhaustion,—which was to him a trance and a vision of Jesus, as distinct as that by which he was first converted.

Writing to the Corinthians, he said, "Boasting, indeed, is of no use to me, but I will come to visions and revelations of the Lord. I know a man in Christ, who, above fourteen years ago (whether in the body, I know not, or out of the body, God knoweth) was caught up to the third heaven, and I know of such a man (whether in the body or out of the body, I know not, God knoweth); that he was caught up into paradise, and heard unspeakable words which it is not lawful for a man to utter." (2 Cor. xii. 1.)

If this epistle was written A.D. 53–4, as I believe, the vision it relates would synchronize with the trance in the Temple, and we should thus obtain some inkling of the unspeakable things as having reference to the commission to preach to the Gentiles.

Whatever may have been Paul's tendencies and predilections before, it seems manifest that between pique and indignation, excitement and enthusiasm, they at this time settled into a resolute determination,—that determination that throughout all his tackings and accommodations in his after troubled course, never leaves doubtful for a moment the large catholicity of religious sympathy and connection which he aims at and hopes to bring about.

He now vanishes for a time from the narrative of Acts, and the interval is filled up with various progresses of Peter, his miracles, and especially the incident of the baptism of the Gentile centurion Cornelius, and his household; and the eating with them, which is related as bringing on a discussion with the purists at Jerusalem—easily overruled by throwing the responsibility upon the Holy Ghost.

From its position in the historical sequence, this anecdote assigns to Peter the honour of giving the first precedent for a Gentile church and gospel. Yet we find that the principle has to be debated again and settled again at a future time, as if Peter's precedent were none at all, and the sanction had only held good for the special case. Still, I am not prepared to deny for the narrative all foundation in fact, and for reasons that have appeared and will appear.

The next great incident in the history is, that of those who were scattered by the persecution about Stephen,—some being men of Cyprus and Cyrene, came to Antioch and "spake to the Greeks; preaching the Gospel of the Lord Jesus."

The news reaches the Church at Jerusalem, and Barnabas is dispatched to the spot; he promotes the movement with hearty sympathy, and, what is most remarkable, flies to Tarsus to seek Paul as an ally and coadjutor,—aware, apparently, how entirely he was in agreement with the development.

It is of course quite possible that Barnabas may have learnt for the first time at Antioch, and at second-hand, in what direction Paul's view of the Gospel had expanded; but in my judgment it is far more probable that he was previously cognizant of some of the fruits of the trance in the Temple, and that to him and to his connection Peter also, whether he had baptized a centurion Cornelius or no, the outburst at Antioch was as little unexpected in its nature as in fact unwelcome.

Whether Barnabas had been sent in the first instance merely to confirm or to report, he did not hurry back to Jerusalem. He remained there with Paul for a whole year, and it was only on the occurrence of certain critical incidents that he returned; and then, Paul went up with him, and this time under more favourable auspices, and with a definite plan.

"And in these days prophets came down from Jerusalem to Antioch. And there stood up one of them named Agabus, and signified by the spirit that there was to be a great dearth through all the world; which came to pass under Claudius. And the disciples, each as he was able, determined to send relief to the brethren dwelling in Judea; which they did, and sent it to the elders by the hands of Barnabas and Saul (xi. 27). . . . And the word of God grew and multiplied. And Barnabas and Saul returned from Jerusalem, when they had fulfilled the service, taking with them John, who was surnamed Mark" (xii. 24), who shortly after starts with them on their first joint missionary journey.

This, according to Acts, is Paul's second journey to Jerusalem after his conversion; but, as the text of Galatians stands, his second was fourteen years after his first, which disagrees with the date given by the famine.

We are here involved in very important questions of dates and times; I insert the following chronological notes as general indications of a few certified points; little more is to be had:—

Pontius Pilatus was Procurator of Judæa from A.D. 27 to 36, and within this interval occurred the crucifixion of Jesus Christ. The consent of tradition assigns to the incident the particular date A.D. 29, the year of the consulship of the two Gemini.

During the whole of this period Herod Antipas, a son of Herod the Great, was tetrarch of Galilee, and his half-brother, Philip, tetrarch of Ituræa, the district beyond Jordan. A king Aretas reigned at Petra as capital of Arabia, and no mention occurs of a state of affairs at Damascus that precludes his having such an interest there as we find ascribed to a king Aretas a little later. Herod Antipas married his daughter, and became embroiled with him by divorcing her in order to marry Herodias, his own niece, and wife of another half-brother,—the scandal of the Baptist.

In A.D. 36 Pilate, at the complaint of the Jews, was removed by Vitellius, the President of Syria, and sent to Rome to answer their accusations before Tiberius; the Emperor, however, had died, 16th March, A.D. 37, before his arrival; why this was so tardy there is no account. Vitellius himself visited Jerusalem at the passover, substituted Jonathan, son of Ananus, for high-priest, and returned to Antioch.

Vitellius followed up this indulgence to the Jews with others, on his visit to Jerusalem along with Herod the tetrarch and his friends, at the ensuing passover, A.D. 37. He remitted certain taxes, and allowed to the priests the custody of the sacred garments which, from the time of Herod the Great, had been retained by the political authority. The robes were indispensable for the performance of certain rites, and the retention of them was a pledge of tranquillity. The Procurator, by command of Tiberius, had an expedition in hand against Aretas in the quarrel of Herod, now in his company; at the solicitation of the Jews, apprehensive of a visit from the idolatrous ensigns, he changed the route of his army.

This was just such a spirit of concession as the Jews were likely to abuse. At a later date, it is in the interval between the death of Festus and the arrival of his successor Albinus, that the Sadducaic high-priest Ananus established a "judicial Sanhedrin," and put to death James, "the Lord's brother," and some others,— violence highly displeasing to a party at Jerusalem that was at once zealous for the law and of moderate political opinions. (Joseph. Ant. xx. 8, 1.)

Any liberty of action that the Jewish priesthood felt able to assume was not likely to be diminished by the news that arrived before Vitellius had been at Jerusalem four days, that Tiberius was dead, and that Caius, or Caligula, had succeeded him. The Procurator proclaimed the new Emperor, and then, giving up the expe-

dition against Aretas,—willingly, it is probable, from a pique he had towards Herod,—he retired to Antioch.

From Caligula, Herod Agrippa, a grandson of Herod the Great through still a third of his numerous wives, and brother of Herodias, received the tetrarchate of Philip, who was then dead; and in two years afterwards, A.D. 39, the dominions of Herod Antipas also, his brother-in-law, who, instigated by his wife, had out-intrigued himself, and was banished to Gaul.

On the 24th January, 41, Caligula was slain,—an immense relief to the Jews, who had been driven almost to desperation by his threatened introduction of the worship of himself into their temple. It was in A.D. 40 that Philo Judæus had undertaken a mission to him from the Alexandrian Jews upon the subject. At this time also, Agrippa, on his way to Palestine, visited Alexandria, and experienced the taunts and insults of the Greek populace, and, indeed, the population generally, who lampooned and caricatured and paraded in effigy the "King of the Jews" in a manner that seems to have furnished tradition with some details for enhancing the humiliations of Jesus. They enthroned a wretched idiot—from his name, Carabas, probably a Jew,—on a lofty seat in the gymnasium, enrobed him with an old mat, put a crown of paper on his head, and a reed in his hand for a sceptre, and bowed the knee before him and hailed him as King of the Jews.

In the first year of Claudius, however, A.D. 41, Agrippa received Judæa and Samaria, and his rule then comprised all the territories ruled over by his grandfather. He endeavoured to emulate him in magnificence of architecture and public festivities,—by extending the fortifications of Jerusalem, as well as by erecting theatres for musical exhibitions,—by savage gladiatorial shows in the amphitheatre at Berytus, and by the entertainment at Tiberias, of an assemblage of related or allied or subordinate kings.

But his position was not that of his grandfather;—a notice from the Prefect of Syria obliged him to desist from his plans of fortification, and at a word from the same intrusive Marsus, his regal congress was broken up, and Herod, king of Chalcis, his brother; Antiochus, king of Commagene; Cotys, king of the Lesser Armenia; Sampsigeranus, king of Emesa; and Polemon, king of Pontus, betook themselves to their own homes.

Gladiatorial shows were for his Greek or Roman subjects; to ingratiate himself with the Jews, he put to death James, the brother of John, and with so much success that he imprisoned Peter in order that he also might furnish a like spectacle to the people, when the moment should arrive that would give it most effect. Peter, however, helped or unhelped, effected an escape.

Agrippa died A.D. 44, after a short illness, which attacked him at a pompous festival at Cæsarea, and Jew and Christian, Josephus and the writer of Acts, were equally prompt to interpret the act of the finger of God, as it might best flatter their several self-importances and the dignity of their religious persuasions.

The dated death of Agrippa is the very pivot of the chronology of the New Testament; the narrative of Acts avers that it occurred while a famine was upon Judæa, or at least impending,—for only so can we interpret the mention of the anxiety of envoys from Tyre at this time, to conciliate the King, "from whose country they were nourished." How this should be is another question; but the thought of the historian is clear when he interpolates such a note between a mention of Paul bringing relief to the starved by famine at Jerusalem, and the account of his return to Antioch after fulfilling his mission.

But Paul, in his Epistle to the Galatians, enumerates his early visits to the Apostles at Jerusalem, and gives some note of the intervening years; and thus, if Paul's text and the statement in Acts are accurate, we may count back towards the date of the conversion and Stephen's martyrdom. We shall find on trial that the two authorities are absolutely at variance. According to Acts, Paul visited Jerusalem for the second time after his conversion, A.D. 44. But the Epistle says that this visit was fourteen years after his first return, which was three after his conversion. But this would carry his conversion back to A.D. 27, which is quite impossible. Something, therefore, must give way; either it is by error that Paul was said to have gone up at all, A.D. 44, or he was mistaken or inaccurate in speaking of fourteen years, or the text is corrupt and some other term was originally written, which is quite possible.

The conclusion I have come to—that I came to on what still appear to me sound grounds, twenty years ago—is, that Paul wrote not *fourteen*, but *four* years. Thus he will state that his first visit to Jerusalem after his conversion was after about three years, and his second four years after that. The manuscripts are unanimous, but they may all be derived from one single faulty copy.

This would bring his conversion and the martyrdom

of Stephen, which must have very closely preceded it, to A.D. 37 or 38, the very period when, as we have seen, the relaxed policy of Vitellius would account for the liberties and violences the Sanhedrin allowed themselves.

I am quite aware of the gravity of my postulate; but what results from the alternative course of identifying the seçond visit mentioned in Galatians with the third mentioned in Acts? The second visit of Acts must then be condemned as unhistorical, and excised along with a group of very coherent and natural incidents; at best it could but be regarded as a blundering version of the visit resulting in the decree. The narrative of the visit and discussion about the decree, must be treated almost as severely, before it will correspond with Paul's Galatian narrative; but this, strong in corroboration, resists such treatment, and the impeachment of it threatens to compromise the pledged candour of Paul himself.

How many other probabilities are conciliated by the proposed solution, we shall find as we proceed.

CHAPTER VII.

GENTILE CHRISTIANITY.

I. THE PRIVATE COMPACT OF PAUL AND PETER.—II. THE PUBLIC ALTERCATION AT ANTIOCH.—III. THE APOSTOLIC DECREE OF COMPROMISE.

I. THE PRIVATE COMPACT OF PAUL AND PETER.

I HAVE assumed, then, without hesitation, that for fourteen, as the word stands in the Galatian record, we should read four years. Holding over this concession, let us see how far other things are coherent.

"Then, after *four* years, I again went up to Jerusalem along with Barnabas, and taking with me Titus also." That mention of Titus is absent in Acts, where omissions are so numerous and constant, makes no difficulty; and especially as it appears presently that the motive for taking him was not generally promulgated. "And I went up by revelation, and communicated to them the Gospel which I preach among the Gentiles, but privately to them that were of reputation, lest by any means I had run, or should run, in vain."

The revelation may refer to the prophecy of Agabus, but more probably to a particular experience of Paul himself. By the "Gospel which I preach," we are to understand the conception of the Gospel, that Paul is insisting upon to his correspondents; the theory of Christianity, as bearing upon the relations of Jew and Gentile, the law and the traditions."

It thus appears quite plainly that Paul acted upon a policy at this early date, which was the same in principle that he carried out in his latest journey to Jerusalem. He seized as an opportunity of getting Apostolic sanction for the Gentile Gospel, the moment when he was conveying a contribution from Gentile converts in aid of the necessities of the poor saints—the Ebionite Church at Jerusalem, with which the Apostles were most immediately connected.

Cavillers disposed to interpret the transaction harshly might have said, and may still say, that Paul came with money in his hand and promise of more; and, by the corruption of a portion of the leaders of a pauperized sect, bought a recognition of his own Apostleship, and a promise of connivance at innovations in the Christian system, that were quite out of consistency with their declared opinions. On the other hand, we reply that Paul saw in the necessities of a starving Church, an opportunity of convincing it of the truly Christian charity with which uncircumcised Gentiles could commiserate and relieve a community of Jews. The spirit may have been much the same as that in which large subscriptions have been collected in England to relieve the sufferings from flood or fire, of communities in France that habitually breathed hate and rancour against our country. This is the spirit in which the Indian famine has been made an opportunity of heaping coals of fire on the heads of a recently-insurgent population,—in which hordes of starving repealers and shouters against the Saxon were comforted during the failure of the potato crop. Corruption is a word that has here no place. That a purpose of conciliation may be promoted along with a work of charity is, of course, not absolutely out of view; but as little is it the sole—least of all can it be called, an unworthy motive.

The charity was given, I have no doubt, without a stipulation. I have no doubt also that Titus, the uncircumcised disciple, was brought forward in such a light and such a position throughout the transaction, as to make it impossible for the Apostles not to recognize the compatibility of the best Christian graces with independence of Jewish rites; so in his later journey, in charge of another and probably a larger contribution, Paul carries up the Gentile convert Trophimus.

"But not even Titus, who was with me, though a Greek, was forcibly urged to be circumcised; (but it was because of the false brethren who had slipped in, who crept in to spy out our freedom which we hold in Christ Jesus, that they might enslave us; to whom we yielded subjection not for an hour, that the truth of the Gospel might remain unto you.) But of those who seemed to be somewhat, whatever they were, it is no matter to me, (God accepteth not man's person;) for to me these seemers added nothing; but, on the contrary, when they saw that to me was entrusted the Gospel of the uncircumcision as to Peter of the circumcision; (for He that wrought in Peter toward the apostleship of the circumcision wrought in me also toward the Gentiles;) and when they perceived the grace that was given unto me, James and Cephas and John, who seemed to be pillars, gave to me and Barnabas the right hands of fellowship, that we might go to the Gentiles and they to the circumcision; only they would that we should remember the poor, the very same thing that I also was forward to do."

From this it appears that James, Peter, and John, who were of leading influence in the Jerusalem church, were prepared or induced to sanction the discipleship of Gentiles, without imposing upon them the rite of circumcision; but that in this respect they were so far in advance of many of their adherents, and probably also of colleagues, that it was not safe to promulgate the compact. It remained at this time a private agreement, and, as usual in such cases, various complications arose in due time, and at last came an explosion.

It is not clear whether the James who was a party to this secret compact was the James, the Lord's brother, who had seen Paul on his return the first time, and is found long after at the head of the Hebrew church; or James the brother of John. I suspect the latter, notwithstanding the name being placed before Peter and disjoined from John. I think so on two grounds; first, from the position that the brothers James and John take along with Peter in certain mythical stories in the Gospels, which, I believe, are derived from these later transactions; and then from events that are recorded in Acts as following close upon these negotiations. Before the return of Paul and Barnabas to Antioch is recorded, we have to read in Acts that Herod Agrippa killed James the brother of John with the sword, and, to please the same party, seized Peter also. We seem here to have an indication of the sympathy of this James with the actions and opinions of Peter; whether we think it worth while further to conjecture or no, that intercourse with Paul had stimulated their enthusiasm to speak more boldly than usual upon some of those dangerous topics that had been before them; and that they had thus excited a popular rage, and exposed themselves to fatal catastrophe.

It is after the return of Paul and Barnabas to Antioch that we first hear of their proposed missionary journey, as if it were then thought of for the first time, and might even have originated independently of them. It is, however, probable enough—it is most probable —that the negotiations at Jerusalem had been pushed on and planned, with the special purpose of settling an advantageous basis, on which to proceed in this very enterprise. The opening there might be for success in such an undertaking, was sufficiently evinced by what was done and doing at Antioch; and the events of the famine fell out just in a way to invite to some preliminary conference with the recognized heads of the Church. It is likely enough that it was with distinct reference to the mission that John Mark, who afterwards was associated in it, came down with Paul and Barnabas; his participation would not be without significance and aid, in the event of opposition from that very likely source, brethren of the Hebrew church. A certain not unworthy end might also be answered by indoctrinating Mark himself with sympathy and interest for a Gospel more liberal.

His mother Mary—sister, or sister-in-law of Barnabas —is named in Acts. Peter, on his escape from prison, proceeds to her house to notify his safety to the brethren, of whom there are many assembled there praying.

Peter, James, and John were treated more confidentially than the rest of the Apostles; but, such are the difficulties of men who are beyond and before their time, that it is quite possible that even to these Paul did not at this time venture to disclose what he would call " the whole counsel of God."

Mark, the cousin of Barnabas, (Colos. iv.) starts with Paul and Barnabas on their journey, but after they have passed through Cyprus, the native land of the latter, from Salamis to Paphos, and thence crossed over to Perga in Pamphylia, on their way to Pisidia, "Mark went not with them to the work, but departing from them returned to Jerusalem." I think it quite possible that he may have had scruples as to the course the teaching was taking. Paul, on independent and original ground, is likely enough to have spoken out about the Law; about not only its non-obligation on Gentile converts, but even its abrogation for Jews, in a way to startle Mark, cognizant though he might be of the private compact, fresh as he even might be from the liberal church of Antioch.

Two incidents related on this journey will have to be considered, as the subjects of the two next Cartoons. At present, I pursue the series of events of which we have witnessed the significant commencement.

That Paul's Epistle to the Galatians was addressed to churches founded by him on this first journey is not absolutely certain, though, I think, highly probable; but however this may be, it shows clearly what was the Gospel he was at this time disposed to preach, and did preach.

He inculcated the faith that Jesus was the Messiah, and the Mediator who would reconcile all men to God; and this faith and its implications he upheld as superseding all Jewish ceremonialism. He not only did not impose the Jewish law on his heathen disciples, but he warned them against it as slavery unbecoming free men; as weak and beggarly elements contemptible to the instructed. He was prepared, not only to denounce the observance of sacred days, months, seasons, years, but to deter from circumcision, by declaring that it rendered the whole law obligatory,—the whole law, which even the circumcised Jew did not and could not keep.

He magnifies the exclusive merit of Christian profession to such an extent, as to find that the balance of privilege is with the unprivileged. Not for nothing had he sat at the feet of Gamaliel; and he evinces his proficiency in the acquirements which his opponent—"some contentious Jew," would most respect, by the fatal dexterity with which he knows how to "entangle him in the web of his own Rabbinical conundrums." With admirable audacity, he even ventures to make out Esau to be the Old Testament type of the truly privileged; and Isaac, the legitimate son of the Patriarch, the progenitor of all Israel, to be the personification of the outcasts. "Agar is Mount Sinai, that is Jerusalem, inasmuch as Jerusalem is in bondage with her children. But Christians have a Jerusalem in heaven; a free mother therefore; therefore Christians are the true representatives of Isaac, the child of promise; and, like him, they are persecuted by the child of the flesh,—by the Jew now, as Isaac of old by Esau. What, then, says the Scripture? 'Cast out the bondmaid and her son, for the son of the bondmaid shall not be heir with the son of the free woman;'" that is, let the Gentile Isaac repudiate the Jew Esau. Surely this is ringing the changes to some purpose.

Touching the outcome, however, there is no ambiguity. "Now that the faith is come, we are no longer under a schoolmaster.... There is neither Jew nor Greek, there is neither slave nor freeman, there is neither male nor female: for ye are all one in Christ Jesus." (Gal. iii. 25–28.) "As many as wish to make a fair show in the flesh, they force you to be circumcised; only lest they should be persecuted for the cross of Christ. For neither do they who are circumcised, themselves keep the law; but they wish you to be circumcised, that in your flesh they may boast. But far be it from me to boast, save in the cross of our Lord Jesus Christ, by whom the world is crucified unto me, and I unto the world. For in Christ Jesus neither is circumcision anything, nor uncircumcision, but a new creation. And as many as walk by this rule, peace be on them, and mercy, and on the Israel of God." (Gal. vi. 12–16.)

Barnabas is referred to more than once in this Epistle, and in a manner that seems to imply that he was known to the Galatians: this is a point in favour of their church having been founded on Paul's first journey, when Barnabas was with him; and I think also, that the words, "that the truth of the Gospel might remain unto you," must be taken to imply that the Galatian church was already in possession of immunity from the customs, when the discussion that imperilled the privilege arose at Antioch.

II. THE PUBLIC ALTERCATION AT ANTIOCH.

Let us now follow forth the consequences of the secret compact, according to the terms of which,—as Paul, at least, chose to interpret them,—he proclaimed a conception of Christianity as large as charity, and only disgraced by being supported by a class of arguments from Scripture interpretation, that he himself always puts aside at last, as if ashamed of them while he is using them.

The all-important chapter (ii.) of Galatians must be our chief guide. Here Paul speaks, as we have seen, of a transaction effected privately with certain leading Apostles at his second return to Jerusalem; the purport of which is significantly shown by the Gentile convert Titus, whom he took up with him, not being required to be circumcised. This demand was made indeed, he goes on to say, but it was under other circumstances and on another occasion; it was made by "certain false brethren who had slipped or crept in to spy out our freedom which we hold in Christ Jesus, that they might enslave us; to whom we yielded subjection not for an hour, that the truth of the Gospel might remain unto you." This paragraph clearly anticipates the order of time; Paul has not yet finished his story as to the understanding he came to with the Apostles on his second visit, in respect of the division of the field of labour; but he is led aside to intercalate the notice of the circumstances under which the conditions of Titus came to be challenged.

No result could be more natural; a latitude in observances, or the neglect of them, was being indulged in by Paul and his adherents, of which the Church at large—the Church at head-quarters at Jerusalem, especially, was not publicly cognizant. Sooner or later, of course, the fact got wind, and equally of course the laxity would be challenged by bigots in the most offensive and violent manner possible. False brethren and sneaks are the best names that Paul has to bestow on them in return, and such in spirit they may probably have been, though we cannot be surprised that the discovery should have produced an indignant explosion.

Apart from the tale of years,—which, as we have seen, must be revised, the order of events in Galatians is quite in agreement or in harmony with the order in Acts. It is there related that it was after the return of Paul and Barnabas from the mission to Pisidia, that "certain men who came down from Judea—some of the sect of Pharisees who were believers—taught the brethren at Antioch, Unless ye be circumcised after the manner of Moses, ye cannot be saved." These are manifestly the false brethren, the creepers-in, who called in question the position of the Gentile Christian Titus, and such as Titus. That Titus and that the private compact are not mentioned in Acts makes nothing against this; such omissions do not impugn facts otherwise authenticated: the true moral of such a difficulty is to set us upon the inquiry how the knowledge of the writer happened to be so scant: his judgment in selection so perverse; or, lastly, how he was influenced in the case by party spirit, or individual bias and plan.

"When, therefore, Paul and Barnabas had no small disagreement and dispute with them, they settled that

Paul and Barnabas, and some others of them, should go up to Jerusalem to the Apostles and elders about this question." (xv. 2.)

There were, however, other elements and parties to the dispute, that are not adverted to by the writer of Acts. Let us again hear Paul.

"But when Peter came to Antioch, I withstood him to the face, because he was blameable. For before certain persons came from James, he ate with the Gentiles; but when they came, he withdrew and separated himself, fearing those of the circumcision. And the other Jews dissembled with him, so that even Barnabas was carried away with them in this dissembling. But when I saw that they walked not level with the truth of the Gospel, I said unto Peter before them all, If thou, being a Jew, livest as do the Gentiles, and not as a Jew, how forcest thou the Gentiles to live as Jews?"

The James in question here is not the brother of John, who was at this time dead. There can be no reasonable doubt that the "certain from James," referred to by Paul, are to be identified with the brethren of the sect of Pharisees spoken of in Acts, who, coming from Jerusalem, are chargeable with exaggerating the terms of a commission, or perhaps with inventing one, from the James whom we find presiding over the Church at Jerusalem, who disowns, or at least is represented as disowning them.

According to the narrative, two points come into question: the obligation of the Law and the customs, not only on the Gentile disciples, but also on the Jewish—certainly to some extent, and perhaps absolutely. For the course of events necessarily opened the entire question. The common meal was the custom, if not institution, of the Church; but in a mixed society of Jews and Gentiles it became an impossibility, unless some of the most inveterate Jewish prejudices respecting meats and persons and ceremonial qualification were given up, or else imposed on and submitted to by the Gentiles. Even if the question of circumcision were conceded, quite enough remained to break up the Christian communion into separate messes, and thus to vitiate the very principle of charity, and countervail the progressive tendency to turn the special distinction of the sect into its single essential,—to make Christ all in all.

By whatever process, by original disposition or persuasion of Paul, Peter had adopted the most liberal view. He had given his authority to the private understanding concluded between Paul and Barnabas and the Apostles, or certain of them, at Jerusalem; and by public and unrestricted association at Antioch, he added his personal sanction for the largest interpretation. On the appearance of the Pharisaic rigorists he went back, and with him Barnabas, who was still more deeply committed. Then came the rebuke of Paul; then came the great occasion of a stand made in the very gap.

The best liberties of the progressive section of mankind were depending at that moment on the resolution with which a firm position should be asserted, and plain words spoken, over a dinner-table at Antioch; and, let us say also, on the candour with which a false step might be retrieved, and half-abandoned boldness resumed.

III. THE APOSTOLIC DECREE OF COMPROMISE.

For the next stage in the story we must again transfer our attention to Acts.

Paul and Barnabas and others proceed to Jerusalem. "And the Apostles and elders came together to consider of this matter. And when there had been much disputing, Peter stood up, and said unto them, Men and brethren, ye know that in the days of old God made choice among us, that by my mouth the Gentiles should hear the word of the good tidings and believe. And God, who knoweth the heart, bare witness for them, giving to them the Holy Spirit even as to us, and put no difference between them and us, purifying their hearts by the faith. Now, therefore, why tempt ye God to put a yoke upon the neck of the disciples, which neither our fathers nor ourselves were able to bear?

" But through the grace of our Lord Jesus Christ, we have faith that we shall be saved, even in the same manner as they."

The last clause of this speech appears to be a distinct enunciation of the principle accepted by Paul, that not only was faith in Christ, without the observances of the Law, sufficient to save the Gentile, but it was sufficient to save the Jew also, who was thus, at last, released from a burden that had depressed the race for generations.

The tenor and the term of Peter's speech, it will be observed, are perfectly in accordance with what we have gleaned from Galatians,—that the discussion had involved the question of the obligation of the Law on Jews, quite as distinctly as its imposition on Gentiles.

If we accept the record, Peter nobly recovers himself after his temporary vacillation, and does his very best to obtain public sanction for even a fuller application of the Gospel than he had at an earlier date promoted privately.

It will be noticed that the question of Jews eating with Gentiles, which brought on the discussion at Antioch, is the very same that, according to Acts, had been provoked and settled after Peter's conversion of Cornelius. The whole story of Cornelius may easily be a mythical transformation of the Gentile conversions and discussions at Antioch. Who shall say? I remain, however, with a distinct recognition in any case of the primary and ultimate liberal spirit of Peter,—his vacillation notwithstanding.

Paul and Barnabas say their unreported say, and then the result is given by James as an authoritative compromise. The Gentiles are relieved from the odious and oppressive customs, with certain reservations to alleviate the difficulties of association and common table. "I conclude not to trouble those of the Gentiles who turn to God, but to enjoin them to abstain from things offered to idols, and from fornication (an ill name probably for marriage with unbelievers), and from things strangled, and from blood." As regards Peter's movement for relief to the Jewish disciples, it is either disregarded, or put aside with a blunt reference to their opportunity of hearing the law of Moses read in the synagogues every Sabbath day, all the world over. The decision is embodied in an epistle, or rather a decree, in which the high tone is assumed of conceding out of mere condescension, and imposing without appeal: it "hath seemed good to the Holy Ghost, and to us, to lay upon you no greater burden than these necessary things," etc. The congregation keep reverential silence during the debate, as might be expected under such a president, but the mandate purports to emanate from the Apostles, elders, and whole church, being of one mind; the disturbers are disowned; Paul and Barnabas, on the other hand, are recognized with high commendation, and to them, along with two special envoys, is entrusted the delivery of the decree.

The decree, it is said, was read at Antioch, and found consolatory. Paul, when he proceeds to confirm the churches that he had founded on his first journey, is said to give them these *dogmata* to observe, and James refers to them as the constituted and unaltered rule when Paul goes to Jerusalem for the last time. That the rules were promulgated with authority is clear from many allusions,—in Revelation and in the earliest Fathers, Justin, and so forth; it is no less clear that they could not have satisfied Paul even if they did Peter. His Epistles disregard them; he gives instructions to the Corinthians that directly disallow them as imperative and contravene their tenor; and he holds no measure, in writing at least, with the permanence of Jewish ceremonialism. Hence it might well be reported at Jerusalem, as James declared to him, that he taught the Jews everywhere that they should no longer observe the Law.

But the motive for the secret compact in the first instance—concealment of full designs from the multitude, lest his ministry should be brought to a violent and premature end—was still as operative as ever. Hard necessity! This is ever the dilemma of proselytizers that are beyond their age, and Paul might learn from bitter experience that the unsteadiness of Peter was not without palliation.

The enthusiast, like Stephen, declares, denounces, defies; the end comes early,—he is stoned. Prudence is taught, and the next innovator advances more cautiously —so cautiously, that he makes no considerable way; then comes the policy of bold advance and as sudden retraction, and then bold advance again; the assertion of a startling principle, the qualification of it till it is reduced to inanity; then the return upon the enunciation to secure its admission in part while the first alarm is set to sleep by seeming withdrawal,—the speech directed one way, action facing directly the other.

Hence it is not impossible that Paul, having done his best at the conference, acquiesced in a resolution which he could not resist, and which at least gave him somewhat. He set some value on what was obtained, and took his own counsel as to where and when, and how far, he would give effect to the remainder. Many very equivocal things are told of him in Acts,—how he even circumcises Timothy; how he goes up to Jerusalem to keep a feast as a matter of urgent moment; how he shaves his head in Cenchreæ, having a vow, and so forth. We may question the truth of these tales if we please, but the fact remains that he goes to Jerusalem several times, when, if his real written opinions were plainly declared there, the city must have been too hot to hold him for a day. This was the concession in action, that he was equally forced to make in argument; when he was compelled to insinuate, to suggest,—to qualify his most positive opinions, as the only means of getting a hearing or a chance of acceptation at all.

Hard, indeed, must it have been for a man of dignity to have "to hedge, to shuffle, to lurch," after this fashion; but the times were against him; the harmlessness of the dove would have perished at once, and the good cause with it, but for the safeguard of a serpent's wisdom. He was beset on every side; in perils by false brethren, he was driven to reservations and inconsistencies; in peril from the bigoted Jews, he was driven to fight them with their own weapons, and take the readiest way to his hand to set Pharisee and Sadducee by the ears; in peril from the authorities, he made the best of his privilege of citizenship, and took every advantage of opportunities; and exerted his eloquence with every aid from rhetoric.

He fought long and boldly a perilous and difficult fight; but amidst all his concessions and all his inconsistencies he kept his great ends in view,—the emancipation of Christianity in the first place from the trammels of Judaism, and then the emancipation of the Jew from his confirmed and deadening ceremonialism, by Christianity.

His patriotic endeavours to save his people, his country, were frustrate; but even as a patriot, his name should be held in honour by Jews for evermore.

To Paul as a Jew, and with a heart that retained a Jew's sympathy for his countrymen, the Apostolic rescript which sealed their continuance in bondage to the Law, must have been a deep source of regret and disappointment; it is clear from his Epistle to the Romans that he retained to that late date in all their entirety, all his principles of Christian freedom for both Jew and Gentile, and his resolution to promote it with all his art and energy. But others may have been less persistent. If Peter's Epistle could be relied on as genuine, he himself, for all his predilections, would have seemed to defer to the majority, and to have held by the decree as the basis of the faith for both Jew and Gentile. On the other hand, some teachers of Gentile blood may easily have acquiesced still more readily; the imposition upon the Gentiles, except in principle, was slight, and involved little inconvenience; their section of the Church was gaining in relative importance every day; and every day it had less and less sympathy with the members of the Jewish section, or the grievances that any portion of them might be sensible of under their share of a convenient compromise. Numerous Jewish and Gentile teachers alike, therefore, would co-operate in giving effect to it, and its influence is traceable far and wide. Even the author of Acts seems to treat it as definitive, and might, if we were off our guard, be interpreted as willing to promote its acceptance for the sake of harmony and peace. But his record contains enough to indicate that he held it as only the best arrangement that was obtainable at the time, not the best that could be desired. When a battle has been lost, a treaty which secures much of what was contested, will always be thought by many of the vanquished not only worth having, but even worth resting upon finally; but I cannot accept such a position of premature finality as being that of the compiler of Luke and Acts; who manifests such sympathy with the expansive tendency of the Gospel,—an idea that his materials show was already most definite and pronounced.

In the Book of Revelation, as well as Peter's Epistle,

—an Epistle as little written by Peter as the Revelation by John,—in Justin and the Clementine Homilies, we find the authority of the decree vindicated, and the contravention of it by Paul adverted to with acrimony. We may gather also from Pliny's Epistle to Trajan, that in his time the abstaining from flesh that had formed part of heathen sacrifices, was a test of Christianity in the communities of Bithynia. Hence it is very significant that while a considerable literature is positive and vehement in citing the authority of Peter for the restrictions of the decree, the author of Acts represents him as overruled in the matter, and never introduces him afterwards, and makes all his authority previously, tell the other way.

Nowhere else in the Acts of the Apostles is the principle of the supersession of the Law by Christ, enunciated so unequivocally as in the sentence here put into the mouth of Peter. And yet this is the constantly-recurring gist of Paul's teaching as we have it in the most authentic form in his Epistles. This could not be by accident; it could not be by ignorance. Was it that the writer of Acts had come to despair of the speedy realization in his time of the truly comprehensive Christianity; and that while he gave it the best chance of surviving by assigning to it the authority of Peter, he was fain to be content for the time to countervail the prejudice it had derived from, and caused against, Paul, by casting the burden of responsibility on the titular head of the opposite party, and so to help an intermediate compromise?

I am of opinion that the finally dominant idea of the compiler of Acts was this:—to set forth incidentally, the largest principle of a free Gospel, common and sufficient both for Jew and Gentile, independently of the Law, as the true goal of Gospel development,—its natural and inevitable and glorious destiny. He displayed carefully the steps by which this was led up to, and the difficulties and complications in its way; he secured for it the sanction of Jesus in parables of unmistakeable moral, in anecdotes of inevitable significance; and also of Peter, the chief Apostle; at Samaria, at Cæsarea, at the conference at Jerusalem. Then he exhibited the complication that arose with the Jewish Christians, and the enforced compromise of the decree which continued the obligation of the Law for Jews, and imposed sufficient restrictions on the Gentiles to vitiate the principle of freedom, and to be a badge of dependence. This compromise, he sets forth, has a fair trial; it is, he avers rather courageously, respected with loyalty by Paul; but by the incidents that he selects for record, he steadily shows that as a measure of conciliation, its sole apology, it proves a failure, and is moreover rapidly outgrown: the extension of the Gospel among the Jews,—the establishment of a general reception of Jesus as Christ by the Jews on any terms, becomes more and more hopeless; it fails at Jerusalem, it fails finally at Rome; it is among the Gentiles that must be sought at last the leading shoot of Gospel development. With a certain feeling of epic propriety, it is with the arrival of the great Apostle of catholicity at the imperial city that the conclusive break is declared, which extricated the Gospel from the trammels of Judaical accommodation, and in doing so broke off at the same time the dependence of the Church, in which a Gentile element was now so immeasurably preponderant, on a provincial synod,—a Jewish sect. Even Paul, in the end, and after many a struggle, gives up his nation; the compiler of Acts, it is true, does not say in so many words that when he sent away the chief men of the Jewish synagogue at Rome, he declared openly that circumcisions, and shavings of heads, and visits to the Temple, and sacrifices, that he had hitherto demeaned himself by giving in to, in the hope of Jewish conversion, should be denounced openly as the obsolete things they were and that he had long known them to be; Paul is not made to say that let James and the elders at Jerusalem think what they may, his course would be clear to declare to them as distinctly as he had done to the Galatians, that in adhering to the Law they were courting damnation —holding by beggarly elements, drivelling in second childhood. This is not said, but this, I have no doubt, is what the author of Acts intended to convey; and to his contemporaries, reading by the light of passing events, did absolutely and of necessity convey. Events had been ripening long enough. Every chance that the Jews could expect had been allowed to them, every admissible compromise been offered and rejected; and in the history would be seen how it came to pass that there was nothing for them at last but to be left aside, or join Christianity on the terms that Paul, the prisoner, had notoriously preached at Rome,—renunciation of the Law as abrogated, as merged in the superior revelation; and acceptation of Gentile brethren who repudiated both the law of Moses and the decree of Apostles, and were all equal in Christ.

Before this catastrophe, however, there was a very important intermediate history. The trimming decree was reduced in value for the Gentile Christian by the reservations and continued Jewish bondage; ceremonialism was conserved at the centre of the sect, and sooner or later was sure to bear fruit,—to give force to the side of bigotry. But if Paul could see this, it might not be so patent to others whose instincts were not made lively by national sympathies; accordingly, the asserted joy and comfort of the Church at the settlement may have been extensive, and we may understand how these feelings coloured so remarkably the course of Christian tradition.

The grand point of Gentile emancipation from the Law was gained, and lively as may have been the indignation at Peter's vacillation at first, he was held in result to have fully re-established himself; and in this point of view he became the hero of apologetic tradition.

The party of Pharisaical converts, on the other hand, were willingly treated as utterly discomfited, notwithstanding that they had consummated an amount of mischief that was fraught with difficulty and misery untold. Tradition took its own way with them, and when the fabulous narratives of the incidents of the life of Jesus became digested into biographies, in the heart of that portion of the sect where the spirit of expansive Christianity lived on the warmest, the scruples and tyrannies and hypocrisies of Pharisees, were as pointedly brought on the scene, as the hesitations and prevarications and repentance of Peter.

They replied in traditions of their own, represented, as we have seen, in a literature which disowns and disparages Paul, and claims the sanction of Peter for at least the restrictions of the decree,—whether justly or not, I will not venture to say.

CHAPTER VIII.

THE HISTORY OF THE CHURCH, IN THE BIOGRAPHY OF JESUS.

I. THE PHARISEES OF ANTIOCH, IN THE GOSPELS.—II. THE EXPANSION OF THE CHURCH, IN THE PARABLES.—III. PETER, JAMES, AND JOHN AT THE TRANSFIGURATION.

I. THE PHARISEES OF ANTIOCH, IN THE GOSPELS.

A GREAT deal has been done by D. F. Strauss and other critics to elucidate the extent to which anecdotes for the life of Jesus took form by the model of those ascribed to the prophets, especially Moses and Elijah, in the Old Testament. Other materials, it is clearly made out, were derived from the interpretation of declamation as prophecy, and of prophecy as Messianic,—as Messianic according to independent pattern, by processes involving all manner of misconceptions.

The operation of these varied influences can often be traced very distinctly in the features of the resulting mythus, though it may be quite impossible to follow each and every through all their reactions and resolutions. A concurrence of minor influences has often a power equivalent to the grand predominance of one; and a single influence is sometimes predominant in virtue, not of its proper vigour, but by the accident that it operates alone. Jesus is born of a virgin: and the tradition or invention may seem sufficiently explained by the citation of a text, grossly misunderstood, from Isaiah. Yet this mistake concurs with a certain symbolical value for parthenogenesis of the founder, the head, the very object of a religious worship. Jesus, like Moses, was transfigured on a mount, and both prophets alike, on descending, found their adherents at the foot in disorder; in one case actually apostate, in the other nonplussed and confounded; but, after all, the parallelism leaves a large margin of divergence to be otherwise accounted for. This is also the case in abundance of other instances; as in miracles of healing and of raising the dead: special details are constantly introduced, which betray that they are significant, but do not for the most part give up and declare their significance forthwith.

Old Testament literature, and the associations of ancient prophets and of Messianic anticipations founded on prophecy, however irregularly,—these were the fund of lore from which the imagery of the Gospel stories were for the most part drawn; they were combined with some truly historical personal incidents, and they had to suffer the usual casualties of copy and recopy in additions and glosses, false divisions, and mistaken agglutinations. But still, all these influences and operations combined, do not constitute, and do not conduct us to, the germinant principle which governed the form of assimilation. The materials of a structure may be referred most exactly to their sources, and still no explanation of the principle of the design be implied. Take whatever anecdote of the set we please that is of any extent, and, after the identification of all its elements in detail, the grand question still remains—what was the intentional drift, the suggesting purpose, or organizing motive of the conception?

The answer to this question that approves itself to me —approves itself on reconsideration after twenty years— is, that most of the miraculous incidents in the life of Jesus, originated with a section of the early Christians that had little or no direct knowledge, or even information, of the details of his personal career; that they were composed originally with perfect consciousness of a definite, and that, for the most part, a moral or controversial aim. Inasmuch as the authors, most probably Hellenistic Jews, were imbued with Jewish associations, their productions naturally relished of the antecedents and the anticipations of the nation. Strong controversial feelings will ever give an undesigned colour to the most simple-minded narrative; but we deal here with something more, and something much more pronounced. The composers, the poets, the prophets, or prophesiers, as they might call themselves, appear to me to have aimed, in many cases, at illustrating the proper Christian view of a pending controversy, by inventing such an incident for the life of Christ as would apply with cogency as a precedent,—tell with the authority of a decision. In other cases we can trace no motive, other than what we may consider purely poetical. "Christ" is constantly employed by Paul for Christ's doctrine, for Christianity, for all that is good and admirable in Christian graces; he preaches Christ, lives in Christ, dies in Christ; and to fail in duty is to crucify, to betray, to deny Christ. The same poetic or rhetorical figure of speech, taken on base of the letter, relates the fortunes of Christianity as those of Christ; and gives a representation of a crisis in the history of a movement, as an adventure or an action of its originator.

Precepts and parables, therefore, are put into the mouth of Jesus which bear directly upon discussions that, by their very nature, could only have arisen subsequently to his death, and to the changes in the anticipations of his followers that then ensued; or, in other cases, the weight of his authority is borrowed by the ascription of proceedings to him, that have either a direct or symbolical bearing on current difficulties.

Again, but I believe more rarely, without any special controversial drift being in question, the Jesus of the Gospels is a simple personification of the Church, and his fate an embodiment of its trials and vicissitudes.

To proceed to examples:—

The incidents at Antioch, of which we have heard so much, reappear in the Gospels (Matt. xv., Mark vii., Luke xi.) transformed into an incident, of which the scene is laid at Gennesaret, apparently on the western border of the lake.

Matthew and Mark relate it, for the most part, with a parallelism that indicates translation from common authority, with here and there a transposition—here and there a gloss.

"Then came together unto him *the Pharisees* and some of the scribes *who came from Jerusalem*, saying, Wherefore do your disciples transgress the tradition of the elders, for they do not wash their hands before they eat bread? And he, answering them, said, And why do ye transgress the commandment of God by your tradition? for Moses ('God' in Matt.) said, Honour your father and your mother; and whoso curseth father or mother, let him die the death. But ye say, etc. etc.

"*Hypocrites*, well did Esaias prophesy concerning you, saying, This people honoureth me with their lips, but their heart is far from me.

"*And calling to him all the crowd, he said unto them, Hear ye all*, and understand, not what entereth into the mouth of a man defiles him, but what proceeds out of his mouth. . . .

"Then came his disciples, and said unto him, Knowest thou that the Pharisees, when they heard the word, found a difficulty? But he answered, and said, . . . Let them alone, they are blind leaders of the blind.

"*And Peter answering, said unto him*, Tell unto us this parable. And Jesus said, Are ye yet without understanding?"

In Luke xi. we read: " A certain Pharisee asked him to dine with him: and he went in, and lay down to meat. And when the Pharisee saw it, he wondered that he had not first washed before dinner. And the Lord said unto him, Now ye Pharisees cleanse the outside of the cup and the platter; but your inside is full of ravening and of wickedness," etc.

"And he said, Woe unto you, teachers of the law! *for ye load men with burdens grievous to be borne*, and ye yourselves touch not the burdens with one of your fingers. (xii. 2,) First, beware of the leaven of the Pharisees, which is *hypocrisy*."

The great denunciation of the Pharisees in the thirteenth chapter of Matthew is full of innuendos that go straight to the blot of the difficulties at Antioch.

"Woe unto you, scribes and Pharisees, hypocrites, for that ye shut the kingdom of heaven against men; for ye neither go in yourselves, nor suffer those that are entering to go in. Woe unto you, scribes and Pharisees, hypocrites; for ye compass sea and land to make one proselyte, and when he becomes so ye make him twofold more a child of hell than yourselves."

The contest of the teachers at Antioch with the brethren of the sect of Pharisees coming from Jerusalem, who cavilled at the neglect of the customs in the order of meals; who shut the kingdom of heaven against the new converts, and while zealous for converts themselves, would make them slaves and bigots; the separate appeal to the general multitude; the special explanation to Peter and the immediate disciples; the unsparing denouncement of hypocrisy at last,—all this seems to me to bring home to the writer of the Gospel—the writer, that is, of the anecdote wrought into the web of the Gospel—the intention and reference that I have imputed.

All touches very directly the principle of the dispute at Antioch, even when it glances off from the most particular application. Jesus is here not declaring the annulment of the law, or even its non-application to Gentiles; he speaks in the spirit ascribed to the Baptist, as the rebuker of formal religion and hollow ceremonialism. He denounces the traditions; but though it is true that in form he adds sanction to Moses and the Law, he founds his rebuke so preferentially upon simple morals as distinct from preceptive obligation, that the Law suffers in truth little less than tradition.

Had the contents of these chapters been on record at

the time among reverenced archives of the Christian community, they could scarcely have escaped reference and citation; if, indeed, we should not rather say that in such case the community would have been little likely to have included "brethren of the sect of Pharisees" at all.

In the following section, from Luke xv. 1–10, the mention of eating with publicans is brought forward in a manner only explainable by the feeling for an application of the moral, to conditions much later than its place in the history.

"Then all the publicans and sinners were drawing nigh unto him to hear him. And the scribes and Pharisees murmured, saying, This man accepts sinners, and eats along with them." The rejoinder is given in the parables of the lost sheep and the lost piece of money, and the moral is expressed in the terms that there is joy in heaven over one sinner that repenteth. The type of the lost sheep is elsewhere appropriated to the strayed members of the Jewish community—the lost sheep of the house of Israel; and in Matt. xviii. the parable of the lost sheep is introduced as if still so restricted in application; and so Zacchæus the publican, just and charitable, is a son of Abraham, and therefore sought and saved as one lost. (Luke xix.) But, take it how we may, the reply assigned to Jesus fails to give the return to the difficulty of the Pharisees. To the Pharisees, who were the enthusiastic upholders of the kingdom of God, the tax-gatherer, if not the tax-payers too, were sinners, on the ground of admitting and administering an unholy dominion of the temporal power; and these sinners can only be understood as so designated in respect of habitual ceremonial uncleanness, contracted from their consorting with Gentiles. The reply does not contravene the imputation of sinfulness, as being unfairly made on such grounds, nor does it allow it, while showing that such ways are for the future renounced; it ascribes repentance in the general moral sense of which, for anything that appears, this obnoxious class had not more need than any other, and therefore, in such case, would not be in any consistent sense in the position of the single lost sheep.

I believe that these parables, in the form in which we have them, were first designed, like the parable of the prodigal son, to favour the reception of Hellenistic Jews as disciples, and that this present form was assumed after or among several modifications; in some of which the moral of the repentant sinner received the highest generalization, while in others it was directed to apply to the ceremonially-disqualified Gentiles. The Pharisaical murmurs in the Gospels represent, in the first instance, the Hebrew opposition to the deacons at Jerusalem, and to the reception as disciples of the Jews of the dispersion; and then the quarrel of the brethren of the sect of Pharisees with Peter and Paul, for joining tables with "the sinners of the Gentiles" at Antioch. Still, in origin, they may easily have been simple denouncements of the exclusive habits of the rigidly righteous, who would condemn a brother for his profession, or make every lapse in ritual observance fatal.

We are here again upon the traces of the force and value of the ministry and doctrine of John, which substituted repentance for ceremonialism to so important an extent, and thus gave a condition for the union of all classes of Jews.

"And all the people that heard, *and the tax-gatherers*, justified God, having been baptized with the baptism of John. But the Pharisees and teachers of the law rejected the counsel of God within themselves, not having been baptized by him." (Luke vii. 29.)

The narratives in the Gospels that give most distinctly the sanction of Jesus to the reception of Gentiles are, the cures of the centurion's servant and of the daughter of a Canaanitish or Syro-Phœnician woman. In both these cases the benefit is conferred on the ground of meritorious faith—faith, which is the specific qualification of the Gentile disciples of Paul, as repentance of the Hellenistic converts of John the Baptist, or Peter.

"O woman, great is thy faith," says Jesus to the Canaanitish woman: "be it unto you as you wish." (Matt. xv.)

"I have not found so great faith, no, not in Israel," is the observation of Jesus upon the centurion's behaviour; and it is followed by the declaration, "Many shall come from the east and from the west, and shall recline along with Abraham, Isaac, and Jacob, in the kingdom of heaven. But the children of the kingdom shall be cast into outer darkness: there shall be weeping and gnashing of teeth." (Matt. viii. 12.) Luke adds with significance: "And behold, there are some last who will be first, and there are some first who will be last." (Luke xiii. 30.)

Luke vii. has another version of the dinner at a Pharisee's, in which the cavil and reply turn, not upon neglect of personal ceremonial purifications, but on the intervention and reception by Jesus of the services of a woman who is a sinner. The case is illustrated by the parable of the larger gratitude of the larger of two debtors equally forgiven, and the woman is dismissed,— "Thy faith hath saved thee; go in peace." The incident is fixed significantly at Capernaum: cf. Matt. iv. 13.

From the title of faith, I do not doubt that this woman is a type of the "sinners of the Gentiles;" and the whole incident, as it is framed, would have borne application so cogently and specifically in the discussion at Antioch, that I do not doubt that it is an impression sealed from that seal, a precedent made after that fact. Nay, the very name of the Pharisee, Simon, appears to be an innuendo on the Apostle Simon Peter, of whose hesitation as to consorting with Gentiles at meals we have two notices,—that in Acts, at the vision of Cornelius, which may or may not be purely mythical; and that recorded by Paul.

The tender, affectionate, and lavish ministration of the repentant woman to Christ, is then a typical embodiment of that ministration to the wants of the poor saints at Jerusalem by the Gentile converts, which Apostles, indeed, were not backward to suggest or solicit, but which Paul himself was eager to promote as fitting demonstration of pious gratitude.

I think I also detect a bearing upon these complications in the early life of Christianity, which furnished suggestions for filling out the life of Christ, in the parable of the unjust steward. The gist of it appears to illustrate how men of the world are more prudent in their generation than the children of light, and gain their ends by unfair employment of that worldly wealth, which better men have not sense to employ, as they might, both efficiently and legitimately, for better ends. " I say unto you, Make unto yourself friends of the mammon (or out of,—by means of,—the mammon) of unrighteousness; that, when ye are in difficulty, they may receive you into everlasting habitations." (Luke xvi.) I do not know when such an argument,—whatever its value, would apply better, or apply at all, unless in such a case as when St. Paul is urging the Gentiles to be liberal in subscription to the Church of the Apostles at Jerusalem:—" For the administering of this service not only supplieth the wants of the saints, but is abundant also by many thanksgivings to God; while by proof of this ministering they glorify God in the subjection of your profession unto the Gospel of Christ, and in the bountifulness of your distribution to them and to all men, and in their prayer for you," etc. (2 Cor. ix. 12.) This is somewhat circumlocutory, but the end of Paul's policy of conciliation could not be more tersely stated than in the sentence cited from the parable.

II. THE EXPANSION OF THE CHURCH, IN THE PARABLES.

Most of the parables bear on their face palpable evidence of having been, I will not say originated, after the death of Jesus, but so far modified at least that they now can only be fully explained by reference to the conditions of the Church, which only arose after his death, and were quite alien from what we have concluded as to his designs and anticipations.

The disciple is likened to a man who sells all he has to buy a field, in which he has discovered that a treasure is hidden; or he is like a merchant in search of fine pearls, who comes upon one of great price, and realizes all his property in order to purchase and possess it. The first case represents the acquisition of the prize,—the kingdom of Heaven, at a sacrifice which may seem to those not in the secret as unaccountable; while the value in the other case is patent to all, though the merchant alone has the energy or the enthusiasm to deal for it.

These parables may seem to be mere general types of the superexcellence of the Gospel, but I suspect that they had once a reference to the sacrifices of worldly goods made by enthusiastic disciples like Barnabas, in the early communistic phase of the Christian society. To the same period we must refer the parable of the rich man and Lazarus, which connects reprobation in a future state, with prosperity however innocent in this, and makes squalid pauperism not merely a condition, but the very essential of meritoriousness. This is an apologue quite in the spirit of the Epistle of James, and the prepossessions of the eleemosynary saints.

The parable of the seed of the sower, cast upon various ground, and having fate and produce accordingly, appears to be as general a descriptive apologue as can be conceived, and has no characteristics that limit it to the dissemination of Christian doctrines rather than any other. It typifies most happily and expressively the circumstances that qualify the reception of worthy instruction in the world, without bearing hardly, so far as I can discern, on any particular party. Of more special application, but still uncontroversial, is the comparison of the Gospel,—the kingdom of Heaven,—to the grain of mustard, the minutest of seeds, which, when it grows, becomes the largest of the herbs; and the like may be said of the comparison to the leaven hidden by a woman in three measures of meal, and ultimately leavening the whole. These are striking figures of the progress of the Church as it arose after the death of Jesus, but are little applicable to the history of his following and career.

The grain of mustard-seed is in all the synoptics; Mark iv. 26 has also this variation:—"The kingdom of Heaven is as if a man should cast seed upon the earth; and should sleep and rise, night and day, and the seed spring up and grow he knoweth not why. For the earth bringeth forth fruit of itself; first the blade, then the ear, then the full grain in the ear. And when the fruit is brought forth, immediately he dispatches the sickle, because the harvest has come."

A turn is here added to the parable, which gives us the first glimpse of that reflection upon the Apostles, that we have traced in the anecdote in John of the woman of Samaria,—upon the Apostles, who remain for the most part seated at Jerusalem, and send out their envoys to Samaria, to Antioch, probably to Galatia and Corinth, if not Rome, to put in the sickle to a ripe harvest, which has grown up from seed of their sowing truly, but otherwise, as far as their labour or later tending is in question, automatously enough. Thus Jesus addresses the Apostles:—"For herein is the true saying; one soweth and another reapeth. I sent you to reap what ye had not laboured at; others laboured, and ye are entered into their labours." (John iv. 37.)

Still the tenor of the parable, as told, is declaration of matter of fact, as of a law of nature to be acquiesced in, not objected to,—whether this were the primary tenor, or whether an original colour of murmur has been obliterated. In the parable of the pounds, and in that of the servants paid equally for unequal service, we have murmurs more distinctly expressed, but the decision ruled in favour of authority.

The simplest form of the first parable is in Matthew: a man going abroad commits his substance to his servants, in various proportion, according to ability. It is the servant who has charge of least, who neglects to employ the one talent profitably, and renders back the capital alone, with the explanation,—"Lord, I knew thee, that thou art an hard man, reaping where thou hast not sown, and gathering where thou hast not strewed; and I was afraid, and I went and hid thy talent in the earth; behold, thou hast thine own." (Matt. xxv. 24.) The unprofitable servant is cast into outer darkness,— "there shall be weeping and gnashing of teeth."

Luke combines with this narrative a peculiar episode, —the traveller is a man of high extraction, who leaves for a far country in order to receive for himself a kingdom; his citizens,—not the servants who hold his property in trust,—send an embassy after him to repudiate his sovereignty; and after he has on his return dealt as above with his servants, he orders these counter-plotting citizens to be brought out and slain before him. We can identify the suggestion of this incident in the narrative of Josephus of the journey of Herod Antipas to Rome, to solicit the succession to his father's kingdom. How he may have been opposed by his citizens, and how he may have avenged himself, we may infer from the story before us, but have no further information. The political and the private incidents do not fall together happily in Luke; and all we can say is, that the execution of the malcontents enforces the quietist feeling of submission to arbitrary authority. The coherence of the composite parable would require that it should have been some of the entrusted servants who countervailed the purpose of their master's journey, if not employed his means to assert their own independence.

The parable of the labourers in the vineyard seems, in the first instance, to be an assertion of the equality, in the Church, of the later, with the original disciples; as the labourers are engaged at different hours of the day, and labour for very different times, yet the late comers receive as high a wage as was fair payment for those who came earliest. The suggestion of this also may be traced to an historical incident, again supplied to us by Josephus: a great multitude of masons and workmen of building trades were cast idle in Jerusalem on the completion of the works about the Temple; they were a public charge, and it became an object with the authorities to put in hand other works, that would give more than fictitious employment; for, as matters stood, as much was paid to a man who wrought for part, as to one who worked the whole of the day.

The parable does not discuss the fairness of the arrangement, but declares the matter of fact: it is the option of an authority which all are bound to acquiesce in, none are at liberty to challenge as favouritism or caprice. "The first shall be last, and the last first,"—it is the way of the world, the course of nature, a dispensation of Providence.

I cannot, however, but consider that this parable embodies impressions of a time when the original sect at Jerusalem was beginning to lose some of its predominance, in consequence of the expansion of the active Hellenistic and Gentile churches.

The parable of the dragnet brings us to the time when even disciples were fain to admit that there was as great a mixture of good and bad men within the Church as without. "The kingdom of Heaven is like a dragnet cast into the sea, and gathering up of every kind; which, when it was full, they drew to the shore, and, sitting down, gathered the good into vessels and cast away the bad."

The separation of the sheep and the goats at the end of the world, is to the same purpose.

There is something more in the parable of the weeds and the wheat; we are on traces of denunciation of false brethren, of pernicious teachers. "The kingdom of Heaven hath been likened unto a man sowing good seed in his field; and, as the man slept, his enemy came and sowed weeds among the wheat, and went his way." On the report of the mischief to the master, he ascribes it to an enemy, with a peculiar phrase—"a hostile man." The remedy must be left till harvest-time, when the weeds will be separated and burned, and the wheat garnered.

A private explanation for the disciples is added, to the effect, that " he that soweth the good seed is the Son of man. The field is the world, and the good seed are the children of the kingdom, and the weeds are the children of wickedness; the enemy that sowed them is the devil," etc. etc.

I am disposed to think that this interpretation was not in the mind of the first author of the parable, or that, at any rate, he held it concurrently with a design to reflect upon a teacher, or a school of hostile teachers. In fact, we find St. Paul referred to, in the early Christian literature, to the principles and authors of which he is obnoxious, as "the man of mischief" in identical terms.

I have already illustrated the bearing of the beautiful parable of the Prodigal Son upon the reception of the Hellenists. I believe it resulted from the great beauty of this parable, as originally composed, that it has come down to us with little or no alteration. The same remark may also apply to that of the good Samaritan, which sanctions so distinctly the brotherhood of a race peculiarly disliked by the bigoted Jew, and by no means uniformly protected in the Gospels.

The story of the Prodigal Son will bear an application to the Gentile Gospel; but this is much more unequivocally advocated in the parable of the rebellious husbandmen of the vineyard. (Matt. xxi. 33; Mark xii. 1; Luke xx. 9.)

The husbandmen who lease the vineyard, and scourge and stone and slay the summoning servants of the landlord first, and, at last, his son, can only represent the Jewish people, the slayers of the prophets, and lastly, of Jesus Christ. Israel and Jerusalem are typified as vine and vineyard in the Old Testament, and the golden vine of the Temple kept the figure always present in the imagination of the people.

"What, therefore, will the lord of the vineyard do? He will come and destroy the husbandmen, and will give the vineyard to others. And have ye not read this

Scripture?—a stone, which the builders refused, the same is become the head of the corner."

The three first Gospels, which insert this parable with little variation, parry its palpable application to the reception of the Gentiles, by noting it as directed specially against high-priests, scribes, and Pharisees; who were highly exasperated by it, but restrained from violence by the protecting and venerating multitude.

Lastly, I have to cite the parable of the contemned marriage-feast, as a concluding example of document imputed to Jesus, for the sake of reaction upon circumstances and doctrines that did not arise till long after his death.

In Luke it is simply a "certain man" who makes the feast, but in Matthew it is a king, and the story moves on with kingly circumstance. The king dispatches servants to summon the invited, but they are some careless, while some seize the messengers, and ill-treat and even kill them. The king sends out his armies, destroys the murderers, and burns their city,—particulars which argue that the parable took this form after the destruction of Jerusalem.

The feast now, like the vineyard in the last parable, falls to the share of new comers, and servants are sent out to summon guests from the highways. A complication ensues,—the zealous servants fill up the marriage, but it is with guests both bad and good. Participation is still not unconditional; the king, on coming in, espies one who has not on the wedding-garment; the interloper is bound hand and foot, and cast into outer darkness—region of wailing and gnashing of teeth.

This restricting qualification reminds of the conditions which the Jerusalem conclave struggled to impose upon the Gentile converts, even after the large liberality of the first admission. Luke's parable knows nothing of the restriction; on the other hand, he extends still wider, and by a second stretch of liberality, the area of the invitation. First, the servant is sent into the squares and streets of the city, to bring in the poor, the maimed, the lame, and the blind. These I take to represent the ceremonially disqualified of Jewish blood, —the unclean, the misallied, the Hellenist, the Samaritan. "And the servant said, Lord, it is done as thou commandest, and yet there is room. And the Lord said unto the servant, Go out into the highways and hedges,"—thus further afield, as in the extension to the Gentiles,—" and urge people to come in, that my house may be filled. For I say unto you, that none of those men who were bidden shall taste my supper." These, then, are the many from the East and the West that are to recline in the kingdom of Heaven, while the children of the promise are excluded. The absolute exclusion of the negligent first invited, corresponds to the total substitution of Gentile for Jew, or the Gospel for the Law; which seems to be the implication of the parables, that forbid the new wine to be put into the old bottles, or a new piece to patch a worn-out garment.

III. PETER, JAMES, AND JOHN, AT THE TRANSFIGURATION.

The Jesus of the Gospels is, therefore, frequently but an impersonation of his Gospel or of his Church; his preaching and parables often enforce doctrine of which the living career was utterly unconscious, to which it would frequently have been repugnant; the anecdotes that are related as incidents in his life, have constantly in this sense not the slightest historical foundation,—a very important historical significance, however, as the embodiments of the vicissitudes of the Church, its leaders, and its doctrines at a later date; in types of which the stuff is borrowed, ready-made, from the prophets and prophecies and marvellous narratives of the Old Testament.

The greatest crisis in the Church, of which we read in the earlier records that remain to us, is the dispute at Antioch respecting the circumcision of the Gentiles and the imposition upon them of the Law and the customs at large. The authority of the Apostle whose preaching had been most influential with the circumcision, had been gained to sanction the immunity of the Gentiles, by consorting with them at the common meal; the sanction was capable of still further extension to the neglect of the Law and the customs even by Jews themselves. Peter, by a private understanding, to which James and John were also privy, had given the right hand of fellowship in a project which had brought in a mighty accession of disciples; and now, at a time when the idea of a Church of Christ that should be in opposition to the Twelve, was still too startling to be entertained, the cover of Peter's authority seemed about to be forfeited, and so all that had been done to be undone. A plausible show of legitimate derivation from the original Apostles would be valued at such an epoch even by those who repudiated unqualified dependence; and this was brought into jeopardy by the temporary equivocation of the great Apostle.

The history of the Acts, without noticing his hesitation, avers that he urged upon the Church the most liberal emancipation of both Jew and Gentile disciple, but that his authority was overruled, and a compromise decided upon in the terms of the decree,—unanimously accepted by the Church, and cordially acquiesced in by the Gentile churches and their teachers. But, on the one hand, it is certain that a section of the Hebrew Church at Jerusalem continued to insist on the imposition of the Law on the Gentiles; while Paul, at least, retained his resolution to urge on by every prudent and efficient means, the emancipation even of the Jew. Between these two lay the party that accepted the decree, and acted upon it either in a spirit of bigoted adherence, and with animus to resist any further encroachment, or with as much cordiality as consisted with the desire to bring about further relaxation as time and opportunity might present themselves. The first class of adherents to the decree is represented by the Clementine Homilies, which magnify Peter, and are too anxious to make the most of his authority as against the innovating Gentiles, to weaken it by any reference to his vacillation, or even—which they might be more inclined to do, to his reduction of the Jewish claim to such a minimum as the decree propounds. The second class was free from some of this restraint; we have the expression of their feelings in the Gospels; their disappointment at being reduced to a compromise is seen in the numerous allusions to the dullness of the Twelve, to their incapacity to appreciate the mission, the spirit, the plainest declarations and teachings of their master. The Apostles who could not be brought to comprehend the scope of the Christian movement when it was spreading over the world, are figured in the Apostles of the Gospel, who are shocked at the idea of a suffering Messiah, who look for the prompt reappearance of the kingdom of David, who have an eye to the distribution of dignities in the Messianic cabinet, and invariably cling to a carnal interpretation of every speech, neglecting the spiritual, which is indeed beyond them. As compared, then, with the others, Peter, James, and John, with all their shortcomings, were much nearer to true sympathy with their master, and, it is implied, were in fact much nearer to his confidence. Amongst them Peter is singled out for distinction, for regard, as a character which, with all its defects, was on a nobler scale, and,—as capable of a genuine enthusiasm, of a more exalted type. On the one hand, his unsteadiness, which had brought the liberal Gospel in its connection with the original Church into such peril, was not spared; on the other, his fervent zeal is made accountable for much of his tripping, and full honour is assigned to the recoil of his conscience,—the resumption of his better thought.

The bigoted adherents of the decree probably overrated the value, or the finality assigned to it by Peter. It would gratify me much if I could resolve myself as to the real attitude which Peter personally continued to take between the Gospel in favour with the Hebrew Church, and that of Paul.

In the compilations and redactions of Christian tradition and Christian apologue, which we have in the form of the Gospels, the privity of Peter, James and

John to the enlarged conception of the Church as presented by Stephen or Paul, is represented in their selection by Jesus to be the sole witnesses of some of his most remarkable works and manifestations. This admission to what is typical of the inner counsel of God, of the Saviour, is constantly accompanied by an injunction to secrecy, which is unintelligible enough as the incidents stand. There may be some appearance in a few instances that this is a gloss; designed, at the time the story was first published, to account for its not having been heard of before: but in other cases, it is mentioned at once that the attempt at concealment failed, and I infer that the incident was borrowed from the characteristics of the really historical basis,—the private compact with Paul. The parallel is then closely pursued in the zeal, the professions, the trepidations, and retreats of Peter, followed up by revival of sense and courage, by repentance and reparation.

The review of some of the incidents, however, will enable them to speak best for themselves.

At the Transfiguration (Luke ix.; Mark ix.; Matt. xvii.), Jesus takes Peter, James, and John up a high mountain alone and apart, and was transfigured before them; his face became other than it was,—it shone like the sun,—his garments were of supernatural whiteness and brilliancy; and two men were seen by them talking with him,—who were Moses and Elias—that is, Elijah.

The parallel story proceeds,—" And Peter said to Jesus, Master, it is good for us to be here; let us make three tabernacles (or tents), one for thee, one for Moses, and one for Elijah. And while he yet spake, a cloud overshadowed them, and lo! a voice from the cloud saying, This is my beloved Son, hear ye him. And, lifting up their eyes, they saw no man, but Jesus only. And as they descended from the mountain, Jesus commanded them that they should tell no man until the Son of man should be risen from the dead."

According to Mark and Luke, Peter made his proposal, not knowing what he was saying; Mark adds, " for they were afraid."

In Matthew, it is at the voice of the cloud that the three are alarmed, and fall to the ground on their faces, till Jesus comes and touches them, and says, " Arise, fear not."

In Luke, the narrative takes much of the colour of the agony in the Garden; the ascent to the mountain is for prayer; the visionary men speak with him of his departure that he was about to fulfil at Jerusalem. In the meantime, Peter, and they with him, are heavy with sleep, and it is on awaking—spontaneously for what appears, that they witness the group. The incident of their alarm is not left out, but it is assigned to the moment that they enter into the cloud. Luke also has to say, " they kept silence in those days concerning what they had seen," but he does not advert to a command.

Moses and Elias are most obviously types of the Law and the prophets,—the representatives of the Old Testament. I think it not unlikely that Elias here is also to be recognized as the representative of the adherents of John the Baptist and the Essenes, as Moses of the strict adherents to the ceremonial Law. The wild, unconsidered project of Peter to establish three co-ordinate monuments of recognition, is apparently a type of some

scheme of recognized classification and division in the Church, on the occasion when he drew off from association with Gentiles. Paul only implies two separate tables; but there may have been easily the same motive for division that afterwards made parties call themselves after Paul, Apollos the disciple of the Baptist, and Cephas.

The divine voice directs attention only to Jesus; and when the temporary cloud disperses, Jesus alone is seen, —a divine intimation of the unity of the Church,—of the all-sufficiency of Christ.

The voice from the cloud, especially as reported by Matthew, is parallel to a like incident at the baptism, according to Mark; a form of the anecdote, in which the motive to connect the mission of John with that of Jesus, but at the same time to keep it subordinate, again becomes patent.

It is on the descent from the mountain that Jesus cures the demoniac boy possessed by a deaf and dumb spirit, which his disciples alone had vainly endeavoured to cast out. It may be that the conjunction of the stories may have occurred by casual association of the dumb spirit with the enjoined silence of the Apostles: the Gospels abound in sequences held together by no more logical a link. I am half-inclined to think, however, that it is not by accident that such a miracle is the first ascribed to the transfigured Saviour, the type of the Church at a new stage of development; when many things long thought of had come at last,—by miracle, indeed!—to articulate declaration.

The Transfiguration was the subject of the last picture that Rafael lived to paint; he included in it the double incidents, at the foot and the summit of the mountain.

The glory and the lightness of the hovering figure of Christ, and of the prophets who regard and adore him in the air, is inconceivable. Moses holds the book of the Law, but holds it so that his hands keep it closed; and he has the air as though he were bringing it to lay it an offering at the feet of the Saviour—concluded, superseded, obsolete.

The three disciples—the chosen witnesses—are prostrate. John screens his downcast eyes with his hand as he falls; James cowers behind Peter; Peter, who, first to fall but first to recover, is just looking up, as if to ask his bold although bewildered question.

For the group at the foot of the mountain a second horizon is taken, and thus the abbreviation of distance marks itself as symbolical.

The remaining nine of the disciples are grouped in a half-circle on one side the boy,—his father and friends are on the other. The mother kneels in front, with her back to the spectator, so that a vacant space is left in the centre of the ring. The vertical circle, which comprises the groups upon the summit of the mountain, is thus associated with groups in the foreground, which arrange themselves upon a circular horizontal plan—an artifice of composition, I suspect, as original as refined.

The only trace that Rafael paid attention to Mark's notice, that scribes were disputing with the disciples, is, that he has given a book to the disciple in the foreground, suggestive of search for formulas and exorcisms.

The boy is represented at the moment when seized by the fit or demon; it "tears and rends him, so that he foams and grinds his teeth." I desiderate further information as to the pathology of Rafael's subject. Sir Charles Bell is referred to on the subject.

Only Mark speaks of the spirit as dumb. I think that Rafael has held this characteristic in mind, leaving aside Luke's statement, that the demon "cries out."

Matthew says that the patient is lunatic, and often falls into the water, and often into the fire. The edge of a pool is introduced at the left-hand corner of the picture; the foot of the disciple in front is reflected in it, and he sits upon logs that I have no doubt, cavil who may, were intended just to suggest the idea of firewood. The sudden gesture of his left hand crossing his body expresses, I think, his apprehension lest the sufferer, in his spasms, should fall into the water beside him.

In the father's countenance distress and affection are beautifully blended; and the introduction of the agonized and appealing mother, not mentioned in the story,—together with, I think, a sister, completes the exhibition of a passion of domestic affections.

The inability of the disciples to cope with the enemy, is expressed with perfect force, yet with the rarest delicacy. The appeals, the supplications of the family of the boy, are most distinct and touching; but we see that, with every indication of interest and sympathy, the disciples already feel that they are reduced to spectators; that they have done their best, and in vain, and have now not to interfere, but to wait. One of them, however, who is, indeed, from his expression and place in the composition, most conspicuous, points upwards in the direction of the summit of the mountain—a clear intimation from whence is to come the help.

The serenity of the upper, the divine portion of the picture, wonderfully contrasts with the spectacle of calamity and perplexity below. Even the prostrate and dazzled three are in positions and in movements that harmonize with the predominant feeling of loftiness and dignity.

The triad of disciples, nevertheless, serves to soften the transition to the group below; and the four disciples here immediately under the centre, are treated with a certain tenderness and repose that still further assist the graceful development of the combination.

The true ethical secret of the combination is in the gesture of the pointing Apostle. In the feeling that dictates this movement is conveyed an echo of the voice from the bright cloud, that is so important in the narrative: "This is my beloved Son, in whom I am well pleased: hear ye him." The action suggests obedience, as if by sympathy, to the divine injunctions; and also indicates the source of the relief which is to complete the history of the demoniac boy. The parental love, again, of which the boy is an object, is not insisted upon so emphatically, without a feeling that it heightens the contrast to the recognition of a glorified Son by his heavenly Father, above on the mount.

The indicating hand and arm of the disciple convey to the mind the sentence "hear ye him," as distinctly as if notified by label or inscription; and thus is given to the heart an assurance of the endowment of the world with a healing power that will dispel the very elements of moral and physical disorder, and cheer the lacerated feelings of paternal affection by blessings fresh from the creative energy which is itself the parent of love and of all living.

It was not without intention—felt, at least—that Rafael brought the pointing figure into such direct contiguity and contrast at once, to the seated disciple who holds the open book. They are so composed that comparison is inevitable: above the veteran,—the inveterate expositor of preceptive if not ceremonial wisdom, rises the nobler figure, who directs to the better dayspring from on high, and thus we have a parallel here to the secondary place of Moses, with his volume, in the upper design.

The time has arrived for the letter to give way to the spirit; and the Transfiguration of Christ is an image of that metamorphosis of mind and heart by which, of old time, the habits of rituals, and the reliance upon them, were cast off, and text and gloss and pedigree were cast aside by the energy of regeneration from within, and the best spirit of the unwritten word took possession of the place and functions of any Testament whatever, either new or old.

In the work of D. F. Strauss will be found, as usual, a full and acute exposition of the Old Testament materials that have found their places in the story of the Transfiguration. The most important combination is the comparison with the ascent of Mount Sinai by Moses, accompanied by chosen servitors; his glorified countenance; his indignation, on descending, at the disorder of the people; his interposition with authority to repress, to regulate, to save.

Besides the Transfiguration and the Agony, there is another scene to which Peter, James, and John alone of the Apostles are admitted—the raising from the dead of the daughter of Jairus; and the narrative finishes again in Mark and Luke, with an injunction to tell no man.

Jairus is called a chief of the synagogue, and any symbolical import of the miracle, it would seem, therefore must apply to the relief, not of Gentile, but of Jew, and probably to liberation from the Law. The miracle embodies the expressive metaphors, "for I through the law am dead to the law, that I may live to God; and I myself no longer live, but Christ liveth in me." (Gal. ii. 19.) "Wherefore, my brethren, ye also are become dead to the law through the body of Christ; that ye may belong to another who is raised from the dead; . . . . but now we are delivered from the law, being dead to that wherein we were held; so that we may serve in newness of spirit, not in the oldness of the letter." (Rom. vii. 4.)

An episode to this miracle is the cure of the woman with an issue of blood, who furtively touches the Saviour's garments as he passes through the crowd. I do not doubt that we have here a type of the Gentile disciples, whose liberty proceeded by even step with that of the ritual-galled Jew. This is intimated by the notice of her vain recourse through many years to physicians who had tortured and ruined her, and left her worse rather than better; and then, by the decisive sign that the blessing is ascribed to the faith of the recipient: "Daughter, thy faith hath saved thee: go in peace." In fact, we seem to have, from the parallelism of expressions, but another form of the deliverance of the Syro-Phœnician woman; and the stealthy toucher of the health-giving robes of the Master on his way to recall life to Judaism, is in substitution of the dog, the type of heathendom, that pleads for at least the crumbs that fall from the table of the children of the chosen race, and on the ground of faith is allowed.

Peter, James, and John are the witnesses of the miraculous draught of fishes, which is only related in Luke, where Andrew, Simon's brother,—who in Matthew and Mark is called along with him to be a fisher of men,—is omitted. The significant reference of the miracle to special participation in the arrangement for evangelizing the Gentiles, I do not doubt, explains this omission. The large influx of Gentile disciples was, in fact, the miraculous draught of the fishers of men when Christ,—when the Gospel, rightly conceived, became an associate in the enterprise previously but scantily successful. Simon Peter is more than astonished—is alarmed—at his own success, and, falling at the knees of Jesus, cries, "Depart from me, for I am a sinful man, O Lord." He recovers himself, however, at the encouraging word "Fear not," and leaves all, and follows Christ.

Peter appears again as a fisherman when, at the command of Jesus (Matt. xvii.), he casts his line into the sea, and in the mouth of the first fish he draws up finds the coin, the stater, required to pay the tax of the didrachma, both for his master and himself. The sum agrees with the sacred tax of half-shekel, that by the Mosaic law was payable to the Temple. (Sharpe's 'Critical Notes,' p. 14.) I suspect a symbol of the rate in aid of the Jerusalem church, that was part of the understanding with St. Paul—contribution for a sacred purpose from the fish of Peter's divinely-sanctioned haul.

The general import of the contents of the dragnet has already been remarked upon.

To the accounts of Jesus calming the tempest and walking upon the waters, which are common, with little variation, to Matthew, Mark, and John, the first, or Matthew, adds another expressive particular. The disciples, overtaken with rough weather, are alarmed to see Jesus walking on the sea. He declares himself, and bids them be of good cheer, and fear not. Peter replies, "Lord, if it be thou, command me to come to thee on the waters." He said, "Come." Peter descended from the vessel, and walked to meet Jesus. He lost heart, however, at the violence of the wind, and began to sink, crying, "Lord, save me. And Jesus immediately stretched forth his hand, and caught hold of him, and saith to him, O thou of little faith, wherefore didst thou doubt? And as they entered into the ship, the wind subsided." (Matt. xiv. 31.)

Here, again, I do not doubt that we have a type of the participation of Peter in the great critical agitations of the Church. The ship of the Church, tempest-tost among the dissensions at Antioch, gains sight at last of the Saviour walking in dignity over the troubled waves; then ensue the prompt forwardness of Peter; his failure of heart on the rising of the wind after his first few bold steps; his timely rescue and recovery by aid of an arm extended to help, but not without rebuke for lack of faith. The place of the lecturing and expostulating Paul,—Paul regarded by the first author of the apologue as representative of the Gospel—of Christ, is assigned here in the usual spirit of an apologue, to Christ himself.

In other directions I have seemed to recognize traces of transferences, to the factitious biography and memorabilia of Jesus, not only from the history of the Church at large, but from the particular biography of Paul. Among these, which it may scarcely be in our way to notice hereafter, I have been accustomed to consider the weeping over Jerusalem and the terms of the lament, consistent with Paul's circumstances at his last visit, scarcely with those of Jesus.

There is an appearance of design, in the incidents typical of the Gentile Gospel and of the discussions, not to say dissensions, that it caused, being for the most part localized to the north of Judæa,—the parts about Tyre and Sidon, the Lake of Tiberias or Galilee, and the districts beyond the lake. The suggestion may fairly be traced to the association of this general vicinage in a conspicuous text of prophecy, with Gentile occupation.

In Matthew iv. 12, we read: "Now when Jesus had heard that John was delivered up (*i. e.* John the Baptist), he withdrew into Galilee." His course has been previously traced "from Galilee unto the Jordan, unto John (placed, iii. 1, in the desert of Judæa) to be baptized by him," and thence into the desert, being led by the spirit." It is only in Matthew that this retirement to Galilee has assigned to it a reference to the captivity of John; and it reads to me much like a special parallel to the migration of the Hellenist Church under pressure of the "persecution that arose about Stephen." However this may be, a citation of prophecy follows that bears upon the principle of the Gentile Gospel of the Hellenists, and becomes explanatory of the assignment of the types of it occurring in the life of Jesus, to a sojourn here rather than elsewhere.

"And leaving Nazareth, he came and dwelt in Capernaum by the lake, in the borders of Zabulon and Nephthalim: so that it might be fulfilled which was spoken through Isaiah the prophet, saying, Land of Zabulon, and land of Nephthalim, by the way of the lake, beyond Jordan, Galilee of the Gentiles; the people sitting in darkness saw a great light; and to those that sat in the region and shadow of death a light arose. From that time Jesus began to preach, and to say, Repent: for the kingdom of heaven is at hand."

The conduct ascribed to Peter, on the occasion of the betrayal and examination of Christ, is but another version of the same events. Peter again is forward with a profession,—whoever else may desert his master, he will be faithful; he does, in fact, thrust himself forward much nearer to harm's way than the rest of the Apostles; again finds himself unequal to carry through the enterprise he had boldly embarked in; and at the challenge by attendants about the fire in the atrium of the highpriest, three times he denies his master. "And while he yet spake, the cock crew. And the Lord turned, and looked on Peter:" a touching incident in Luke's account, but which renders the reminding cock superfluous: "and Peter went out, and wept bitterly." (Luke xxii. 60.)

The same collections of traditions that characterize Peter so significantly, ascribe to James and John, the sons of Zebedee, an ambition for first places in the kingdom of heaven,—which seems to smack of the hierarch; and something of the hierarch's readiness to resort to fire from heaven to rebuke the inhospitable Samaritans. It is John again (Mark ix. 38) who would have checked one who, not following the Apostles, presumed to cast out devils in the name of Jesus, but is bidden by the Master to offer him no impediment.

In Mark the ambitious petition is direct; in Matthew it is transferred in tenderness to the ill-guided affection of a kneeling mother. (Matt. xx. 20; Mark x. 35.) The question arises, whether tradition may not have made one of its slips, and transferred the domineering spirit of the James of the Council to his namesake the son of Zebedee, who seems to have been, along with his brother, on the side of liberal opposition. It is quite possible, however, that, to the followers in opposition, these two, their leaders, may have seemed too much disposed to arrogate authority, even in the enterprise of attacking authority. In Matthew xviii. the disciples generally—that is, the Apostles—are introduced as eagerly interested on the subject of primacy, and rebuked by Jesus, who calls to him a child, sets him in the midst of them, and declares that "whosoever shall humble himself as this child, the same is greatest in the kingdom of heaven."

This subject was painted by Mr. C. R. Leslie. Jesus and the Apostles were resting, as having come into the house after the journey to Capernaum (Mark ix. 33), when he questioned them as to what it was they disputed of on the way. He was beckoning to him the exemplar child, and the moral of humility it was to exemplify was indicated with delicate invention in the simple bashfulness, not shyness nor alarm, with which it was leaning against its mother's knee, and showed, by constraint in attitude, that it was only gradually gaining courage.

CHAPTER IX.

ELYMAS STRICKEN WITH BLINDNESS.

I. PAUL AND BARNABAS IN ROMAN CYPRUS.—II. THE CARTOON OF THE REBUKE OF ELYMAS.

I. PAUL AND BARNABAS IN ROMAN CYPRUS.

WE have wandered forward in the Apostolic history in our later exercitations; we must now return to the occasion when, as we have seen reason to conclude, Paul and Barnabas, having come to a private understanding with the leading Apostles as to a basis for the Gentile Gospel, returned to Antioch, intent on taking advantage of it with energy and enterprise. John, who was surnamed Mark, went with them from Jerusalem. The narrative proceeds: "Now there were at Antioch, in the church established there, certain prophets and teachers; as Barnabas, and Simeon who was called Niger, and Lucius of Cyrene, and Manaen, foster-brother of Herod the tetrarch, and Saul. And as they ministered to the Lord, and fasted, the Holy Spirit said, Separate me Barnabas and Saul for the work whereunto I have called them. Then, having fasted and prayed, and laid their hands on them, they sent them away. So they, being sent forth by the Holy Spirit, went down to Seleucia; and from thence they sailed to Cyprus. And when they were at Salamis, they preached the word of God in the synagogues of the Jews: and they had also John as an attendant. And when they had gone through all the island unto Paphos, they found a certain magus, a Jewish false prophet, named Bar-jesus: who was with the proconsul, Sergius Paulus, a man of intelligence; the same sent for Barnabas and Saul, and desired to hear the word of God. But Elymas the magus (for so is his name interpreted) withstood them, seeking to turn aside the proconsul from the faith. Then Saul, (who is also called Paul,) being filled with Holy Spirit, set his eyes fixedly on him, and said, O full of all craft and all mischief, child of the devil, enemy of all righteousness, wilt thou not cease from diverting the straight ways of the Lord? And now, behold, the hand of the Lord is upon thee, and thou shalt be blind, not seeing the sun for a season. And immediately a mist and a darkness fell on him; and, turning about, he sought some to lead him by the hand. Then the proconsul, when he saw what was done, believed, being astounded at the teaching of the Lord.

"Now when Paul and his companions sailed from Paphos, they came to Perga in Pamphylia; and John, departing from them, returned to Jerusalem." (Acts xiii. 1.)

However the terms of the narrative may read, it is quite open to conjecture that the expedition was a much more independent enterprise on the part of the missionaries than the terms in themselves imply. They first direct their course to Cyprus, the native country of Barnabas, and nothing is said of the tenor or success of their teaching until their encounter with Elymas. The connection of this man with a proconsul has abundant parallels in Roman story. Josephus, Ant. xx. 7, mentions a Simon, a magian of Cyprus, who is in a similar position of influence with the procurator Felix. Jewish cultivators, on private behoof, of the prevalent addiction to superstition and miracles, infested the Roman world; and while some deceived and preyed upon the vulgar, the more artful or accomplished flew at higher game. Apollonius of Tyana, and the Alexander of Lucian, furnish types of the more ambitious class, to which Simon Magus seems also to have belonged. The wandering Jewish exorcists, the sons of Sceva, of Acts xix., are cattle of the same horn, but of inferior breed.

With one or other of these classes, Christian missionaries, of Jewish blood or association, with their outbursts of enthusiasm, their pretension to miraculous power and interpretation of prophecy, and their indiscriminate, if not preferential, appeal to the weak and the ignorant, were liable to be most offensively, but not quite unnaturally, confounded. The misapprehension was the more embarrassing, as the Christian would not deny the reality of the wonders worked by these impostors, but only questioned the agency, and claimed to have the power of controlling it. Miracle was opposed to miracle, as in the court of Pharaoh,—white magic to black,—and the teachers, who were imbued with a conviction that they belonged to the prophet class of which the Old Testament gave the type, were not themselves inclined to disparage the powers of opponents for whom it was their boast to be an overmatch. Hence there was motive abundant, if not for inventing, at least for imparting, more or less consciously, such colour to questionable incidents as resulted in popular stories, like the discomfitures of Simon or Elymas, or the ludicrous defeat of the sons of Sceva, and the change wrought upon the girl who had a spirit of divination, at Philippi. The contest was regarded as waged, not with flesh and blood, but with the prince of the powers of the air, and the work was often difficult accordingly. The miracles of the Man of Sin of 2 Thessalonians ii. 8 are not denied, but ascribed to Satan; he is the prototype of the marvel-working idolatrous beast of the Apocalypse, xiii. 11; and so Elymas is denounced by Paul as " a child of the Devil."

The special notice, that the Proconsul was "a man of sense," "a man of reflection," is rather remarkable; it seems intended to parry the natural inference to the contrary from his entertaining such a creature as Elymas. For the rest, the general outline of the tale is probable enough. Rulers in our own time, who have certainly not wanted of reflectiveness, have some listened, and some been suspected of listening, with deference and curiosity rather too concentrated, to a nervous illuminate, or even to a vulgar spirit-medium. It is perfectly consistent with such disposition, that the Roman Sergius should wish to hear more of the new comers, as belonging to a class that he did not disesteem—perhaps stood in some awe of. That Elymas in one way or other should be discredited when pitted against the heartfelt and impressive exhortations of Paul, is quite conceivable; and even very moderate favour and acquiescence on the part of the Proconsul—and there is no reason why something more than moderate might not be in question—would easily be interpreted as belief, conviction, conversion.

He is said to have believed, being astounded at the teaching of the Lord. The teaching of the Lord is scarcely an equivalent expression for a miraculous deprivation of eye-sight, but the deprivation is not declared in perfectly unqualified terms. "Mist and darkness" denote rather weakness than extinction; and at last the infliction is only declared to be temporary. Had the entire story been pure invention, there would scarcely have been a motive for economizing marvellousness, and making the sign less than conclusive, the blindness less than absolute. We have here probably an indication that a limit was given by notorious fact, to the liberties that might be taken by tradition. So in the case of the easiness with which Simon Magus is let off,—it is difficult to think that mythical variation, not to say indignant invention, would have treated such an offender so mercifully but that his later story was too well established to be tampered with, and in fact it happens, that we are in possession of independent proofs of his later notoriety.

It was after this journey that Paul and Barnabas, with the strongest possible motive to make much of their doings and divine favour, set forth at Jerusalem what signs and wonders God had wrought among the Gentiles by them. In such discourse a metaphor, a little loosely defined, easily slides from a potential to an actual miracle. Self-deception is but too accommodating in such instances; and Paul and Barnabas may have been as ready, not to say as willing, to believe that the failing sight of an impostor was due to their malediction, as Salmasius to congratulate himself on having conduced to the blindness of his opponent, Milton.

After the palpable transformation of Paul's vision of a great light at noonday into an actual interview with Jesus risen in the flesh, it is really unnecessary to postulate a very long time or very numerous interchanges to produce such a version as we have before us of the Cyprian miracle, and that, after all, equivocal. We must therefore not hastily assume that the historical record is very remote from the date of the event recorded, merely because a non-historical colour has been imparted to it. Still less are we entitled, on the ground of even large predominance of non-historical elements, to disallow its claim to be an historical record of considerable value.

It would be the most natural accident possible, time and circumstances being duly appreciated, that in the course of tradition and delivery—in the very process of earliest tradition—Elymas or Bar-jesus should be said to be struck with blindness, while at the best the affliction may never have existed at all in any other sense than an inability to see his way to a refutation of arguments involved by a pupil of Gamaliel, or to discern the superiority of Paul's holy spirit to his own. Even if the fiction, or the misconception, were traced up to the averment of a contemporary, it would be a very insufficient reason for the abnegation of all groundwork in matter of fact. I have already hinted at local associations that might qualify the growth of the mythus.

The matter of fact that we can rest in at last may seem to be not worth very much. It may amount to this: that all that proved worth relating of this missionary journey through Cyprus, was certain intercourse of Paul and Barnabas with a Roman proconsul credulously inclined to Eastern superstition; and a certain advantage gained by them over his previous professor of supernatural influence.

When we take the incident, however, on this very circumscribed ground, it is replete with significance. It was not with those in high stations,—stations that are usually seized and garrisoned by unenthusiastic men of the world,—that the Christian teachers had, in the beginning, the most declared success. The qualities that conduct to posts of power are not usually those that conduce to, or are even compatible with, the cordial acceptation of new truth or new semblances of truth. Nevertheless, speculative zeal and truthfulness are not absolutely incompatible in a certain class of minds—by no means of the highest order, with possession of those capacities for administration and ardour for public business that, under concurrences of fortune, carry them high in the state or in the army. The spirit of the men of the world, of this world, and the men of the next, the children of light, are in such natures in strange alliance; and the impulse for personal advancement and the restraint of conscientiousness live on together, sometimes by means of compromise and mutual concession, more frequently by each finding a field for itself or occupying the same ground in alternation, often ridiculously and miserably enough. In such examples, habit and education and routine are on one side, and a germ of uneradicated original character on the other. Praying soldiers and pietist money-lenders and maundering statesmen have not been so little abounding in one country or another, and more or less near to our own time, that we may not comprehend such a position and moral constitution as those of Sergius Paulus, even if we interpret them strictly to the letter.

As time went on, and the Christian community gained numbers and force, spreading widely below, and then gradually rising upwards, it came ultimately to pass, that even the most rational, even the most coldly self-seeking Roman could see that the adoption, that is to say, the profession of the new doctrine, had become even for worldly wisdom only a question of time. The step might easily be precipitated if the conduct of the crisis fell to a man not absolutely superior to the spiritual apprehensions inspired by fanatical proselytizers. All the conditions for the mounting of Christianity to the leading places of the Roman Empire, are set before us in the incident of the conversion, more or less pronounced, of this Cyprian proconsul: nothing more was required for the catastrophe of one dispensation of mythology and the inauguration of a new with a long history of development before it, than the accident that such a man, neither more nor less intelligent, should hold the military force of the empire in his hand; so soon as the empire should have become fully subjected to that systematic indoctrination which Paul and Barnabas only quit the prætorium to help very importantly to carry out.

The religious history of ancient Rome—the history of the religious sentiment among the classes that were the source and the seat of her political power—has, I believe, still to be written. The final establishment of Christianity was the great climax of this history; in progress to which it passed through many an intermediate crisis. The settlement of the properly Roman worship and rites in relation to the foreign superstitions, came within the organizing operations of Augustus; after his time we may trace a series of licenses and innovations by the military emperors, usually explainable by tendencies of the quarter of the empire with which the legions they relied on were chiefly connected; this inquiry, however, must be for others, and at another time.

It is in the narrative now in question that the change of the ordinary appellation of the Apostle is made from Saul to Paul; this was connected of old with the similarity of name of the Proconsul: "Apostolus a primo ecclesiæ spolio, Proconsule Sergio Paulo, victoriæ suæ trophæa retulit, erexitque vexillum ut Paulus ex Saulo vocaretur" (Hieronymus). Probably there is no more in it than a coincidence, and perhaps dependent upon a change here of the source of tradition which may be connected with the retirement of Mark. Beyond this, the Apostle is now in the way to address Gentiles particularly, though not exclusively, and to become to them by the usual, and, in his case, avowed policy of the seekers of proselytes, as much like one of them as might be. There was quite sufficient motive here for his habitual adoption of a Gentile name,—a constant practice with his countrymen of old, as now; and of old, as now, the secondary name was frequently adopted for the sake of a certain assonance with that which it superseded.

We may be allowed to wonder, but it is of little use to inquire, what was the motive of the retirement of John at this point, just after a marked success; it is alluded to afterwards as if it were a flinching from labour or fatigue. Could it be that he was in truth not overmuch in sympathy with the freedom with which Paul gave signs of his intention to interpret the secret compact?—Who shall say?

With the retirement of his cousin, Barnabas loses his place of precedence in the narrative; we read thereafter of "Paul and Barnabas," an order in accordance with the representation of Paul as the chief speaker and worker of signs; and a certain Hebraistic tone, not unfrequent before, is now lost almost entirely. Henceforward, it may be said, the history of the Acts proceeds as if the development of Christianity were bound up with the life and the labours of Paul, and concludes as if it reached its completion, with the arrival of Paul at Rome. Such, in a most important sense, it cannot be doubted was the case; the arrival at the metropolis of the world of the Apostle of the Gentiles, the great vindicator of a free Gospel, of the new religion under conditions that made it susceptible and worthy of universalism, was in itself strikingly impressive; it would have been so, though his career had then come to an end forthwith. This, however, was not the case; for two whole years at least he taught, without let or molestation, which he could hardly have done in any other place, however far less important. What the result of this teaching may have been, the historian forbears to say; but he concludes, as upon a keynote, with an enunciation of its purpose, and both must have been notorious to his immediate readers. He breaks off with what is equivalent to an expressive aposeiopesis. For what further he and his Roman readers might have in their minds,—is it not all expressed at large in the Epistle to the Romans, the completest, the most definite, the most liberal and practical exposition of the noblest aspect of Christianity from that day to this? Here, with whatever of brotherly tenderness, the Jew is bidden to recover himself from his hallucination of privilege, and here the Gentile was bidden to recognize his obligations to Judaism at the same time that he held fast by his freedom, —noble lessons in application as in spirit. Alas! that from that day until this present they should have been taught in vain.

The blinding of Elymas, considered as one of a series of tapestries for the Sistine Chapel, is a Pauline miracle of a severe type parallel to the Petrine subject of the destruction of Ananias. In the Acts of the Apostles a still exacter Petrine parallel is furnished by the humiliation of Simon Magus; it is one of a system of parallels in the Apostolic history that has given rise to much speculation—in Germany principally. In England we have turned away our faces from such suggestions, or have affected to regard them, while, at the same time, we were winking hard,—or have looked on, indeed, with sober sincerity and simplicity, but with an innocence of intelligence, as well as of heart, truly infantine. If the Germans have erred sometimes in their conclusions after labouring exhaustively upon the evidence, I think it has mostly occurred from indulging to excess an appetite for the discovery of the unhistorical,—an avidity for discrediting every shred of original evidence, in forgetfulness that the highest rarefaction must depend on a certain basis of molecular solidity after all.

True, however, it certainly is, that for every Petrine

narrative or miracle in Acts, there is one of Paul as a parallel, or *vice versâ*. A man "lame from birth" is cured by Peter at the Beautiful Gate; by Paul, at Lystra: the very shadow of Peter carries health and healing; and, as if Paul could of course be not less salutary, kerchiefs that he has worn restore the sick: Peter raises Tabitha from the dead, and there is at least goodwill to convey that Paul did as much for Eutychus: and if Peter has to protest his humanity to the devotional Cornelius, Paul likewise only escapes divine honours at Lystra by proclaiming that he also is a man.

This parallelism may be partly due to that feeling for repetition and antithesis that in its best form, as in Rafael's selection of subjects, is truly artistic; in its inferior, it is simply an expedient to save expense of inventive effort. Otherwise, no doubt, it may easily have had a certain controversial root in a design to vindicate the co-ordinate authority of Peter and of Paul. This latter suspicion opens an inquiry as to which were the original stories; were Paul's invented to vie with Peter's, or did the adherents of Peter struggle to cap Paul?

But there is another very important and antecedent source of such parallelism, and that is the existence in the minds of both Apostles, or the historiographers of both, of a common model. Both would expect, not to say claim, and from both it would be expected, that they should display the proper signs of Apostleship according to the accepted precedents,—the signs and wonders wrought by the prophets in the Old Testament. To this cause I am disposed to assign very extensive influence; in the first place, however, the correspondence of incident may have been heightened by the bias of the compiler when he came to select from an accumulation of traditions.

II. THE CARTOON OF THE REBUKE OF ELYMAS.

Again we recall ourselves, and this time to the Cartoon.

To the poet-painter any license is allowed that he can vindicate, not by verisimilitude merely, but by significant effect; and to Rafael we permit, without grudge or cavil, that the blindness of Elymas shall be actual, not potential,—shall be sudden and total; and the conversion of the proconsul equally instantaneous and absolute.

We must read the narrative as illustrative of the picture, with this heightening conception; and by such a light, how shines forth the expressive force of the Cartoon?

The scene is a marble-paved hall, and in front of the raised tribunal of the proconsul. This is exactly in the centre of the picture; the divisions of the inlaid pavement correspond with its position, and behind it,—behind the curule chair of the magistrate, is an apse or coved niche, flanked by shafts of coloured marble. On either side of the tribunal an open arch admits a view different on either side, of other columns and other arches, conveying the impression of an extensive palace or public building. Still beyond, also on both sides, we gain that glimpse of open country and sky, which is provided in every one of the Cartoons, whether the incident represented takes place withindoors or without.

At the right of the picture are apparently seen the

jambs of a doorway, but through this also the strong daylight penetrates into the apartment.

The Proconsul is seated on his tribunal, wearing laurel crown, and the robe and ornate sandals appropriate to his rank. To his right another Roman stands, also conspicuous in dignity of toga; to his left, on the steps ascending to his seat, the fronts of which are ornamented with piles of arms and trophies—among them, expressively, shields charged with the head of Medusa—stand two lictors, bearing the axes and rods, the symbols and the instruments of the power of life and death.

Thus surrounded by all the indications of dignity and power and pre-eminence, the Proconsul, on his very seat of state, is starting in unfeigned and scarcely checked astonishment at a punishment inflicted by the exertion of a power as different as it was superior to his own.

Paul and Elymas stand out confronted, leaving a clear space in front of the Proconsul, and every pictorial aid is given to heighten the effect of the implied moral contrast.

Paul stands firm and erect, and extends with decision his denouncing arm and hand, which are caught by the bright light that falls on him from behind. His face is in dark shadow, but his expressive profile is seen in distinct relief. His right hand grasps a book, —the Scriptures, doubtless; an indication that his controversy was with a Jew, and that the perverting efforts of Barjesus had been met by exposition of prophecy. The book and the controversy are closed, and Barjesus receives the punishment of the sophist who will not admit recognition of the most manifest fact; who will not allow a passage for argument along the course of the directest sequence. In the English authorized version we read by habit, without noticing the gratuitous incongruity, that he went about seeking some one to lead him by the hand. In Rafael's more accurate interpretation, whether of Greek or Vulgate, he stands helpless, stricken, and groping. With spread feet, and with one leg bent and one advanced, he stoops his body and throws back his head instinctively, to enable him to preserve his balance in case of unexpected impact. His blindness is made manifest by the strong light falling effectless upon his closed eyes; by his stretched hands and feeling fingers, of which the very tips are recurved in agitation, and his utter unconsciousness of the proximity of the man who avoids touching the wretched reprobate, but is otherwise as close to him as he can be.

This man, of somewhat plain and commonplace and common-sense aspect, looks with fixed and glaring eyes of inquiry at the closed lids of the Jew; and in his raised and displayed palms we read conviction of the certainty. There is a certain clumsiness in the configuration of his hand and fingers—I once thought he had gloves on—and in the hard creases of the skin, that gives great force to the tremulous sensitiveness of those of the sorcerer.

Again; while Elymas feels his way with his forward foot, and so retains the other below his bent knee, as to enable him to redress his balance on the instant, this peering neighbour throws all his weight upon one erect leg without hesitation; and while his other foot—visible beyond the gaberdine of Elymas—just touches the ground, he leans so far forward that, but for his having all his senses about him for safeguard, a single touch would throw him forward on his face.

The simplicity of the majestic drapery of Paul contrasts, not without meaning and effect, with the complicated, and at the same unhandsome, array of his opponent,—a palpable reminiscence of the sempiternal systems of bodily enfoldings, of the Ghetto. There appears to me to be a peculiar quivering effect given to the lines and lights of the drapery over the arms of Elymas, as if his upper extremities were all a-tremble.

I scarcely venture to make an attempt to define in words his marvellously characteristic face. There is a certain vulgarity in the nose, a confidence of loquacity about the mouth; but the features and brow taken together are, perhaps, more expressive of impudence than incurable depravity, and certainly of astuteness rather than stupidity; a very "child of craft and of dexterity in management of mischievousness."

In the face and gestures of Sergius Paulus we see conviction and astonishment; we see, at the same time, an angry expression of contempt, which may be partly for the quelled deceiver, and just a little, perhaps, may be contributed by self-reproach for having allowed himself to make a guide and a confidant of such a shiftless impostor. His friend beside him may have been intended as the introducer of the Apostles; certainly he is independent of a surprise, and turns his head with a flexibility and freedom that give force to the rigidity of Sergius. He speaks over his shoulder to one in the background, while he extends his arm in the direction of the victim with unmistakable indication of all being over. The tenor of his words is further gathered, and his composure illustrated in turn, from the expression of the face behind, which is that of one shuddering and aghast.

Behind Elymas we see the general crowd of attenders of the Proconsul's hall of audience, and amidst it a dialogue proceeds, which is easily interpreted. A female, whose head appears above Elymas, seems hurrying in, and points to Paul, while she turns with a scolding look of nervous excitement to one of the immediate bystanders. The man appealed to points with right hand to Elymas, and approaches the index-finger of his left to his own eye, in evident illustration of the nature of the catastrophe that has occurred. In the Cartoon there is a little confusedness in the position of this left hand, or, at least, of the arm, and the drapery it belongs to,—an unpleasant uncertainty whether it may not belong to the aged man beyond. I do not doubt that this equivocal effect is entirely due to the drapery of the sleeve at least, having been first ruined, and then repainted. The drapery is certainly continuous with the mantle of the man who points to Elymas, but it has not at this part the fringy edge and patterned border that are distinctly marked at the other parts: the modelling has vanished, and flatness and emptiness remain.

The appropriation of the hands, as given, is quite borne out by the tapestry at Mantua; on another point this authority seems at fault. The toe of a boot just visible below the skirt of the sorcerer is made blue;— I do not doubt by mistake, and that it ought to match the other red boot of the glaring figure next to him.

The woman we may probably regard as the sorcerer's

wife. As to her informant, I think, to judge from Dorigny's engraving, he by no means expresses compassion, nor, as it seems to me, very much astonishment. I am almost disposed to think that he feels some of that gratification which Rochefoucauld says we afford in our misfortunes to the best of our friends—the Tubal of an ancient Shylock.

A group of heads still further back have their eyes directed to the illustrator, with a fixedness of gaze that helps the realization of the pertinent ideas of the force and value of vision.

The manner in which the figure of Elymas stands forth detached upon the pavement, is admirably managed. His back is in deep shadow, and the dark outline from shoulder to heel gives that one long line of marked definition in the picture upon a lighter background, upon which Rafael constantly relies as an element of vigour. The upper outline of the raised arm of Paul is the converse and correlative definition of a considerable illuminated line upon a darker background.

It is observable how the force of Paul's erect figure is assisted by the strong shadows cast upon the pavement, at an exact right angle to it.

Over the right shoulder of Paul we see the head of Barnabas—"a good man, and full of faith"—lighted up with devout satisfaction as he raises his joined hands in adoring thankfulness. Beyond, there appears another sympathetic face, which is doubtless Mark's, not pressing forward with eagerness, but accepting the result from the denouncement, and expectant in gathered seriousness of the further consequences.

Intermediate between Mark and the Proconsul are

the lictors; and one head behind is seen with the lion scalp, which denotes the wearer to be a Roman soldier. The lictors, notwithstanding that they preserve their formal station, and continue the unrelaxed grasp of their fasces, seem to press together with a shuddering recoil, and turn their heads; one, I think, not without a touch of brute compassion, the other more distinctly in dismay.

The group to the left of Sergius Paulus is thus made up entirely of the ministers of his executive authority, and the members of the Christian mission; an omen of the consummation that was preparing; of the tendency of which his conversion prefigured the end in the alliance of the temporal force of the empire with the new spiritual power.

In the meantime, the superiority of sanction derived immediately from God may be taken as symbolized in the arm with which Paul deals out the delegated authority, being shown in relief upon the background of the forms of the appalled lictors.

I observe that all the Romans introduced have a somewhat commonplace type of head and feature, and they remind me of the figures upon Trajan's column. How better could be indicated the peculiarly administrative genius of the people,—that genius which is ever disposed to boast as its greatest triumph of success the keeping down all spontaneousness, which delights to depress and trample out every germ of personal and political independence and intellectual originality. It succeeds for long, but its time comes.

In Pistolesi's engraving from the tapestry he shows behind Paul a broad pilaster, parallel to the plane of the picture, and reaching to the top, with a niche in which is a statue. I am not certain, without further examination, that this is not to be taken as an integral portion of the picture. I observed this addition in the Mantua tapestry also. The statue is a hooded female; the base is supported by Bacchic terms; upon it is sculptured a battle of Tritons.

CHAPTER X.

THE SACRIFICE AT LYSTRA.

I. THE MYTHOLOGY OF OVID, IN ACTS.—II. THE CARTOON OF THE SACRIFICE AT LYSTRA.—III. TIMOTHY OF LYSTRA AND ACCOMMODATION.

I. THE MYTHOLOGY OF OVID, IN ACTS.

I BELIEVE that the story of the sacrifice at Lystra is a very remarkable example of a genuine mythus; but we must beware not to adopt the uncritical canon sanctioned by the high authority of Grote, and conclude that, because a mythus, it has therefore "no historical value whatever." A mythus that obtains wide acceptation is itself an historical event of no slight consequence. By the study of it we may chance to learn,— and it may be, indeed, our single chance of learning,— the characteristics of the period that produced and accepted it; and an age is not prolific in producing myths, and eager to invite or entertain them, without having characteristics of history that are worth studying, and are necessary to be studied. And a myth that professes to be historical may, probably enough, have historical value, not only in reference to the times that produced it, but also to the times that it, however fancifully and fabulously, refers to. Human invention is not usually so spontaneous as to make something out of nothing,—least of all will it make the endeavour, when a fund of material is to be had, with no conditions to shackle treatment. It will not hesitate to cover a blank page with figments transferred and transposed from all quarters; but if the page be not absolutely a blank; if it still retain some trace of genuine, though half-obliterated, records, these which are in possession have a better opportunity than any others of becoming the stems of mythical grafts, which may then, no doubt, branch forth and bear fruit diversified and wonderful enough.

So, I believe, it will prove that the story of the attempted sacrifice to Paul and Barnabas at Lystra is as mere a fable as can well be imagined; and yet, that by an analysis of its import and origin, we shall find that it attaches itself very significantly to something of historical fact worth the saving.

We are returning upon our steps, it will be remembered, to the first missionary journey pursued under the terms of the secret compact, and anterior to both the dispute at Antioch and the congress at Jerusalem.

From Perga by the coast, having left Cyprus and now lost Mark, the mission passes considerably inland to Antioch of Pisidia. Here it is represented that the Jews and the Jewish religion have much the same degree and kind of important influence that Josephus ascribes to them at Damascus. Numerous Gentile devout men, proselytes of the Gate, or equivalent to what are known as such, frequent the synagogue, some of them leading men in the city, and, as usual, a still larger proportion of Gentile women, all devout and many honourable,—that is, of superior station.

It was perfectly consistent with the theory of Paul that he should commence his labours in the synagogue, and on the Sabbath. His letters sufficiently show how his Hebrew nature yearned for the attachment of his countrymen; how he would make for it every sacrifice, even of consistency, but the last. A sermon is ascribed to him here, which seems peculiarly addressed to Jews, and to Jews fully imbued with hopes and anticipations of the restored temporal kingdom of David. The sting of it, however, is in the declaration of the insufficiency of the law of Moses: "He, whom God raised up, saw not corruption. Be it known, therefore, unto you, that through him remission of sins is announced to you; and from all those for which ye could not be justified by means of the law of Moses, every one who believes in him, is justified." This corresponds very exactly with the passage in the Epistle to the Romans, where Paul presses the alternative between the Law and Christ, as between the flesh and the spirit; and urges the argument with what care and caution he may, until the inference that the Law was become superfluous must have been inevitable. In the present instance, the manner in which Jesus recognized by John, is presented as typical substitute of David anointed by Samuel; and the corruptible kingdom is superseded by an incorruptible, has a closer parallel in the argument of Peter's early speech in Acts.

The facts, indeed, at least as related, seem to imply even more of outspokenness than stands on the record. The ministry is continued through the week-days, and with an effect that is easily conceivable after the experience the Apostles had acquired in Syria, in bringing their doctrine to bear upon the minds both of proselytes and of purely Gentile hearers.

On the next Sabbath there was a great uproar: the Jews had taken alarm at the influence exercised by preachers, who brought almost the whole city about the synagogue, but brought it, as the alarm shows, by promises and by incitements that the synagogue was not disposed to sympathize with. Thus it was that these opponents were enabled to gain the assistance of the Gentile adherents to the synagogue, male and female, in a persecution of teachers, who only commenced with scrupulous citations of the Prophets and the Law, in order presently to promote a society which, in respect to Gentiles, dispensed with the Law altogether; and, as regarded Jews, at least indoctrinated them with principles that very moderate perspicacity might suffice to discover, presupposed its abrogation.

Paul and Barnabas retire before the clamour to Iconium, where like causes produce like effects; and thence they move on to "the cities of Lycaonia, Lystra, and Derbe, and the neighbourhood, and there they preached the Gospel."

"And there sat a certain man at Lystra, impotent in his feet, a cripple from his mother's womb, who had never walked. The same heard Paul speak: who steadfastly beholding him, and seeing that he had faith to be healed, said with a loud voice, Stand upright upon thy feet. And he leaped up and walked. And the crowd, seeing what Paul had done, lifted up their voice, saying in the language of Lycaonia, The gods are come down to us in the likeness of men. And they called Barnabas, Jupiter; and Paul, Mercury, because he was the chief speaker. And the priest of the Jupiter, that was before the city, brought oxen and garlands to the portals, and would have sacrificed with the crowd. And when the Apostles, Paul and Barnabas, heard, they rent their clothes, and sprung into the crowd, crying out, and saying, Men, why do ye these things? We also are men of like passions with you, and we preach good tidings that ye may turn from these vanities unto the living God, who made the heavens, and the earth, and the sea, and all things that are therein: who in the generations past suffered all the Gentiles to walk in their own ways. Nevertheless even so he left not himself without witness, doing good, and sending to you from heaven rains and fruitful seasons, filling your hearts with food and gladness. And so saying they scarcely kept the multitude (populace, more correctly) from sacrificing unto them.

"And there came Jews from Antioch and Iconium, who persuaded the multitude, and stoned Paul, and drew him out of the city, thinking that he was dead." (Acts xiv. 8.)

It would be too much to say, considering what is known of the sympathetic effect of mental excitement and contact with the excited on the ailing and the cripple, that a very wonderful recovery of muscular energy may not have occurred to a hearer of Paul, and that undesigned exaggeration may not have transformed the marvel easily into the cure of a man who had never walked from birth. There is the highest probability that these early preachings were attended by all the convulsionary phenomena familiar in modern religious revivals; but however this may have been, there are, in the story as it now stands, verbal coincidences with the curing of the lame man by Peter and John that forbid us to take it out of the class to which that narrative has been deliberately consigned. The cripple of Lystra, like the lame beggar at the Gate of the Temple, is, in identical terms, "a certain man lame from his mother's womb;" attracts the "fixed gaze" of the teacher; and, at a word from him, jumps up, and "leaps and walks." The Lystran cripple, therefore, like his compeer, I conclude to be nothing more than a type,— a metaphor made into a matter of fact, of a class of converts rescued by the Gospel from a congenital disability; the excluded heathen in this case as the carped-at Hellenistic Jew in the other.

We are then told that the Lystrans, who honoured Jupiter as the tutelary god of their city, still retained a living faith in a legend, of which trace is found in classical literature, that Jupiter and Mercury (Zeus and Hermes) had visited their region once in the form of men, and that it was not impossible they might repeat the visit again in like masquerade. Such a faith, it is true, smacks of much earlier times, of the times not even of Homer and Hesiod, but rather of the times that they looked far back to; it is in every respect a primitive tale, not more gross and simple than has been entertained far down into civilized times by Italian peasants or Welsh mountaineers, but that jars upon our associations when we are bidden to accept it as rife in the imaginations of a considerable city under Claudius. Ovid tells the tale in the 'Metamorphoses' with a great many pleasing and natural touches, for many of which he probably had to thank a Greek original. To him, or to his original, may be also due a good deal of the finished air it possesses. But it must not, after all, be overlooked how we constantly find in the tours of Pausanias under Hadrian, that legends which had been furbished up, and made correct and artistic even in the time of Homer, still lived on, in a popular and religious sense, in their native localities; and that fables there still excited awe, still brought respect and revenue to priests and temples, that in poetry were reduced only to gratify the purest taste and most cultivated imagination. It is therefore probable enough that Paul found indeed at Lystra a still subsisting faith in the possibility of a visit from a god in human form; and, at least, no mistrust whatever that such visits had been paid, with incidents common to patriarchal tradition, of rewards and punishments to the insulting and to the hospitable, —the inhumane and the warmhearted.

The tale for which we turn to Ovid, is localized in the neighbourhood of Tyana and the hills of Phrygia. Tyana is on the borders of Lycaonia and Cilicia, and but little removed from the position Lystra must have occupied,—a site which modern travellers have not yet, and which it is highly desirable they speedily should, discover. The peculiarities of the locality might throw light upon the story. I should anticipate that a lake would be found near the site of Lystra, helping the explanation of its sympathy with the Tyanean legend. Tyana seems far enough away from Phrygia, according to later political geography, but I have no doubt would be comprised within the great central plain of Asia Minor in days when the mythus originated. Otherwise, we have but to impute a lapse to Ovid, which indeed, in itself, is probable enough. .

Here, then, adjacent to wooded eminences, was a marsh that once had been habitable and populous, but had become the haunt of such birds as the stork, that modern travellers in Asia Minor see " feeding and fishing more than a hundred together in the space of an acre : "—

> " Haud procul hinc stagnum, tellus habitabilis olim ;
> Nunc celebres mergis fulicisque palustribus undæ."
> OVID, *Met.* viii. 624.

Hither, on a time, came Jupiter and Mercury in mortal form, and from the multitudes of households sought reception and rest, but in vain, till at last they applied at the small and rustic cottage of an aged pair, Baucis and Philemon. The simple, honest, and warm-hearted entertainment of the disguised stranger by Goldsmith's Hermit of the Vale, seems to owe some touches to the description that ensues,—

> " Super omnia vultus
> Accessere boni . . . . "

The marvel of the widow's cruse follows; and it seems as though the gods, who in a search for virtue would even waste good appetites upon a poor dinner, could not bring themselves to pollute their lips with bad wine, or put up with a small bottle ; even as at the marriage of Cana,—

> " Interea quoties haustum cratera repleri
> Sponte suâ, per seque vident succrescere vina."

Why did not Rembrandt depict the next scene,— Rembrandt who etched the visit of the angels to Abraham to promise him legitimate offspring;—winged, but also bearded worthies they are, fit prognosticators of the birth of an ancestor of chapmen to supplant the generous Ishmael, who already is practising within their sight the free exercise of archery, genuine promise of a life at large, of vigorous sport and daring. The last, the only goose of the household is to be slain in honour of gods so miraculously declared; but active with foot and feather, it eludes the chase of the feeble old folk, which is still persevered in till at last—

—" 'twixt the knees of Jove it saves its life
From old Philemon's hospitable knife."

The gods command the couple to attend them to the top of the mountain; there, turning round, they see the impious vicinage submerged in a lake, their own cottage only remaining. The cottage becomes a temple by a transformation that gives good account of the origin of many details in marble architecture; they themselves become its priests; and in good old age, even as they stand in front of it, still gossiping of the judgment, they are transformed into trees, and the intertwined trunks remained to be cited long after as evidence, quite as good as any other, of the miracle and the story.

"Ostendit adhuc Tyaneïus illic
Incola de gemino vicinos corpore truncos."—V. 720.

Need is not to do more than allude, but it would be rather scandalous not to allude, to the parallel of the retreat, conducted by the angels of the Lord, of Lot and his daughters to the mountains, and the punishment they at last look back upon, after it has been fulfilled, of the grossly inhospitable cities of the Plain. The semblance of fiery visitation here, I suspect, suggested the sin that was to be punished.

The story from Ovid, then, is worth relating in outline, as probably embodying some genuine Lycaonian elements, whatever additions he may have imported into it from his own imagination, or from other local legends. It bears an extraordinary resemblance to a great number of parallel stories, of all ages and regions, respecting submerged cities—inhospitable cities submerged by angry divinities, who have proved them by visits in person, but disguised as wanderers and strangers. A collection and comparison of these will be found in the Transactions of the Royal Society of Literature, vol. vi., part 3,—a collection amusing for what it includes; amusing, nay lamentable, for the omission with dignified hardihood of the capital instance of all,—the story from the Pentateuch.

Many a fertile plain has vanished indeed by sudden flood, or by gradual subsidence in the course of ages; and the tradition and the ruins together would be quite sufficient to suggest, as a theological explanation, that the scene of agricultural productiveness could only have been desolated so suddenly and irrecoverably by the gods, in punishment for some overweening pride of wealth, some ungrateful or grudging ways in the enjoyment of the God-given fruits of the earth, unknown to the poorer colonists of higher ground. The source, from the heavens direct, and the great suddenness of the mischief done by inundations in the neighbourhood of mountains, or of rivers that swell very suddenly without visible cause, —from rainfall on mountains at some distance, have always caused superstitious populations to regard this class of affliction as peculiarly marking divine wrath. We find the indications of the feeling throughout Roman history, and down at least as late as the odes of Horace. In districts of peculiar conformation, where plains are entirely surrounded by hills, and only preserved from being lakes by the water-drainage finding subterranean outlets, any solid obstruction of such channels, or even their insufficiency at a given time from an unusual rainfall, has constantly produced the most serious disasters, and turned plains into lakes for a time, or even permanently, if the obstruction continues. Such localities are numerous in Greece, especially in Bœotia and Arcadia. The little valley of Pheneus, which Colonel Leake, in 1806, found drained and well cultivated, was, in 1828, in consequence of obstruction in the Katabothra, covered by water to the depth in some places of 150 feet. The valley of Stymphalus presents the same conditions, and both valleys had their mythical stories in antiquity, and even in later times; giving certain explanations of the phenomena as connected with the demons or divinities for the time in vogue as angry or as appeased. The Alban lake in Italy was in a position that would quite agree with such an origin; and there is no improbability at all that, as Diodorus and Dionysius averred, and as even Niebuhr the questioner accepted, remains of spacious buildings might not be discoverable at the bottom during extraordinary droughts. Such incidents actually occurring in some places would readily be transferred to others where lakes had existed from all time; and the agriculturist, who found his operations upon desirable land limited by an encroaching lake, which was more extensive than he would have wished, might readily enough conclude that the water had once been sent in divine anger to deprive the earlier impious cultivators of an advantage that they had abused.

"Where the lake of Alba now lies,—the tourist divine from England was told by his mule-boy, there once stood a great city. Here, when Jesus Christ came into Italy, he begged alms. None took compassion on him but an old woman, who gave him two handfuls of meal. He bade her leave the city: she obeyed; the city instantly sank, and the lake rose in its place." (Dr. Thirlwall, Trans. R. S. L., *ut sup.*) The boy's ancestor, in Roman times, had told how it was the palace of an impious king that had been swallowed up,—I do not doubt for some similar breach of hospitality and compassionateness.

A judgment upon pride and inhumanity, as exhibited in denial of relief in food, was ever for the simple-minded the inconsequent interpretation of a wide-spread and utter devastation of food-producing land, and the homesteads of its wealthy masters.

The following story was found by Major Harris among Christians in the highlands of Ethiopia:—"Of yore, when the spot now inundated (by the lake Alobár) was *terra firma*, the Virgin Mary is said to have appeared in the house of its wealthiest cultivator, residing in the many flourishing villages that then existed, and to have addressed herself to the mistress, saying, 'I am hungry, and have nothing to eat; give me corn, and I will grind for wages.' A vast heap of grain was pointed out, sufficient for a week's labour; but no sooner had the Virgin touched it than it was miraculously converted into meal. The inhospitable master now refused the pittance claimed, nor would the 'Four Chairs,' before whom the complaint was carried, give redress until a poor shepherd had become mediator. As a mark of the displeasure of Heaven, the scene of this offence against the mother of Christ was forthwith converted into a lake, which has since formed the abode of the lord of all the gins and evil spirits in the land." The quotation does not assign a reward to the just shepherd, but no doubt this was provided in the legend.

As much further down in Africa as between the eleventh and twelfth degrees of south latitude, Dr. Livingstone heard this account of the origin of Lake Dilólo, which every year rises in flood over the valley on its banks:—"A female chief named Moéna (lord) Monénga came one evening to the village of Mosógo, a man who lived in the vicinity, but had gone to hunt with his dogs. She asked for a supply of food, and Mosógo's wife gave her a sufficient quantity. Proceeding to another village, standing on the spot now occupied by the water, she preferred the same demand; but when she uttered a threat for their niggardliness, was taunted with the question, 'What could she do though she were thus treated?' In order to show what she could do, she began a song in slow tune, and uttered her own name, Monénga-wŏŏ. As she prolonged the last note, the village people, fowls, and dogs sank into the space now called Dilólo. When Kasimakata, the head man of the village, came home and found out the catastrophe, he cast himself into the lake, and is supposed to be in it still. The name is derived from *dilólo*,

Despair, because this man gave up all hope when his family was destroyed. Monénga was put to death."

See 'Once a Week' for 13th June, 1861, for a pretty version of this staple tale, accounting for—it is said, according to a local tradition—the origin of the lake of Gidlen in the island of Rugen, in the Baltic.

It is represented, then, that at Lycaonia Paul found the Lystrans still apt to believe that the gods whom they worshipped had of old,—wherefore might they not again?—come down amongst them in human shape to test and to descry their ways.

As the story now reads, the expostulation of Paul is directed to correct the error of the populace in taking men,—himself, namely, and Barnabas,—for gods; I suspect that in the original account, the argument that was at least ascribed to him, aimed simply to discredit the superstition that Jupiter and Hermes were gods at all, or had ever, as the hearers supposed, come amongst them as men. In contrast with such "absurdities" is put forth the doctrine of the living God, to whom, indeed, were due those very benefits with which the Tyaneian legend connected the visitants from Olympus,—"who made the heaven, and the earth, and the sea, and all things that are therein;" who for the generations hitherto had allowed the Gentiles to take their own courses with no personal interference, but still had not "left himself without witness, doing good and sending from heaven rains and fruitful seasons, filling hearts with food and gladness."

This in some original record may very easily have been a summary of the argument by which Paul was represented, nay, may even have been truly recorded, as seeking to divert the Lystrans from their idolatry and idolatrous sacrifices. That the sacrifice in hand was a sacrifice, not to their established gods regarded as former visitors, but to their present visitors regarded as gods, I take to be a change that supervened upon the story, at the same time that the conversion of Lystrans came to be narrated as the miraculous cure of a man, by virtue of his "having faith to be saved,"—a proper sign of moral vigour, not of muscular,—of a lameness from birth, so that he who had never walked in his life at once stood up erect, and walked about and leapt.

It may be said that we know nothing of the extent or moral condition of Lystra, and that such a besotted blunder may not be beyond probabilities in a secluded provincial town at that time, any more than the reception of Mad Thom as a prophet by the be-squired and be-rectored peasantry of Kent in our own. Perhaps not; but likely sources of misconception in the case are suspiciously near at hand. It is said that the crowd declares the divinity of the Apostles in the Lycaonian language; this seems apparently intended to explain how it was that Paul and Barnabas did not interrupt the preparations for sacrifice until it was on the point of being consummated, but it brings us to the difficulty—how, then, did the crowd understand the Apostle's rebuke? No doubt many of these Asiatic towns were as fluently bilingual as settlements of French creoles on the banks of the Mississippi; but, then, they need not have chosen just the language the Apostles did not understand for proclaiming their veneration.

Really, as the narrative stands, there is an opening for the imputation that the Apostles were over-hasty in snatching a compliment that was never intended for them. "The priest of Jupiter that was before the city, brought oxen and garlands to the pylons (of the sacred precinct, we infer), and wished to sacrifice with the crowds;" but it might be suggested that only want of knowledge of Lycaonian, would justify the Apostles in supposing that the worship was intended for themselves.

I am inclined to suspect, however, that an original narrative, whether in the fullest sense authentic or not, related how Paul and Barnabas preached the Gospel to heathen idolators in Lycaonia; setting forth the arguments by which they endeavoured to sap a predominant local superstition of the gods Jupiter and Mercury having founded their temple, when visiting the earth in human form. It might further proceed to declare how, encouraged by success, even among the priestly class as well as the multitude, they had ventured to expostulate on an occasion of public sacrifice to these anthropomorphist gods. Successful or not successful, a riot speedily ensued, which would be ascribed to the malignity of Jews by those who were inclined or accustomed to trace this malignity everywhere, but might very easily have arisen on such an occasion independently of any cause but the zeal of the Apostles. They had reason to feel that they had overrated their influence, for, by a reaction, Paul was mobbed and pelted, perhaps stoned, and very narrowly escaped with his life.

When the establishment of a Lystran church came to be narrated as a miracle of healing, it was a very natural jumble for the interrupted sacrifice to the pair of deified men or humanized gods, to be interpreted as intended for the Apostles Paul and Barnabas, who had just displayed the possession of supernatural power in working such a marvel.

Thus much of truth there may be latent and overlaid in the narrative, but thus much of fable at least there must be, and very possibly a great deal more.

II. THE CARTOON OF THE SACRIFICE AT LYSTRA.

The scene of the picture is laid in a public place,—the agora or forum of Lystra, amidst an assemblage of stately public buildings, and on an area paved with geometrical slabs of marble; large dark octagons, with intervals filled with small diamonds of white marble. Niches on the walls and between the columns of one of the buildings are filled with statues, apparently not of divinities, and suggestive of the readiness with which such honours were accorded in this city. The usual glimpse of country and open sky is obtained in the background, and against the open sky is seen relieved a statue of Mercury Caducifer upon a lofty pedestal; an indication of the special regard of the Lystrans for the god,—the god of interpretation and of eloquence.

The pylons of the text seem to be conceived as the entrances to a temple or sacred precinct, and are indicated by the portal of the building seen at a distance to the right, through which a lounger advances leisurely; and by an entrance nearer to the front, on the advanced step of which Paul is already standing, while Barnabas descends upon it with hasty bound from within.

In front of this entrance, a little aside, is an enriched altar of square, not triangular, plan, and placed with one angle directly fronting the spectator, so that two of

its sides are equally displayed. The opposite angle is obscured by the interposed flame, but both the tapestries and perspective declare for a square abacus; boys with incense-box and pipes are ministrant, and to this is brought the sacrifice by the priest of Jupiter with full attendance and apparatus of divine service, while the crowd presses on behind, and the cured cripple rushes in with every sign of activity and of gratitude.

Paul, in grief and indignation at the impiety of which he has been the unwitting cause, is rending—at least disordering his garments, and looks down with repudiating look at the man crowned with leaves, who has brought in the ram intended as appropriate sacrifice to him as Hermes, god of flocks, and who returns the look with questioning surprise. The caduceus of the statue of Hermes "dressed" with fresh foliage, denotes that it is his festivity.

One of the bulls, for Barnabas as Jupiter, is just on the point of being slaughtered by the priest of Jupiter, the leader and promoter of all, and towards this group Barnabas, who "leaps" forward, according to the text, and descends on the ball of his foot, is looking out.

One priest on his knees retains the head of the bull, and looks up with eyes full of reverence at the Apostles; a second wields the poleaxe. His right hand grasps the extremity of the helve, while the left slides upward towards the head, soon to descend, and the instrument has just taken its full swing to the left preparatory to the blow. The axe, as it is shown in engravings, and, as far as I can discern, in Cartoon and tapestry, would give no fatal blow to sacrificial ox; it lacks the spike that, not alone in modern slaughter-houses, penetrates through the forehead to the brain, but that is shown no less, sometimes slightly recurved, in all the Roman bas-reliefs that I have seen of this sacrificial group; there is one at Mantua, another at Florence.

Behind the kneeling priest are two other garlanded devotees, also on their knees, and looking up with like engrossment of concentrated interest. Beyond the striking priest are two other officials, officially serious and hooded and stoled. Their formality might be taken to represent the stolid impassiveness of the hackney priests who fill the choir and mumble the chant with equal indifference in whatever service, to whatever god; there is, however, in the expression, of one especially, more of the ironical self-restraint of augurs, who cautiously avoid to intercross their glances on such an occasion lest they should laugh in each other's faces. Senile concurrence in one face displays the irony in the other,—a much younger, but experienced man. Rafael must have had ample opportunity for studies of both kinds. The heads of two others are just visible behind.

At the left corner of the picture, the right of the unreversed Cartoon, the cured cripple hurries in with hands lifted and eyes sparkling in grateful adoration. On the ground lie his abandoned crutches, and we behold his leg restored to usefulness, with foot planted flat and firmly upon the ground, if even yet it seems scarcely to play with the elasticity that will come with practice. An old man following lifts the margin of the scanty and sordid skirt to examine it more nearly, and the gesture of his disengaged hand shows his marvel and conviction. A younger man and a youth partake of his curiosity, and press to look over his shoulder.

Above these heads are two female heads, which, by the direction of their gaze and in their expression, connect the marvel of the miracle with Paul. One is an aged and toothless, but vigorous and shrewd-looking crone, who screens her eyes and looks towards Paul with the same glance and gesture that Dante ascribes in a simile to his old tailor threading a needle; the other female is young, and, with head erect, looks steadily and without effort, in the same direction. The aged dame is not introduced without a special purpose, and it is not for nothing that the curious scrutinizer of the recovered limb is so well stricken in years. These are the very oldest inhabitants of Lystra, and in their testimonial astonishment we have vouchers for the previous lameness of the man, by evidence that would easily reach backward to the date of his birth.

Rushing and driving through the close crowd, and with eager arm reaching across the broad back of the sacrificial bull to stay the stroke of the priest, we see the eager young disciple Timothy;—to obtain this character for his dramatic scene, Rafael had to read on in the Acts of the Apostles beyond the chapter that describes the superstitious sacrifice. His arm comes in front of the two down-looking haruspices with much of that gain of expression which the arm of Paul, in the scene before Sergius Paulus, gains by being relieved against the upright forms of the guarding lictors. The head of Timothy is so inclined as to aid the full extension of his arm, and we see his excitement not only in the strain, but in the open and fluttering fingers. Close to his youthful and ingenuous face, but on the opposite flank of the animal, appears the face of a female, older, and yet still young,—still young, though her head be hooded with her mantle, matron-like, perhaps widow-like. I do not doubt that this is the believing mother of Timothy, who is mentioned in Acts, and has a name, Eunice, in the impugned Epistle to Timothy. She looks towards Paul with a tranquil air of affectionate reverence, that bespeaks her a disciple in Christ, not sharing the madness of the crowds. The grandmother Lois I prefer to miss entirely, rather than to identify her in the peering crone at the extreme left.

A second bull is being brought along by other attendants, who also wear the wreaths of festive ceremony.

Rafael adapted the group and details of the sacrifice from certain well-known works of antiquity, and, like the architecture introduced, they imply a pomp and profusion somewhat beyond the proprieties taken strictly, of a simple-minded and secluded population.

The design, however, not the less remains a significant embodiment of the event,—the earliest type of the influence of Christianity and of the rhetoric of Christian missionaries upon Pagans and upon minds that, in respect of culture or acuteness, are semi-barbarous. We have here a very significant illustration at an early date, of the opportunities of influence and power that lie in the way of those who devote themselves to evangelizing the heathen,—the temptations and the abuse of zeal which has sometimes turned missionaries in our own colonies into land-speculators, sometimes erected political hierarchies, as in Paraguay. Here we have a prospect which might warm the ambition of a college *de propagandâ fide* ; the sequel of the story, the reaction which led to the stoning of Paul, gives a warning that was as little

thrown away, that if the promise is to be made the most of, and the career of success to be uninterrupted, the new doctrines and superstitions must not be too eager or too scrupulous in renouncing relationship with those that are to be superseded; that means must be found for softening off the shock of change, even though it should happen, as happened too surely in the Roman world, that when the change was rested in as complete, the new doctrine proved to have consented to incorporate a large proportion of all that was most mischievous in the old.

This is the lesson that priestly astuteness might derive for itself,—it is not that which Rafael sets forth. The incident, as he displays it, inculcates the beauty of Apostolic humility as impressively as it illustrates Apostolic power, let Pope and Cardinal read it as they might.

The perspective of the picture is rather peculiar in the nearness of the point of view.

The converging lines of the pavement give us the point of sight, and thence the horizon. The distance along horizon from point of sight to point intersected by prolongation of one side of the base of the altar,— the diagonal of a square,—gives distance of eye from the picture, and this proves to be less than its breadth. I suspect that Rafael made his adjustment to suit a predetermined angular presentation of the altar.

III. TIMOTHY OF LYSTRA, AND ACCOMMODATION.

It was, as I have inferred elsewhere, after Paul and Barnabas had returned from the present journey to their starting-place at Antioch, in Syria, to report of marvels wrought, and churches founded among the heathen, that the discussion with Peter occurred, and the dissension with the Pharisaic brethren, as to the very principle and basis of the success; the council at Jerusalem; the compromise of the decree;—the Galatian letter, with its unabated resolve, dating, in the interval, between the dissension and the enforced compromise, and before Paul had returned a third time to Jerusalem.

It was after that crisis, which we have already considered, that Paul again visited Derbe and Lystra; this time it was in company with Silas, an elder of the church at Jerusalem,—one of the envoys, indeed, to whom the Apostolic decree had been committed; and, accordingly, we read that "as they passed through the cities they delivered them the *dogmata* that had been sanctioned by the Apostles and elders at Jerusalem, for them to observe." Can this be true? we ask ourselves; and how far is it compatible with the strenuous principles of his Epistles to these very churches? But this was not all; we read further: "And he came down to Derbe and Lystra; and, behold, a certain disciple was there, named Timothy, the son of a believing Jewess and a Greek father, who was well reported of by the brethren at Lystra and Iconium. Him Paul wished to go forth with him, and took and circumcised him, because of the Jews who were in those places, for they all knew his father that he was a Greek. And as they went through the cities they delivered to them the decrees to observe that were ordained by the Apostles and elders that were in Jerusalem." (Acts xvi. 1–4.)

It is at least in accordance with such concessions that this time we hear nothing of mobbings and persecutions in these parts. But not alone the consistency of history,—the consistency of Paul is at issue. Paul, if indeed we may trust the history that he acted thus, must have been doing violence to his feelings, and scarcely less in delivering the Apostolic decree, to the fundamental principle of which he was so utterly opposed. How far would the concession in this instance, if justly imputed, compromise principle as well as feeling? Let us hear more.

It would appear, in the first place, that the fact that the father of Timotheus was a Greek was presumption that he himself was not circumcised; and the fact that he was of Jewish blood by the mother's side rendered circumcision, according to the prejudices of the Jews, obligatory upon him. Half-blood made him a Jew, not a Gentile, in the eyes of the Jews at large, and probably would have done so in those of the church at Jerusalem, and thus would debar him from the privileges in respect of the customs, conceded by the decree to Gentile converts.

James, in his authoritative decision and decree, parries the liberal motion ascribed to Peter, and leaves the Jewish brother with an unqualified responsibility to the law as weekly expounded; and, at a later date the church at Jerusalem assumes that upon this point there is no question even with Paul,—and so that church continued; as to the Greek, the decree at least released him from circumcision, though insisting upon some other limitations of dangerous tendency.

Had Timothy, therefore, been unequivocally a Greek, Paul, by subjecting him to circumcision, would indeed have been very grievously receding from the position he had successfully maintained in the case of Titus, and that had since been sanctioned by the decree. But if he was bound, or felt bound, or, under a difficulty, admitted himself bound to regard Timothy as a Jew, how stood the case then with his consistency? In Galatians he states his compact with the Apostles to have been that he should address himself to the heathen, and they to the circumcision; but this distribution could not have been understood on either side as exclusive, and as we cannot suppose that James, Peter, and John, however liberally disposed, were then prepared to go the full public length of denouncing the Law as not only unnecessary for Jews, but the observance of it a breach of Christian duty, so Paul, too, may reasonably be supposed to have made the concession to weak brethren of his nation; or even to the bolder, who were hedged in by difficulties and dangers insuperable, unless by temporizing and some little reticence. That he had already made up his mind that the Law was an obsolete and dangerous abuse, abrogated to all intents and purposes—once and for ever, I do not doubt; and writing under excitement, not to say irritation, to the Galatians, he does not hesitate to say as much; nevertheless, considering how much was at stake for the internal cordiality and union of the church, it is to me quite conceivable that uncompromising words were qualified in act by such charities as he inculcates on the Corinthians in respect to scruples about meats and days; and, that while he communicated the trenchant Apostolic decree, he did not withhold from such qualifications as we find him allowing to the same Corinthians in respect of mixed marriages and things offered to idols, etc., as would leave little value indeed for the original Apostolic authority and sanction.

Is it quite impossible that he may have submitted to the sacrifice, and shall we disallow the historical fact entirely? I think we should be rash. The record itself clearly implies that Paul acted under a compulsion; the writer is cognizant of the direction of his sympathies, and admits implicitly that, if he could have kept the Greek paternity or the uncircumcised condition secret, Paul would have done so; and *à fortiori*, that had he been able with prudence to declare openly his repugnance to the rite altogether, whether for Jew or half-Jew, he would have spoken out with alacrity and joy; but we have Paul's own admissions how far he could carry accommodation when driven by the dire compulsion of "needs must."

This anecdote is but one of the many instances by which the compiler of Acts seems willing to exemplify the serious, if not questionable concessions that even an Apostle would make—might be reduced to make with whatever repugnance, for the sake of concord; and the management that was necessary, and therefore, it is implied, allowable, in dangerous times for the sake of avoiding the machinations of enemies, or escaping a fatal catastrophe.

There is much appearance that at the edit date of Acts, the passion for inviting martyrdom, or the scrupulousness as to temporary concession or even caution for the purpose of escaping it, were rising in the Church, and that tact in slipping through such complications, is set forth by high example in place of counter-argument. The amusing comedy of the riot pacified by the town clerk of Ephesus is scarcely more relished by the writer, than the dexterity with which Paul foils now a captain, now a Sanhedrin, and now an oratorical Tertullus, and, as I suspect, on occasions like the present the very Apostles themselves; he has a manifest bias of his own to inculcate prudent, temporizing, even shifty accommodation;—does he impute actions to Paul falsely or negligently, to favour his bias? That Paul himself avows how far in action he qualified stringent principle by policy, makes this difficult to determine;— a dangerous admission, apt to be abused by smaller minds without the compelling occasion, and too often staining a party or a Church with the last disgrace,— worse than pusillanimity,—of dishonourableness.

Such, however, are the conditions of our moral being when we move for the furtherance of great, of noble enterprise, beyond the easy and the beaten track where every duty is preceptively defined and reason never called upon to arbitrate in conflicts of obligation; and when right election at last must be left to the impulse of overruling feeling which may have its full justification, but possibly far beyond the ken of the agent himself, and giving him up sometimes not merely to the imputations of the envious—that is a little thing —but to his own most unmerited remorse.

CHAPTER XI.

PAUL IN THE PRISON AT PHILIPPI.

THE CHRISTIAN APOSTLE IN ORPHIC THRACE.

"At the time of the earthquake. The earthquake is personified by a giant who has torn an opening in the earth. Behind the grate of the prison the Apostle is seen in prayer; in front are the guards. (A very small tapestry: the cartoon does not exist.)"—Kugler, part ii. cap. iv.

The above extract, for want of more detailed description and in the absence of an engraving, must be my text for what observations I can offer on the pertinence of the design. An engraving of the giant, of little value, is to be found among Rogers's engravings after the ancient masters.

It is on St. Paul's second missionary journey when he is accompanied by Silas and Timotheus, that he crosses over from Troas to Neapolis, in Macedonia, and thence passes on to the neighbouring Philippi, the chief city of its district and a colony. The privileges of a colony had been granted to the city at no very remote date by Augustus, in commemoration of his victory over Brutus and Cassius, the closing disaster of the history of republican

Rome. The region has associations of interest with a much earlier history; the portion about Philippi is a plain lying between the ranges of Mounts Hæmus and Pangæus, a large level of fertility and verdure, bounded by ranges of snowy summits and by slopes native to the blushes of the rose. In earlier geography the country belongs to Thrace—to the Thrace of the Pierian worshippers of Apollo, to the Thrace of Orpheus, minstrel and mystic priest, magian and orderer of pure and philosophical life.

The story of Paul's sojourn at Philippi, as we now read it in the Acts, is wonderful enough: neither marvels nor enhancements of marvels are spared. Still, I am disposed to think that though here, as at Lystra, we have to do with a legend, the legend is again not without some obligations to an original and authentic tradition of his movements and adventures as well as to a fund of local associations.

The account of the circumstances of the imprisonment is introduced just after the commencement of the personal narrative of Acts (xvi. 11); but the first person is already dropped, not to be resumed till the history has passed over some years, and then again at Philippi (xx. 5, 6).

Whoever this personal narrator may have been,—and I am not disposed to give him up as a mere invention, for why, then, was not the invention more sustained and definite?—whoever may have been the companion of Paul, whose personal notes seem to have been incorporated with the Acts, he in no instance commits himself as an authority for a miracle that will not explain itself easily, though at the same time he gives pretty clear indication of a relish for the miraculous when it may be come by without much risk or violence. Thus, at a later date he records Paul's visions and revelations, the recovery of Eutychus, and the not very wonderful incident of the chilled serpent at Melita. At Philippi he narrates in direct phraseology the casting out of the spirit of divination from the soothsaying damsel; this is just such an occurrence as might and does occur within the range of the most critical observers of mesmeric phenomena. Abstraction being made of all that is demoniacal—mere technicalities of the time, nothing remains either in the excited demonstrations of the girl or in her settled tranquillity after commanding and confident rebuke, that they who are curious in such matters may not hear of or be witnesses of, in any metropolis in Europe in our own day.

The narrative tells of a damsel "following Paul and us," and as the collective pronoun must include at least two persons, the presumption is in favour of the two companions named as in his company, Silas and Timotheus. That Silas was not the narrator seems proved by his being forthwith spoken of along with Paul in the third person (xvii. 10), and that in a section which there is no particular reason for supposing interpolated. We are then cast upon Timothy; but (xvii. 14–16) Timothy is joined with Silas in the third person, and he also seems to be excluded. Yet it were possible that this might be a hasty conclusion. We shall see reason to consider that the incident of the imprisonment at Philippi has been tampered with, to say the least, and that here, as in some other cases, foreign materials have been interpolated in the personal narrative. To this class of interpolations, authentic or not, I assign the section of Paul's residence at Athens, with a report of his speech there while he was waiting for Silas and Timothy. The continuity of narration would have been too grossly damaged had the introduction to the incidents (xvii. 16) run thus:—" While Paul waited for us to arrive, he delivered this address to the Athenians," and the person may have been changed accordingly, to accommodate the inserted paragraph. But no such explanation will remove the incongruity which would attend another reappearance of Timothy, on the supposition that he is the personal narrator. He is one of a list of seven of whom it is said:—" These went on before us and tarried for us at Troas, and we sailed away from Philippi after the days of the unleavened bread, and came unto them to Troas" (xx. 6). It seems to me therefore not probable, though I will not repudiate a possibility, that the personal narrator could have been Timothy. In any case I do not hesitate to disallow that either one or the other could have been the compiler of the third Gospel and of Acts. To increase the confusion, the narrator dissociates himself from Paul in the journey from Cæsarea to Jerusalem. Whoever he may have been, he is not implicated in the account of the incidents in the prison at Philippi, which came from another authority, or passed through other hands that obliterated the stamps of the original author.

Nothing is directly stated of the Apostles having extended their ministry at Philippi beyond the Jewish community and its immediate adherents, but when the masters of the divining girl, incensed at the loss of their profitable oracle, raise a disturbance, the accusation before the magistrates runs, that "these men, being Jews, are introducing discord and teaching foreign superstitions." The crowd are clamorous; the magistrates, as represented, are very pliant and very summary, have the prisoners stripped, beaten with rods and cast into prison; the next morning, as though the punishment inflicted was considered at least sufficient, came the order of release. There is no great difficulty in accepting all this as matter of fact, and we may find as little in supposing it possible that the protestations of the prisoners that they were Roman citizens, or at least one of them, were disregarded at night, but came to be considered more seriously in the morning, and were made the ground by the sufferers, of exacting from the officials something very like an apology. Unless there were some cunning policy in saying nothing about the citizenship, when it was not inquired about, we must conclude that the story lapses when it implies that the first the captains heard of it was the next morning.

By the side of this tolerably consequential and at least natural series of events, we have the supernatural series very slightly connected, which furnishes the subject of the design for the tapestry, for the lost Cartoon. "And when they (the captains) had laid many stripes upon them, they cast them into prison, charging the jailor to keep them safely: who, having received such charge, thrust them into the inner prison, and made their feet fast in the stocks. And at midnight Paul and Silas prayed, and sang hymns to God; and the prisoners listened to them. And suddenly there was a great earthquake, so that the foundations of the prison were shaken; and immediately all the doors were opened, and every one's bonds were loosed. And the jailor awaking, and seeing the prison doors open, drew his sword, and would have killed himself, believing that the prisoners had fled. But Paul cried with a loud voice, saying, Do thyself no harm: for we are all here. Then he called for light, and sprang in, and trembled, and fell before Paul and Silas. And he brought them out, and said, Sirs, what must I do to be saved? And they said, Believe on the Lord Jesus Christ, and thou shalt be saved, and thy house. And they spoke the word of the Lord unto him, and to all that were in his house. And he took them in the same hour of the night, and washed them from the stripes; and was baptized, he and all his, straightway. And bringing them into his house, he set out a table, and rejoiced, with all his house believing in God."

There is of course nothing impossible in the coincidence of an earthquake with the time of the imprisonment, and nothing in the influence it might have had upon the superstition of a jailor; but I think we should be wrong in accepting even thus much for history; and besides the implied dependence of the two events on each other, which is self-condemned, I very much doubt whether all the rest of the section just extracted is better than pure mythus from beginning to end; or if not pure, mythus heightened by conscious elaboration.

The ordinary precautions of Roman prisons might have been trusted to detain the prisoners; and only an intention to give force to a miracle required the introduction of the special charge to the jailor, the inner prison, and, even within that second and interior dungeon, the stocks. So in the tale of the miraculous jail-deliverance of Peter, precaution is heaped upon difficulty, the captive has chains on his hands, sleeps between two soldiers, keepers before the door kept the prison, and the rescue has to pass the first and second ward, and after those the iron gate opening to the city.

The secondary improbabilities are abundant and salient enough. How it came that the jailor alone slept while the prisoners were all waking, if not kept awake by the prayers and hymns of the Apostles;—why his desperation should be so hasty as to proceed to the extremity of suicide before making any examination whatever;—how Paul in the dark could have answered for the presence of the other prisoners as well as himself, or have known what the jailor was about with his sword;—what could have been the nature and value of the belief in the Lord Jesus Christ which the jailor had an opportunity of entertaining between the interval of midnight earthquake and little beyond midnight bath and meal;—what the value for the jailor, and what for his household whose belief is either taken for granted by Paul as following the master's, or is claimed as a bye-stipulation that a little improves a bargain;—how the jailor reconciled it with his responsibility and the special charge, to transfer his prisoners from the cells of the public prison into his own house, adjoining though it might be,—all these are questions which involve an army of improbabilities. History the most veracious is no doubt made up of improbabilities, and historical truth is never obtainable by a mere balance of probabilities in the absence of positive evidence which no improbability can discredit. The possibility might therefore be admitted that some of these unlikely details are founded on fact, or easily might have been; but we are bound no point beyond. The earthquake is represented as a miraculous interposition; the circumstances that precede it are manifestly adjusted to give relief and effect to the deliverance; and so, for the incidents that follow, we may with confidence declare that, whether by fiction or by colouring, they are combined for the purpose of giving lustre to the characters and function of the Apostles, to illustrate their dignity and the spontaneous vigour with which the Gospel that they preached, won upon the veneration of even the class to which the jailor would belong, and carried over whole households suddenly and enthusiastically to the Church.

Besides the parallel to the delivery of Peter from the prison of Herod, this Philippian incident has certain points of resemblance to the conversion of the centurion Cornelius, the baptism of himself and his household, and that implied entertainment by him of his Jewish converter which, it is related, opened the question of the relation of Jewish ceremonialism and Gentile conversion, in the first instance.

Of these parallel deliverances, who shall say which is the earliest in date,—which lent, and which was the borrower of characteristic inventions? There may have been intermediate legends and forms of legend that are now lost,—who shall say? In respect of marvellousness there is really not much to choose between the two stories; but we may justly inquire into the cause of the difference of the machinery,—how came another narrator, or the same, to employ a natural agency in one case, a spiritual in the other, when in neither was there any scruple as to economizing the supernatural? Why, when the scene was at Philippi, was it elected or suggested to expend an earthquake for the same service for which at Jerusalem it was preferred to detail an angel? Does the difference imply that the delivery of Peter is more directly from a Hebrew source, or that at least a certain feeling of local keeping and poetical propriety made an angel of the Lord a very plausible agency in Judæa, and above all at Jerusalem, but nothing less than an incongruous intrusion elsewhere?

In point of fact, I have no doubt that a like sense of local propriety governed the introduction of the earthquake of Macedonia. We have seen that the same spirit of legend that brought angels into play in Judæa, caught up the local mythology of Lycaonia,—Pagan though it might be,—to elaborate marvels for Paul and Barnabas at Lystra; and even so again at Philippi, not much perspicacity, and only so much candour as ought to be matter of course, are required to detect or identify in the miracle there, the modified forms of old local fabulous associations. The key to the mystery is in the notice that the earthquake takes place with all the implication of an effect following a cause,—upon the fettered Paul and Silas praying and singing hymns to God, while all the prisoners listen. We do not meet elsewhere in Acts with notice of the singing of hymns as part of usual devotional exercise; and the sudden and supernatural effect that ensues in this instance transforms the hymn into something of the speciality of an incantation. Even so; we are now in the primitive region of Orpheus, the ancient reputed author of a fund of holy and mystic hymns, and had Pausanias fortunately included this tract of Thrace in his description of Greece from personal visit, we should probably have found among his gleanings, from rites and monuments, from administrators of local sanctities and sanctuaries, that traditions from primitive times still lived on here, as in Attica or in Bœotia, unsuperseded by Roman encroachments or by the elegant transformations of the refined age of Greek poetry. The lyre,—the hymns of Orpheus, were fabled to have drawn not only savage men and animals, and even trees, but rocks themselves obeyed its influence (Apollodorus), just as at the sound of the lyre of Amphion the rocks rolled together and fitted themselves in even piles to form the walls of Thebes. Pausanias has a strange story to tell of a disastrous inundation which befell, in agreement with a prediction, when the bones of Orpheus were exposed to the sun. This condition he relates to have occurred when his monument was overturned,—an accident which was due to the song of a shepherd, who, as he slept reclining against it, was inspired by song, and gathered round him such an eager crowd, that their pressure overthrew the fatal basis. This legend is itself probably very corrupt. It reads as if originally the fall of the monument and urn must in some way have been due to the inspired song, and an inspired singer with closed eyes suggests a Thamyris or a Homer,—a blind minstrel; and we ask, is not the legend one of the same class as that which threatened that Bacon's mansion would fall when a greater than he should pass by it?

However, for our present purpose we are only concerned with the traditional influence of the song of

Orpheus over even unorganized nature,—the influence that was likely enough to be in favour in the confines of Mount Pangæus, rich in mines and active in mining operations:—

> Αὐτὰρ τόν γ' ἐνέπουσιν ἀτειρέας οὔρεσι πέτρας
> Θέλξαι δοιδάων ἐνοπῇ ποταμῶν τε ῥέεθρα.
> <div align="right">APOLLON., <i>Argon.</i> i.</div>

The song of Paul to the true God was thus vindicated as at least equivalent to the chant of Orpheus upon his own ground; it moved the subterranean powers no less; no less it humanized the severe and even the depraved; and thus is explained the import of the otherwise enigmatical and irrelevant notice that, as the divine hymn went on, the prisoners listened, and even when their prison was opened remained as spell-bound. The circle of entranced prisoners is the equivalent of the circle of listening emblems of ferocity, amidst which Orpheus is so frequently represented in ancient poetry and art:—

> "Sylvestres homines sacer interpresque Deorum
> Cædibus et victu fœdo deterruit Orpheus;
> Dictus ob hoc lenire tigres, rapidosque leones."
> <div align="right">HORAT., <i>Ars Poet.</i></div>

The miraculous release from chains is also an Orphic incident; it is among the manifestations of divinity of Orphic Dionysus in the Bacchæ of Euripides. (Compare also the Orphic incantation that promises to make the torch automatous.—Eurip. Cyclops, 639.)

Even the midnight hour, the darkness, the demand of a light by the astonished jailor, seem not to be without mythic root in the suggestive story of the minstrel who carried harmony down to the shadows of the underworld, who charmed the guards of the great prison-house, and suspended the torments of the condemned. I perceive even reason to suspect that the recovery of Eurydice by Orpheus must have been represented in some forms of the legend as exacted rather than solicited, and Pluto and Persephone were probably as importunate to the intruder to withdraw,—to take his Eurydice and go, as the Duumvirs of Philippi are represented to have been to Paul and Silas,—were therefore represented to have been,—to accept an apology and depart:—

> "Quod si fata negant veniam pro conjuge, certum est
> Nolle redire mihi." OVID, *Metam.* x. 38, 39.

Even the previous distinctly personal narrative is not without certain appearance of Orphic association. Thracian Orpheus, who was believed to have originated religious initiation (Paus. ix. 30), purification from sinful deeds, the healing of diseases, and the averting of divine anger, seems to reappear in the teacher who promises redemption, who threatens with a futurity of punishments only too like the Orphic hell, who draws after him crowds, and heals and remedies the defects of body and of mind. The description is particularly lively of the enthusiastic girl who follows on the heels of the Apostle exclaiming, until he turns round suddenly and rebukes and expels the divining devil that did but tell the truth. The picture calls up at least the image of the shade of Eurydice following the trace of the great master of love, theology, and song, until he turns, in this case for himself too soon, and the charm is at an end.

How much of all this is coincidence, merest casualty; how much is due to the habit of mythical exposition having developed illstarred ingenuity in recognizing false analogies, in making legible inscriptions out of figures in sand, the writing of the wanton winds,—I am not prepared to decide positively. I am content here to originate a speculative view, and to record a strong opinion that it will prove not destitute of fact for its foundation.

I refer to Lobeck, Aglaophamus, p. 295 f., for citations respecting the prevalence of Bacchic or Orphic orgiasms among the women of this region from earliest times.

To Orpheus, says Creuzer, from the spirit of many so-called Orphic verses, a certain Christianity was ascribed, and his lyre was employed as a symbol of the might of the Gospel. He refers to Aringhi, 'Roma Subterranea,' t. 11. p. 296 *seq.*; also to Fr. Munter, 'Sinnbilder der alten Christen,' s. 89, taf. 111. p. 64.

The transference of association was in truth very natural and easy,—how much so I have indicated in an essay on the paintings of Polygnotus in the Lesche at Delphi, where Orpheus was painted harping to heroes in the underworld. Orphic marvels, Orphic rule of life and the Orphic scriptures in which it was inculcated, the descent of the hero into hell for the redemption of Eurydice, all furnished characteristics that were readily seized on. It seems clear that much that was lofty and refined, and certainly much that was subtle in systems of theology and severe in morals, had taken fixed association about the name of Orpheus in the later days of Paganism. Hence the importance ascribed to the name and the school it represents by such writers as Proclus and Porphyry and Plotinus, in their endeavour to elaborate a system of faith and morals that should save the world from the infatuations that were clustering about Christianity in their time.

How readily parallel associations intertwine in the poetical and enthusiastic imagination may be illustrated here from the application of the fable of Orpheus by an adherent of revived Platonism in Italy,—Lorenzo de' Medici:—

SONETTO.

"Fugiendo Loth con la sua famiglia
La città, ch' arse per divin giuditio;
Guardando indietro, et visto el gran supplitio,
La donna immobil forma di sal piglia.

Tu hai fuggito, et è gran maraviglia,
La città, ch' arde sempre in ogni vitio;
Sappi, anima gentil, che 'l tuo offitio
E non voltare a lei giammai le ciglia.

Per ritrovarti il buon pastore eterno
Lascia el greggie, o smarrita pecorella,
Truovati, e lieto in braccio ti riporta.

Perse Euridice Orfeo già in sulla porta
Libera quasi, per voltarsi a quella;
Però non ti voltar più allo inferno."

Otto Venius seems to have had this sonnet in his mind, though it is not cited in his text, in one of the designs of his 'Emblemata Divini Amoris.' Here the little damsel that personifies the soul hastens over a causeway from a city that is seen in the background overwhelmed with fiery rain from heaven. She is supported and encouraged by Divine Love,—the Eros with bow and quiver of Greek mythology, and with the halo of the Saviour, with whom he is identified throughout. The Soul bears a bough, reminiscent of the charm of golden twig that carries Æneas safely past Cerberus, and the shadows of the pair falling behind them are

seen on the ground transfigured to a pair of furies watchful with snaky hair and with snakes in their hands, —the expectant fiends that wait in hopes of a second lost Eurydice. Orpheus and Eurydice contribute, with Lot and his wife, with Æneas and the Sybil, to the symbolism of the dangers of the soul and its rescue by divine love,—love of which the most comprehensive personification is carried up as to its home, to the Pieria and the Thrace of Orpheus. It is but frigid entertainment when, after these imaginings, we are referred by Venius (p. 56) to a homily of Chrysostom for the moral that, as the shadow is constant to the body, so in this world is the persecution of Satanas; or when we find our own way to an antithetical couplet of Pope,—

"Envy does merit like its shade pursue,
But, like the shadow, proves the substance true."

Thus far, then, have we wandered away.

I have no proof that Rafael had even a suspicion of the pertinence of this Philippian subject of the tapestry, to Orphic legend; at the same time I should not be at all surprised to find that it had been discerned by the Platonic Academy, and was thus on the ready highway to reach the friend of Castiglione. Certainly it is remarkable that precisely in this design he should have introduced a personification,—a giant,—an earth-brood, that owns so direct a relation to heathen mythology, and is so utterly alien to Jewish. The coincidence warns that we may not be yet at an end of our pictorial analysis.

There is indeed another type among the Orphic legends

of the environs of Philippi, that in some respects more exactly corresponds with Paul praying, singing, and influencing elemental powers, though bound with chains and stocked. This is found in the tale of Silenus, himself a son of earth, who was captured by Midas, son of Gordieus, in the rose-gardens of Mount Pangæus, and sang in his bonds prophetically of another world, of the commencement of all things, of the preferableness of death to life. (Creuzer, Symbolik and references; Herodot. viii.; Virgil, Ecl. vi. etc.)

For the origin of some other very circumstantially narrated incidents we have to turn, not to primitive tradition, but to the pages of all but contemporary Roman history. We might be disposed to suspect that the jailor, of whom it is told that he drew his sword to kill himself, had no other intention with his weapon than to threaten or to slay an escaping prisoner,—the other version being mere hasty assumption. But we cannot safely venture even so far in historical concession in a case where so much is manifestly convicted mythology. We may more justly pause upon the coincidence with the self-slaughter of Brutus and Cassius, last of the Romans, on this very plain of Philippi. The motives that present themselves in the suicide of Cassius are particular characteristics in the incident of Acts. It was in premature and mistaken despair that he closed his career "in the high Roman fashion." He misconstrues the course of his friend and messenger Titinius, misinterprets and interchanges the signs of his captivity or freedom, and turns to self-sought death in the agony of sudden grief.

So positively does the narrative of the planting of

the Gospel at Philippi relish of the place, its most subtle poetry and most tragic prose.

The picture, then, taken by description, stands as a link between Christianity as originally Jewish and Asiatic, and now, for the first time and expressively, European. In the peculiarity of its treatment I am disposed to regard it as a specific enunciation of that sympathy between moral and physical convulsions, which, as a belief at least, has had no little force in every historic crisis and catastrophe. "The stars in their courses fought against Sisera." The history of the decline and fall of the Roman Empire, catalogues stages of physical as well as moral decline; what might not the history of Europe have been but for the storm that damaged the Armada; for the dearth in France before the Revolution; for the unusual severity of the winter when Napoleon invaded Russia?

CHAPTER XII.

PAUL PREACHING AT ATHENS.

I. THE CARTOON OF PAUL PREACHING AT ATHENS.—
II. CHRISTIAN PROMISE AND GREEK CULTURE.—III. THE
HARMONY OF THE REVERENTIAL AND THE RIGHTLY
REASONABLE.

I. THE CARTOON OF PAUL PREACHING AT ATHENS.

IN the scene of Paul preaching on the Areopagus at Athens before groups of philosophers, Rafael found the subject for his last Cartoon, or rather tapestry,—the close of the Biblical series of the Sistine Chapel,—the expressive type of the crisis in the history of Christianity, when it at last confronted the highest intellectual culture previously attained by man, and avouched its ability to hold its own. The Cartoon, like the history, does not hesitate to aver, that whatever secondary points of agreement there might be between the new religion and the old philosophies in certain principles, the spirit and the promises of the two were very positively in opposition. Philosophy, in the condition that it had now become reduced to,—at least is represented to have become reduced to,—in the Roman empire, is declared to be out of sympathy with Christ, and more likely to come off worsted in a conflict than to unite in common cause. The narrative in Acts which supplies the theme, sets forth enthusiasm, a spirit of devotion and enlarged philanthropy on one side, in contrast, on the other, to gossiping disputation, curious subtlety, and general coldness or contempt for devout awe as a motive.

As Rafael has treated the subject, he has asserted for the Christianity represented by Paul, a willingness to be tested, and a claim to be admitted under the strictest examination that intellectual subtlety can subject it to. The Paul of Rafael represents Christianity; but not, therefore, the dogmatic form of Christianity that criticism may ultimately bring forth as proper to the great Apostle. Still less is the assertion made in favour of any later historical symbolon or formula, of council or of papacy; much, indeed, the reverse. Paul, as we see him stand on the steps of the Areopagus in the picture, is the very emblem of Religion admitting the obligation to accept the challenge of Philosophy. We may have our doubts how far the best phase of ancient philosophy is fairly represented in the audience as described; we may doubt as justly how far the special representation of Christianity put in, will hold good for very moderate examination; nay, very serious doubts must be entertained how far the entire narrative in Acts, incident and speech together, can be accepted as explicit history. Fortunately, however, these uncertainties do not affect the expressive value of the picture; and the contrast it embodies, the characteristics it defines, are transcendental in respect of all history; while the fact that Rafael did so embody and define them is an historical fact for his own time, itself one of the most interesting epochs of intellectual and religious history.

The story of the Cartoon is thus read in the Acts of the Apostles:—

"Now while Paul waited for them—Silas and Timothy—at Athens, his spirit was stirred in him, when he saw the city given to idolatry. Therefore disputed he in the synagogue with the Jews, and with the devout persons, and in the agora daily with them that met him. And some of the Epicurean and Stoic philosophers encountered him. And some said, What will this babbler say? and others, He seemeth to be a setter forth of strange demons: because he preached to them the gospel of Jesus, and of the resurrection. And they took him, and brought him to the Areopagus, saying, May we know what this new doctrine, whereof thou speakest, is? for thou bringest certain strange things to our ears: we would know therefore what these things mean. For all the Athenians and the strangers that sojourned there spent their time in nothing else, but to tell and hear something new. And Paul stood in the midst of the Areopagus, and said, etc.

... "And the times of this ignorance God overlooked; but now commandeth all men everywhere to repent: because he hath appointed a day, in which he is about to judge the world in righteousness by a man whom he hath ordained; having given assurance to all men in raising him from the dead. And when they heard of the resurrection of the dead, some mocked: and others said, We will hear thee again about this. Thus Paul departed from among them. But some men clave to him, and believed: among whom was Dionysius the Areopagite, and a woman named Damaris, and others with them."

The scene of the picture is an open space amidst temples and majestic buildings; the statue of Mars on a basis, as an armed warrior, indicates the god of the precinct. To him also seems to belong the circular temple, the door of which he faces: in the niches under the peristyle we see one statue bearing a buckler; another seems to wear the robe and laurel wreath of military triumph; the third appears to be Aphrodite, the paramour of the soldier-god. Statue and architecture alike are of Roman taste and type;—the purer models of the Greek were still to be recovered.

The Apostle stands at the angle of a platform raised above the general level by four stately steps. He has advanced quite to the edge in his eagerness. Impressiveness and dignity breathe from the air of the head, and the composed energy of the entire figure, as with arms extended before him, and hands raised above the level of his head, with a lively force well conveyed by the drawn folds of his sleeve, he seems at this moment to be insisting upon the grand crowning topic of the resurrection. The figure is usually spoken of as an adaptation of a figure by Masaccio, to which, like the Paul in the Cartoon of Elymas, it certainly bears much resemblance. But in each case the force and the definition of expression belong to Rafael. Here, as in the other Cartoon, the face of Paul is in shade; and here also again, and in a still more marked manner, the erectness of the figure is defined by contrast with lines upon the ground, directly at right angles to it.

The back of the statue is turned to the scene of the

sermon; the right arm and the grasped spear are extended towards it, but the face averted looks over the shield another way. There is a certain symbolical antithesis in the lifted right arm of the immobile brazen figure, to the arms of Paul instinct with life, and stretching forth against it in the warmth of his denunciations of idolatry. The remoteness of the statue in the background reduces the contrast to that latent indefiniteness that precludes the offensiveness of a cold conceit.

Intermediate, and in most absolute contrast to Paul, stands the Epicurean philosopher, as erect as Paul himself; but while perfectly attentive, perfectly composed, he takes in the discourse, listening with placid, uncontracted brow; and with arms hanging in tranquillity below the undisturbed folds of a graceful and somewhat delicate robe, he watches the exhorting gestures of the preacher with some of the interest of curiosity, supported by the polite indulgence of a gentleman.

The quietness of his expression is heightened by contrast with the listener close behind him on the left, who, with bent brows and eyes towards the ground, presses his left fore-finger to his lips with the signs less of perplexity of thought than of being stung inwardly by a self-reproach,—by a conviction, if not an alarm of conscience,—a smitten voluptuary. On the other side again of the philosopher of stronger nerve or easier habit, we see behind two youthful curled and pretty-favoured heads,—scholars who are following him along the primrose paths of the garden. Both look towards the new teacher askance,—one with an expression of pert dislike, and one with flippancy.

From the Epicurean group, either way, the circle of

hearers is continued by a group of Stoic philosophers on the right; and, on the left, by a seated knot of eager disputants, whom we shall see reason to regard as Academics. Both these groups give evidence of being deeply affected by the intellectual drift of the discourse, but with a difference that is seen in their contrasted manifestations.

One of the Stoic philosophers props his chin upon his two hands as they rest upon the cross-head of his staff, while he bends his aged, but still piercing glance upon the Apostle. The other has folded his arms in his cloak, and with nearly closed eyes, and chin upon his breast, has the air of abstracting his attention from all but the one subject that tasks his whole powers,— the very impersonation of the obscurity that, no less than dignity, was a leading characteristic of all the writings of Chrysippus. This, the second, is the much more intellectual head and countenance; his older companion we might even be-inclined to identify as the typical Cynic—"quem duplici panno patientia velat" (Hor. Ep. I. xvii. 25. I refer to the note of Orellius on this passage for illustrative citations; Diogenes Laertius, vi. 22, etc.) His dress seems almost sordid, as well as scanty, compared with that of the Epicurean; and the staff was, with a scrip, the ensign of the Cynic. At the same time, he may be but the representative of the Cynical side of Stoicism; the staff is as frequently assigned to Stoic as to Cynic,—

> "Vellunt tibi barbam
> Lascivi pueri, quos tu nisi *fuste* coerces,
> Urgeris turbâ circum te stante, miserque
> Rumperis et *latras*, magnorum maxime regum."
>
> Hor. *Serm.* 1, iii. 135.

Behind these also are to be seen a pair of pupils,—a mighty contrast to the students who have elected Epicurus for their guide. Their physiognomies are significant of steadfast earnestness—the temper that befits the haunters of the Portico,—the admirers of the noblest ideal of human character the world has seen:

> "Secta fuit servare modum, finemque tueri,
> Naturamque sequi, vitamque impendere vero,
> Nec sibi sed toti genitum se credere mundo."

And yet, at the same time, there is a taint of coxcombry even here; and in the set uniformity of the pose of the heads, the fixed brows, the settled drapery, we see hints of that affectation of the school, which offered so fair a mark at this very date to the shafts of Lucian.

There is something in their formality beyond the ordinary preparations expected from a listener,—

> "Audire atque togam jubeo componere" ....
> Hor. *Serm.* 2, iii. 77.

Very different is the genius of the group of seated listeners and debaters. Here, methinks, we see true successors of the groups of mingled elders and youths that clustered around Socrates in eager and equal vivacity, as he went about upon his self-imposed mission to Piræus or agora. Here the younger men are seated regardlessly in the front; and while one turns his head to listen to the discussion of his seniors behind him, another takes part in it uninvited, but unchecked as without hesitation, and is pointing with his left hand towards Paul, while declaring, if not vociferating, his sentiments towards the right.

Of the seniors, one of the chief is enforcing his reasoning by much the same expressive gesture that is assigned to Socrates in the fresco of the School of Athens. He presses the index finger of his left hand to the thumb of the right, as if telling off the stages of a syllogism, or marking how a concession already reserved affects of necessity the conclusions that have been deduced from other premises; his opponent lends an ear to the representation with an air of not unwilling candour; and the third head, visible between the two, is inclined towards him with all the appearance of an appeal, to the effect that the logical necessity, as illustrated, cannot in fairness be declined.

Immediately above the pointing hand of the young man is the head of another youth, who is gazing upon the Apostle, and, as I interpret, with an expression of profoundest awe, which makes him quite unconscious of the discussion going on so near to him; or is the turn of his head given by the motive to catch what the Apostle is saying, by averting his ear from the Babel beside him? This head, remote as it is, is so relieved upon an illuminated background, and so placed, as to be highly conspicuous; and it is of great importance in the ordination of expression. In its terminal position it rounds off the composition, and answers there to the effect at the other extremity of the hemicycle, of the two figures we have yet to observe upon. These are the nearest of all to the plane of the picture, and represent the leading converts, Dionysius the Areopagite, and the woman named Damaris. Their faces beam with conviction, happiness, and joy. The right hand of Damaris, it will be seen, appears below her left arm, retaining her drapery; the arms and hands of Dionysius are beautifully expressive, and gain and give force by contrast to those of Paul. He appears to be ascending the steps; his raised foot would come upon the lowest, or fourth.

There only remain to notice the figures behind the Apostle. Of these, the standing bearded figure in shadow seems to be a Jew,—a great man in the synagogue; he rests his hands on the top of his stick, but appears to draw up his head as if with some recoil from the tenor of the doctrine at the point it has now arrived at. His aspect is that of a man of intellectual capacity, of acquirements,—is it fanciful to say, of learning rather than of investigation and invention, and all dominated by jealousy and pride?

If the Jew draws himself up as the direction of Paul's teaching declares itself, the bulky listener who stands next to him draws back with different, but equally decisive, indications of distaste. He is a fellow of gross habit of body, and girt in vulgar costume significant of commonplace and coarse occupations. His hair is hidden by a cap—perhaps nightcap—which looks as though donned for some protection among dirty work; his slouch paunch is bestowed in a vest retained by the comfortable, but not dignified, invention of a row of buttons,—an acknowledgment of obligation to the mechanical that would be incongruous in the array of a philosopher. His cloak is crossed shawlwise over his shoulders, and kilted skirts leave his limbs unimpeded for the bustle of handicraft, or the general hurry-scurry of business. Lastly, we see the two weighted ends of a sash girdle that is twisted round his middle, and his fat left hand clutching the knot of it with instinctive feeling. The girdle is the purse of this pursy drysalter;

and while what intellectual powers and generous sympathies he has that are competent for such employment, are hovering about the topics touched on by the preacher, he keeps his hand upon a gripe of the coined metal, that a positive sensation may save him from drifting into ideology, may remind him to hold hard by what he is resolute to accept for life as the main chance. He handles his money as if from a fear that others may be looking after it, while he is for once attending to an enthusiast; or as if the eloquence itself might charm his money from his pocket, or the spiritual exhortation end in a demand for money, which he does not intend to part with. He has crept out of his hole—shop or mart, manufactory or counting-house—or has been caught on his way thither; he will be back again there in half an hour, convinced that his time has been wasted for any purpose that need concern a man of business, and will probably wonder at the regard bestowed upon the movement by men whom he knows to be quite as keen and quite as selfish as himself, but whose very selfishness, in virtue of the larger scope on which the keenness is employed, makes the man of business into the man of public business.

This figure is thrown still deeper and more entirely into shade than the Rabbi; had a gleam of bright light been accorded to him, his presence would have marred the sentiment of the entire picture, instead of contributing, as it now does, the last relief,—town as complementary of gown; the most sordid aspect of this world looking in upon the enthusiastic forewarnings of the next.

The uncongenial spirit of these two figures—the

chapman and the Rabbi—brings into prominent effect the sympathetic phase of the third of the group. He is seated on the edge of the same step on which Paul stands, and appears to me intended for his disciple and companion. In the Mantuan tapestry his devout expression is very manifest, and very decided. I apprehend that Rafael intended him for Luke,—as the accepted writer and reporter of the Acts of the Apostles. The speech, according to the narrative, was made while Paul was waiting at Athens for Timothy and Silas; but the terms of the narrative, and the very record of the speech, would be taken as implying that he was not absolutely alone.

In Luke we have the one figure in the composition, to whom the drift and detail of the discourse was not a novelty. His looks are directed, not to Paul, but to Paul's audience; his right hand is between his left elbow and knee, and his attitude contracted, but easy; and inclining in the direction of his master and his master's words, gains force from opposition of the two erect figures beyond him. He partly rests his chin on the thumb of his left hand, and partly seems to press the closed hand against his lips; while his eyes glance, and his brows are arched with some semblance of excitement. Do we not see, indeed, the gesture of a sympathetic listener, who knows that the speaker is advancing upon the very crisis of his argument, which is to decide whether he will carry his audience safely over, or part company with them for ever? Anxiety in such case comes to its crisis also: the ally is somewhat disposed to be apprehensive of the rashness of the orator, and presses his clenched hand against his own lips in the fear that a premature, an inconsidered, a hasty word may, at a moment, undo all the labour of preparation. A certain degree of sacred confidence qualifies the trepidation in this case; but the trepidation, I believe, exists no less.

How many hundreds of proselytizing preachers and missionaries in modern times have drawn their inspiration and braced their energies from the accounts of the labours, the success, the policy of Paul, as set forth in the Acts of the Apostles! This fact will account for many coincidences in practice; but if a Methodist at the present day does not address a group of idlers on a common without having one or two mute companions standing behind him to support him, it is as much by natural suggestion of the situation as with any view to run parallel with Paul, Timothy, and Silas. As a point of natural suggestion it is taken up by Rafael, and he even diverges from the most literal implication of the text to satisfy the requirement of a sympathizer, and of an example of respectful attention and sympathy.

Two figures, at considerable distance, engaged in lively argument even as they walk, may be called Peripatetics if we please, or be taken simply as furthering the illustration how talk pervaded the very atmosphere of Athens.

The steps, at the edge of which Paul is standing, seem to be those of a platform, so treated architecturally as to give special dignity to the central summit of Mars Hill, and assist the suggestion, by the very formality of their treatment, that the Areopagus was a title as much symbolical as descriptive, and conveyed the idea of an institution, of a moral even more distinctly than of a natural elevation.

I have already spoken of the dignity of the figure of Paul; there is interest in observing the artistic resources—and we may almost say stratagems—by which it is enhanced. Dionysius and Damaris are nearer to the spectator, and therefore larger in scale, upon the picture; but, besides the contraction of their attitudes, the whole of their figures is not included within the picture, and thus Paul retains the distinction of being the highest fully-displayed figure in the composition. We shall recognize the value of this distinction if we notice how it is observed, and with what effect, in the other Cartoons. In the Miracle at the Beautiful Gate we have complete view of the erect Peter, while John is subordinated by being partly covered by the cripple. The second cripple and the arm of the Levite come in front of the tripping mother with her infant, as, although somewhat more remote, her graceful stature would have introduced a dangerous competition. In the Blinding of Elymas, the crouching Magus is of course no match for the commanding prophet over against him.

In the Sacrifice at Lystra, the figure of Paul alone of the figures that stand erect is seen from head to foot, without any other object or figure partially interposing. At either end of the picture a figure is introduced nearer to the spectator, but, as in the case of the Areopagite, each of them is stooping, and of each a portion is without the limits of the picture.

In the Cartoon of the Destruction of Ananias, numerous and very important figures are much nearer to the spectator than the protagonist Peter; but Peter, besides his central position, has alone the advantage of the free display of his full height: even his coadjutor, who points to heaven, and seems almost as direct an agent of wrath as himself, is sufficiently kept down by the unceremonious interference with his figure, of the post and rail of the dais.

In the Delivery of the Keys, other figures besides the Saviour are seen erect and uninterfered with—as Thomas and John; and the due subordination is here obtained, apart from distribution of light and all-important expression, by presenting them only in profile.

In the Calling of Peter this rule of subordination deserts us. The design comprises but few figures, and the distribution of light, the indication of personages by conspicuous attributes, the preferential position, and the expression which touches here the limits of all that is possible in art, are quite sufficient to give the superiority to Peter, kneeling and half-hidden though he be, above the more central and more entirely displayed Andrew.

Wonderful ingenuity seems to me to be displayed in the adjustment of the immediate background of architectural details, which relieve the head and expressive hands of the Apostle at Athens. The spring of the unfinished arch, with its interrupted voussoir, gives emphasis to the living lift of the arms of Paul; and these, by their direction, cross and effectually dominate the vertical lines of the architecture. The marked lines of the steps and inlaid pavement, at right angles to the erect preacher but less short than his height, contribute no little to the force of his elevation.

The light of the high sun shines upon the back of Paul, and thus gives full illumination to the fronts and faces of the audience opposite to him. The expression of his own face is fully displayed by his profile falling well defined against the illuminated portion of the sleeve of his right arm. The continued sharp dark outline, of which, as I have noticed before, Rafael constantly avails himself once in a composition, falls here to the front outline of Paul's robe and lifted arm. The general management of the light and shade—the grouping of the figures from consideration of effects of light and shade,—is managed with the seeming simplicity of nature, with all the refined dexterity of subtlest art.

The simplest point of management of all, for gaining effects of distance and distinctness among groups, is resorted to without any dissembling affectation. All the figures are lighted from the same side; but by disposing or viewing them obliquely, the shadowed side of one may be relieved upon the brightened side of that beyond, and *vice versâ*. Thus the back of Dionysius stands off from the robe of Damaris, and by the opposite effect his illuminated features are happily set forth by the dark shadow they fall against, of the robe of the musing Stoic. The right side of the second Stoic is defined upon the left-hand shadow of the Epicurean, and so on. The tameness of repetition is avoided by the blending of the lights on the fronts of the pair of Stoics, where the less marked distinctness required is gained by colour and tone; and then, again, by the arms and hands of Dionysius breaking the lights of their background. Again, in the group of seated debaters very varied effects of light and shadow are introduced,—are caused, we might more properly say, by their varied positions. The light passing through the intervals of the group gives defining background; and each of the front figures from its position casts a degree of shadow upon itself. Linear and aerial perspective co-operate with these adjustments, and give particular value to figures which, like Dionysius and Paul, are relieved upon background and figures of which various portions are at very various degrees of remoteness.

What need is there to notice how the tranquil curves of the drapery of Paul's companion, the curves and eddies of that of the Academic group of debaters, and the lively agitation of the converts, lifting head and hand and limb in sympathy with the doctrine, relieve the erect lines and lights of the preacher and his listeners, and of the columns and arcades around them?

The circular plan of the Temple of Mars is sympathetic with the hemicycle on which the congregation has arranged itself.

The moral triumph of pictorial harmony is achieved by the invention of expressions, gestures, and combined or responsive actions characteristic of the occasion, and by the disposing of them with such cunning naturalness that each seems to fall into its place spontaneously; while each attains its own acme of expressiveness by enhancing that of its immediate neighbour first, and thence, of all.

And now of these matters sufficient.

II. THE CHRISTIAN PROMISE AND GREEK CULTURE.

As regards the general sentiment of the subject of Paul preaching at Athens, Rafael has allowed himself to quit the rigidly historical, as it may be held to stand in the Acts, for the sake of rising to the ideal. The leaders of the Epicureans and Stoics who attend him show no indications of an open sneer, or of politely waving him and his doctrine aside for that future hearing which in such case never comes. Something of this disposition is expressed in the Epicurean students; but that is all, and they are quite subordinate.

The philosophers are represented as candid enough to continue to listen, and the discourse of Paul is favourably represented as of a nature not only to detain and interest them, but to reduce them to difficulty, if not to nonplus.

Rafael chose therefore, let us say, to avail himself of this subject to give a typical embodiment of the first confronting of Greek philosophy taken at its best, with ideal Christianity.

How, then, is such a design, and such execution of it, borne out by sufficient justification? Or shall we find it necessary to admit that, in the superiority claimed for the doctrine of Christianity, we have only to recognize the narrow egotism of a sectary,—we have but the lion conqueror of the man, painted as might be expected when the inferior animal wields the brush.

What was contributed to the world by the Christianity of Paul, what was being contributed, or remained still capable of being contributed, to the world by Christianity in the time of Rafael, that will vindicate him for assigning such dignity to it in comparison with the Greek philosophies?

These questions it will be time to consider when we have disposed of the consideration of the matter of fact of the Athenian discourse, as we read it in the extract from Acts already given.

The narrative indeed, as it stands, is quite as little consistent with itself as any representation of Rafael can be with any part of it. Yet I once thought there was a confirmation of literal exactness in a point that does not at first seem to promise it. The philosophers have their interest shocked or cooled by the doctrine of the resurrection; and this was natural enough, for the resurrection, as conceived by Paul; though otherwise the conception of a future life, was familiar to all the schools, and with some a favourite. What Paul's exposition of the doctrine might have been, we read in the unquestioned Epistle to the Corinthians,—the coming of Jesus in the clouds, the signal trump, the revival of the dead with bodies superior to decay, the substitution of spiritual bodies in place of the material, for the living,— for Paul himself and for his contemporaries, so many of his listeners who believed. Certainly we must ascribe small blame to the Athenians, if they were treated to the subject-matter of these chapters, and demurred to accept either the logic or the revelation. A still more detailed, but scarcely a grosser representation of the last day, is given in the Epistle to the Thessalonians; and the supposition that this was written by Paul from Athens gave some confirmation to the tenor of his Athenian speech, and the peculiar effect it is stated to have produced. This point, however, must stand over; there are more difficulties than Paley saw, or chose to see, in the date of the Epistle; and in the appreciation of some it has become more than questionable,—not only whether Paul addressed the letter from Athens, but whether he ever wrote it at all,—whether it is not altogether a forgery; I may say that, for myself, I retain confidence in its authenticity.

After what we have already seen of the casualties by which the text and composition of the Acts of the Apostles have suffered, we must be open, if not prepared, for finding that the section now before us has its own peculiar difficulties. It is, in truth, inconsecutive enough. The first incongruity it presents may perhaps be got over by a little liberality in translation. Let us consent to read,—" The spirit of Paul, as he waits at Athens for his companions, is excited by the appearance of the city crowded with idols; preaching therefore in the synagogue to the Jews and devout men (on the Sabbaths, is implied) he discoursed also on all the other days of the week in the agora with whomsoever he found occasion." If the speech had followed immediately upon this, it would have been pertinent enough, for its main argument is directed against idols, and temples, and worship by ceremonies and sacrifice. And thus, probably, it did follow originally; and the signs of working up the narrative into a scene are salient in the introduction of Stoic and Epicurean philosophers as inviting the discourse which altogether misses or misrepresents their case; no worshippers of idols they in the gross sense implied, or, indeed, in any sense whatever. In the grouped masters of Athenian wisdom, in the set of scene on the Areopagus, in a certain correspondence between the notion that Jesus and Anastasis were foreign divinities—nothing less is implied by the Greek,—with the charge that was fatal to the greatest Athenian philosopher Socrates, and in the Demosthenic opening, "Ye

men of Athens,"—in all this, methinks, I trace the hand
of the master who hits off the town clerk of Ephesus
with such character and effect, and who certainly was
skilful in the distribution of materials, whatever the
amount of criticism or of conscience he employed in
the collection of them. In the present case, I do not
hesitate to assent to those who find in the traditional
discipleship of Dionysius the Areopagite, the suggestive and sole source of the tradition that placed Paul as
a preacher on the Areopagus. Here, therefore, as at
Lystra,—here, therefore, as at Philippi, local pagan
myths blended with Christian local traditions; and even
the associations of the local notabilities of history lent
some traits of glory to the new protagonist of a power
that already was advancing to the conquest of the
world.

Nevertheless, this section of Acts may contain, as it
stands, much wholesome history, if we can divest ourselves of a false appreciation of detail as of any importance when placed against definition of the inspiring
idea. The fortunes of Christian evangelization at Athens
in Pauline times may be not ill-expressed after all in this
quasi-digest of Paul's reception and proceedings there.
The Greeks required wisdom, as the Jews required a
sign: the speech, in its opening, is no poor attempt at a
refined subtlety, to meet the special requirement. The
end of it, however, was, that not many wise, as not many
rich, became converts. Whatever hearing might be obtained for the inculcation of morality and monotheism,
Paul, by his nature and his prejudices, could only come
back at last to the imminent approach of the judgment,—
the rousing angel, the revived dead, the translated living,

and the avouching of all this by the revival and translation of one man already, even Jesus the coming judge. There were plenty at Athens, and at Rome also, who would mock at this, for it was perfectly safe then, and for some time after, to mock at it; and there were plenty who were polite enough to say they would look into the matter, for the sake of as speedily as possible having heard and thought the last of it.

"Ye men of Athens, I observe general indications of your unusual susceptibility of the religious sentiment; for as I went the round, and viewed your sacred monuments, I came, among others, upon an altar inscribed 'To the unknown God.'" This sentence is full of local colour; it is as characteristic as a chapter from Pausanias; indeed, its expressions curiously agree with the reflections of the Handbook writer a little later, upon the peculiar piety of the Athenians towards the gods, even to the extent of being a little farfetched; an error this, he seems to think, on the right side; as he records that not only had they an altar to Pity, but also to Modesty, to Rumour, to Alacrity. Again, we seem to listen to one who is fresh from seeing the chryselephantine Athene of the Parthenon, in the words "Wherefore we ought not to regard the Godhead as likened to gold, silver, or marble, modelled by human art and ideal conception." Even the Athenian pride of autochthony seems to be glanced at in the allusion to the divine settlement of races of men in special times and given bounds about the surface of the earth.

We may easily admit that the speech may be considerably contracted and condensed; nay, may even be an attempt to compress into one the general substance of many addresses. To this source may often be due—and this it is important to allow for—the resemblance of style in reported speeches, to that of the compiler of Acts and Luke, rather than to that of the author of the Epistle to the Romans. The same cause will account for incoherencies of argument, as well as sudden transitions. Certainly here the argument, as it is given, halts to desperation. "Being therefore of the race of the gods, it behoves us not to regard the Godhead as like statues and works of art." But a better reason could scarcely be found for regarding the Godhead as in form like a man. So Pindar sang, "One is the race of gods and men, and from one mother are we both descended: the difference that divides us is that of mortality and immortality." Perhaps it may be thought that Paul would admit the formal likeness of man to God in his image, and only denounced the veneration of the senseless image as God; but this would be for him to misconceive indeed the intention and the spirit of the sacred and symbolical art of the Greeks.

The authenticity of the abstracted speech rather gains than falters by this inconsequence, for it is another point of agreement with Paul's own epistle to Gentiles, to the Roman Christians.

There was less excuse for Paul, perhaps, than for our contemporaries, in not being able to distinguish an ideal from an idol, especially as among the multitudes of images of gods in Athens, a certain number no doubt commanded from a certain vulgar, the veneration which constitutes its object an idol. Still, his argument loosens its hold in the course of his divergencies and illustrations. He is come to declare the Unknown God, the All-Creator, the Almighty, superior to dependence on ministration of sacrifices, not to be housed in temples, utterly alien to stocks and stones, however cunningly composed and modelled; this is the God who, having made of one blood all nations, scattered them over the earth, and for a certain time left them in ignorance of himself as regards direct information, and left them to help their ignorance as they might by endeavours to feel after him and find him, to divine his existence and nature by speculation or by sympathy. What success the Greeks may have had in the search comes out in the illustrative citation from Aratus, which he adopts, and which commits him to Pantheism of an elevated type. It is with something of the feeling of an anticlimax that we read his next observations, to the effect that such attempts were vague and useless struggles of ignorance, and that the true revelation of the Unknown God comes before the world in the assurance of a Jew, that his nation has been in direct communication with him all along, and that before long every nation everywhere, and the dead as well as the living, will be summoned at the sound of trumpet to an audience and a judgment, the judge being a Jew; and the certificate of all these wonders being that that very Jew has already died, has already been raised from the dead, and—on the testimony of those who knew him when alive, as well as of some others—has already ascended into heaven.

Surely, surely, the men were not hasty who apprehended in all this less the discovery of the Unknown God than promise of much vain babble—dissemination of a very couch-grass and tangle-weed of doctrine,—the establishment of a new Pantheon of strange divinities with a new mythology.

Whencesoever the origin of the Attic section of Acts, it does not unfairly represent the eschatology of Paul; though it postulates rather a Jewish than a philosophical audience,—it provides signs rather than a superfluity of wisdom. "But now commandeth he all men everywhere to repent, inasmuch as he has determined a day, on which he is about to judge the world righteously by a man whom he has appointed, and accredited to all men, by having raised him from the dead." (Acts xvii. 30.)

The full interpretation of this—the extension of its abbbreviated terms—is found elsewhere:—"Behold, I tell you a mystery; We shall not all die, but we all of us shall be changed, in a moment, in the twinkling of an eye, at the last trump: for a trumpet shall sound, and the dead shall be raised incorruptible, and we shall undergo a change. For this corruptible must needs be invested with incorruptibility, and this mortal put on immortality, and then shall the word that was written be fulfilled, Death is swallowed up in victory." (1 Cor. xv. 51.)

The same anticipation occurs in the First of Thessalonians, and constitutes a chief proof of the genuineness of the epistle. No pseudonymist, writing in the interest of Paul after his death (and of such only could there be question), would put into his mouth a prophecy which, even equivocally, by this very antecedent death, would stand as falsified; it would have been more in order for him to have relieved the over-confident representation of Paul by insinuating an apologetic gloss. "For this I say unto you in the word of the Lord, that we who are alive, who are left over at the coming of the Lord, will in no wise anticipate those who have fallen asleep. For the Lord himself will come down from heaven with a shout, with the voice of an archangel, and with the trump of God: and the dead in Christ shall rise first: and then the living who are left will be snatched up along with them into the clouds, to meet the Lord in the air: and thus for ever shall we be with the Lord." (1 Thess. iv. 15.) He proceeds to inculcate prepared vigilance, as the day of the Lord will come suddenly, like a thief in the night, and overwhelm their enemies. So in Philippians: "Let your submissiveness be patent to all men; the Lord is at hand" (iv. 5). It may be that his words do not absolutely imply expectation of the last day before his own death; we may read them as equivalent to "such of us as shall then be left alive;" but no candour, however indulgent, can be pressed to admit that his expectation was not instant, and certainly covered by the current generation. Even in the so touchingly indited letter to the Philippians, in which he expresses a desire to depart and be with Christ, he still retains his ancient expectations: "For our citizenship is in heaven, from whence we expect a Saviour, the Lord Jesus, who shall transform our base body into the semblance of his glorious body." (Philip. iii. 20.)

This is the last opportunity we shall have for inquiring, how far did prolonged experience, and new thought or apprehended revelations, modify his ideas? The Corinthian epistle sufficiently shows that Paul, about this time, believed that the kingdom, with all its supernatural accompaniments, would come presently; and numerous fragmentary evidences of the belief, half-altered, unaltered, are imbedded in the Gospels. This alarming imminence doubtless wakened zeal, and urged activity to carry the tidings as rapidly as possible over the earth. It seemed, perhaps, within compass to get through this work in time, when Jews only were to be addressed; but where was the hope when all Gentiledom was in question? The consideration was not entertained, but all the converts urged on the work, and diffusion and dissemination advanced apace: the word grew; the way of the Lord went right on; the kingdom, as an assemblage of adherents, had its limits widened every day.

The kingdom of God, as announced by John the Baptist and Jesus to be hastened and conciliated by repentance, was still semi-political, and its glories largely borrowing from hope of Jewish deliverance. Time went on, and the hope of speedy restoration of Israel was superseded by the inculcation of patience, along with sobriety and vigilance, as in the parable of the virgins with their lamps; and then by the treatment of the disciples' anticipation that it was to come immediately, as ignorance. Then came in the larger and less purely Jewish idea of a heavenly kingdom—a kingdom not on earth, but involving resurrection; a transformation of mortal bodies into bodies superior to decay and corruption; and a catching up of all into the clouds, the end of this world by a renewed creation. This to Paul was a spiritual conception as contrasted with the fleshly or material ideas of political insurrection—expulsion of Romans from Jerusalem, and so forth. The Jewish section of the Christians took up a form of this to suit themselves, and, dropping the carnal idea of the Jerusalem Temple, looked forward to a quasi-spiritual,—a new Jerusalem in the clouds. They gave up the existing Temple and its rites to adopt the grander notion current; but, as in Revelation, restricted it as absolutely as possible to exclusive Jews, and modelled it on an exclusively Jewish ideal.

As time went on, Paul's spiritual kingdom of saints in the clouds, with etherealized bodies, disappointed his expectations, and reasons to account for delay had to be imagined or invented,—the withstanding sorcerer (2 Thess.), the hardness of heart, etc.; and friends of those who died expecting had to be comforted.

We find traces in the Gospels of all these contradictions, and prophecy comes down to us with a tail of apologies draggling after it,—that the time is not now, but presently; not presently, but unawares, at any rate; not to be brought before its time by looking for it, etc.; and what was once the end is the beginning of the end, and then the introduction to the end, or the proem of the introduction.

I refer gladly on this subject to Mr. Mackay's sketch of the Rise and Progress of Christianity; and they who follow my reference to this and others of his works will be grateful for my indication.

One more step remained, and we have a sign of it in the Gospels. Some were bold enough to say, " The kingdom of God is within you." We have signs of it in the denouncement in the Epistle to Timothy, whoever wrote it, of they who taught that the resurrection is already past.

The progress is insensible, but inevitable; the kingdom of God, at first grossly, a restored dynasty of David in the seat of Herod, is next a cosmical development, catastrophe, conclusion; then the kingdom of God is an expression for the subjects of the kingdom; the kingdom is extended or established as converts are made. At first all are veritable; then, as in the parables of the drag-net, the wheat and tares, the sheep and goats, and the sown seed, the kingdom of heaven includes the nominal converts indistinguishably, and becomes but a provisional expression; then the kingdom consists in the doctrine, or in state of mind, and the last enfoldings of materialism are dismissed, and a steady gleam from the very body of truth reaches us, if but a single gleam, and if but for a moment, as we read, "The kingdom of God is not meat and drink, but righteousness, and peace, and joy in the holy spirit." (Rom. xiv. 17.)

Does the author of the Acts, who follows so many developments, follow on to this? The book scarcely enlightens us; we can only say that he recorded as imbecility the Apostles' expectation of an Israelite kingdom, and showed, without any mitigation, the effect on cultivated Gentile minds of Paul's idea of a somewhat more spiritual kingdom; but he does not seem to have got much further, and the world, on the whole, has not got much further to this day. Perhaps now the prevalent notion is that the day of death is for each the day of judgment—that Christ judges each as each departs; or, there is the notion, unspiritual enough, of long torpor and suspension in the grave until a remote revival, and reunion of families and friends. This is a transference into the skies of earthly affections and relations,—the Jerusalem of our own day; and whether the leading passion be a ritual metropolis, a conditional sentiment, or "the dog, the bottle, and the wife," makes not much difference. Still, there are some who hold by the truer kingdom of God, the true resurrection; for the only resurrection we can possibly have cognizance of is indeed come already, is realized when goodness and truth are wrought for to the best of our lights and our forces, and in reliance on influences, the direction of which in last resort is beyond us. And so Faith in an energy by which such a kingdom can come, brings Hope—only solace of the soul—that it is in us and about us and beyond us, and Charity meanwhile to all who, sincere in aspiration, are fastened unhappily in ceremonial or materialistic slavery, from which may some John, some Jesus, some Stephen and Peter and Paul, happily and in good time release them!

III. THE HARMONY OF THE REVERENTIAL AND THE RIGHTLY REASONABLE.

The Cartoon is so far true to the history, that it claims to embody the antithesis of enthusiastic to speculative religion. Christianity on the one side, and Philosophy on the other, thus seem to express the culminating civilizations of the Semitic and Indo-European races, whose unity is vindicated by their concurrent tendencies quite as positively as by the words of Paul. But in virtue of this very unity, the end of the development must be, not antithesis, but harmony. The devotional, the reverential, and the reasonable instincts of man have to be conciliated, not committed to constant conflict, or with a victory forthcoming either on one side or the other. The happiness and the satisfaction of the mind are to be found, to be advanced, if ever, in the cordial sympathy of the clearest and coolest intellect with the warmth of religious reliance, and in the sustained energy that is born of such a combination.

But the philosophical explorations which date their origin from Greece must aid us in such enterprise; only by their indications and help can we attain to just appreciation of the limits of human knowledge,—an object as important as to pursue whatever can be known within those limits; then at last devotion may be enthusiastic without fear of being absurd; may be reasonable, without mistrust of lapse to indifference; calm yet energetic; sober, yet not selfish—nay, most actively benevolent, sympathetic, affectionate. If such a consummation shall be ever reached, the very apostles of religion will be foremost to declare the limitations of knowledge, and to denounce the wickedness of attempts to impose on the credulous, whether for seeming good or ill, by professed secret and special information as to what has gone on, or is going on, or is to be looked forward to, hereafter beyond them, of which all must of necessity be equally ignorant.

Philosophy must drop of its own accord its search after a theology which is the very philosopher's stone of speculation; must do its best to define the boundaries of the explicable; and, admitting their existence and place, not pretend to explain the inexplicable: it will then be ripe for unblamed co-operation with the spirit of faith, of humility, of devotion, and be more than ever entitled to proffer services to get Christianity, and all other dogmatized forms of religion, out of their difficulties. To the aid of philosophy the better spirit that may be within Christianity must recur—and it will be done with more dignity if done spontaneously,—to purge away its false and ill-conditioned accretions; its codes of dogma and systematized conundrums; its fabulous history, mythical miracles; its prophecies after the fact, and its false ascriptions of prophetical character; its recognition of false prophetical pretence.

Still there is more to be done: Paul denounces symbolism and temple service at Athens; and yet, as these had been applied in Athens, they gave the nearest solution man has yet attained to, of the problem how to find expression and excitement for the religious element of our nature, without the fall to superstition or absurdity in doctrine or rites. To Pericles, centuries before, the great historian had ascribed a claim on the part of Athens, of successfully combining the indulgence of artistic and speculative predilections with dexterity and energy in action. Pericles himself, as orderer of the sacred monuments and celebrations of the state, had done much also to supply the healthiest outlet and discipline for the religious feeling of which the people that he guided was so susceptible. The literature of his age, however, gives abundant indication that the time was not yet for the most important of all consummations. Speculative inquiry had still the work of centuries before it; and what had been acquired was far from being generally diffused. The roots of old superstitions were alive, widely spread, and deeply seated; and the appetite for religious excitement, lively as it might be, was, to a large extent, a diseased appetite, and turned from the lofty and the refined to gorge itself preferentially on garbage.

The very movement that Paul inaugurates had much

the same history before it. It soon sought alliance with all the stage properties of temple service, and was ensloughed in a debasing ceremonialism accordingly. The Beautiful, which is the Divine, vindicated itself at last in Mass and *Miserere*, in all the glories of architecture and of all the arts; but, again, the value of these aids to true devotion was confined in all purity to but a few minds; with the multitude, the symbolism, which is the soul of the combination, escaped apprehension; it was countervailed by traditional association with absurdities most crass, with craft making gain out of ignorance, with luxury availing itself of the manifestations of divine art merely to relieve the tedium of routine, to keep off the inevitable yawn during the interminable celebrations,—instruments of tyranny over men, of which the very weight was all but intolerable to those who wielded them.

Is it the case that, as men and as society are now constituted, as they always have been, and are ever likely to be, the regulating power of religion alloyed with fable and superstition, cannot be emulated by influence at command of any purer form, and can therefore ill be spared? Is it all, and the best that we can do in our difficulty and distress, to deal tenderly with the established,—to let the sleeping dogs of fanaticism lie, if fortunately lie they will, and, in case they are restless, to resort to means of stupefying them? Shall we rejoice to calm religious excitability into drowsiness, by the corruption of preferments and dignities distributed with judgment to those who, displaying power to influence a numerous following, hint willingness to give aid, for a consideration, in hoodwinking opening intelligence, and drugging with opiates the very well-springs of sacred enthusiasm?

It is on some such theory that the man of the world applies himself to the problem of the day; so usually proceeds the statesman, who is the man of the world concerned with politics; and so, still more usually, the hierarch, who is, for the most part, another man of the world, cumbered with the intercomplicated spiritualities and worldlinesses that cling about the administration of a church. Let each, and each will, see to his own; but the very formula is a claim of immunity for one who should make it his own business to think for all. When such arrives, may the claim serve him! It will be well if, in thinking and discoursing in the interest of all, he can protect himself against all, for all are likely enough to be against him.

Even while the colours of the paintings we have been studying were still fresh, the spirit of Paul's protest against superstition, and on Paul's own authority, was re-published to the world, and resounded from the pulpit of Luther. Did the Cardinals, who assisted at mass with this tapestry displayed in their sight, recognize the parallel? To their actions, I fear, we should turn in the last instance, to look for an answer that could satisfy our curiosity. Centuries roll round, and great again is the company of the preachers who profess allegiance to the principles of Luther and of Paul. Which of these successors, however, in England now will dare to ascend his Mars' Hill, and appeal in all frankness, as well as fervour, to the philosophers? Appeals in some form or fashion are not wanting; but the place of Paul would now be among the Epicureans and Stoics of the crowd; and if in his misery, as the words went on, he forbore to mock, I, for one, do not doubt that he would walk away, and not even profess willingness to be a listener at a future time, to soften his leave-taking.

What the world still longs for, and yearns for, is a scheme of theology, intelligent, noble, self-respecting, which shall not take advantage of human credulousness, nervousness, and fright; shall not play tricks with either docile trust or the edified human understanding, by vain pretences, transcending the capacities of our nature, of accounting for the infinite, of revising the relation of those universal postulates that are the conditions of perception, not to say of reason,—which shall not pretend to have satisfied itself, nor claim to have satisfied the understanding of all candid and acutest criticism on all mysteries, when it has only succeeded in hiding question and answer alike in impenetrable haze.

Beyond this, the social, no less than the personal, sympathies desiderate some scheme of religious celebration which shall give expression, coming home to the bosoms of all, of the salutary sense of the common amenability of all mankind to the same ultimate sanction of right and wrong,—the same dependence of strong and weak, of young and old, of rich and poor, of wise and foolish, upon an ulterior Mystery, Power, Existence, —call it what we may, that is ever within reach of our affections, however far it transcends our capacity of intellectual appreciation, or foils our babbling attempts at articulate expression;—before which, if, in our depression and despair, we can only, on the mere ground of common sense and consistency, bow in blind resignation; in hopefulness, which is our health, we may rejoice to rest in confidence for our futurity,—to repose in happiness and faith.

Human life—I need not tell it to my contemporaries, may gladly welcome whatever of consolation, not to say encouragement, it can gain a glimpse of. The ills and accidents and liabilities of our state are too dreary, too dire, too hideous, and too certain, to be made light of by either frivolity or courage. The poetic enumeration of "Labour and penury, the racks of pain, disease, and sorrow's weeping train," leaves still the worst in silence. The mind may sustain the body, but whither shall it fly for refuge from wounds, from diseases proper to itself— from self-reproach, from self-disdain for still recurring weakness—from desolating loss of confidence in mankind, at large and in particular, shaken and gone for ever, and with it all interest in pursuit or study—for what occupation is there of which the condition is not relative dependence on the advantage or the capacities of men?

Wise and good have ere now, and will again, in their unhappiness, desire that they could revert to the blind but passionate confidence of childhood. The cry will go up,—Would that I could recover that faith which idealized in a heavenly father the superior, the unquestioned force and ever-watchful and efficient affection of an earthly father! What would not be my content if I could rely upon an Omnipotence of favour and affection, that, whatever my troubles, my faults, would assuredly see me safely through them; but who will lean with confidence on a reed he knows to be broken

—lie down to rest cheerfully on a mine when he traces the slow smouldering fuse? I can but say that such are the conditions of our life, and we must accept them or resign—we do accept them in every action of our life and exercise of our senses. We cannot vindicate the reasonableness of either hope or despondency, faith or mistrust; but the seal of truth is decided in the struggle for existence—and Hope and Faith, for ever young, reviving ever, receive their justification by nature's own infallible signature of unquenchable and ever-victorious vitality.

THE SPIRIT OF THE NEW TESTAMENT WITHIN THE OLD: JOSEPH AND BOAZ.

THE spirit or genius of Christianity, however we define it, is in as direct opposition and contrast to the spirit or genius of Judaism, as the widest and warmest sympathy is to the narrowest and most restricted reserve—to the coolest temperament for fellow-feeling out of a close limit, and that defined most selfishly. The Jews of old time are confident of being rather the exclusive than the especial objects of divine favour, the channels of divine revelation, the instruments and administrators of all that is divinely good and great, and in place of the eagerness to impart, we find an eager reserve, a selfish jealousy of participants. Compassion on one side is in harsh contrast to contempt on the other; the will to make any sacrifice of self for others' good is opposed to careless disregard of the fate of generations; the desire to break down barriers is met by the bigotry that strengthens them; the motive to unite mankind is opposed by the will to separate them, and to keep them apart.

Still it was from the midst of Judaism that Christianism came forth, and in this there is nothing irrational or opposed to likelihoods;—such a result is due to tendency to reaction, by a law so familiar to the student of history, that it becomes an unconscious process with him when in the neighbourhood of any strongly marked and developed tendency,—bigotry, enthusiasm, energetic and animated exertion, to look about at once for an equal and opposite manifestation. Even sloth and lethargy have a certain disposition to set vivacity and vigilance in motion, though such reagent stimulus is certainly less alert than in more lively combinations.

Hence, the manifestation of Christianism, or the spirit of Christianity, was not delayed till the appearance and ministry of Christ. The conditions of its excitement were in order ages earlier among the Jews, and although its full fervour only appears when those conditions were at fullest, sporadic outbursts and efflorescences are not wanting in the literature that preserves so much of the history of the Jewish mind. These earlier traces are most noteworthy as themselves preparing the way for the later declaration, but it is probable that they do but faintly represent the feeling in its extent and vigour as it originally flourished. Still, beyond the presumptions alluded to, they are our only evidence, and various are their forms.

To the Gentile it might easily appear that the Jews to some extent counterbalanced their uncharitableness towards the rest of the world, their unfeeling disregard, their supercilious contempt or virulent hatred, by as exaggerated sympathy for each other. But in truth intestine divisions were anything but exceptional, and tribe was opposed to tribe and party to party, with a depth of dislike and acrid antipathy that was revolting even after the spectacle of their feelings towards the Gentile. Divisions and civil wars commence early in their history, and when arms are out of reach the clash of dogma is as fierce, and the vengeance of sectaries as prompt and unrelenting.

It is in attempts to soften these internecine animosities, that we trace in the earlier literature of the Jews the indications of that coming sun of Christianism of which the orb itself was still far below the horizon. We find them in detached precepts and glosses of the law, but most remarkably, and no doubt most efficiently in that form of quasi-historical apologue, which, whether in the parables of Jesus or in the memorabilia of his story, has conveyed most forcibly and touchingly the great moral of his mission. The instance I am about to cite of anticipative Christianism has in truth its lamenesses and laxities, but this is characteristic of such prevenient phenomena, and is indeed no more than we find in the march of Christianity its very self, though here the stages of progress pressed on more vehemently.

If the Christian spirit be expressed anywhere in Hebrew literature it is in the touching history of Joseph, which is told in Genesis with a fullness, we cannot say a diffuseness, that suffices to mark it of a peculiar origin as compared with the greater part of the book. Literary criticism traces a mixture of original materials, but to no serious extent, and the story at large belongs to the record Elohim.

The prophecy of the patriarch Jacob on his death-bed furnishes certain negative dates for at least that portion of the story very satisfactorily; we shall see whether the date of composition thus indicated throws light on the moral and purport of the narrative at large.

Judah is addressed as the head of a royal tribe, and supreme over his brethren or having been so; the passage therefore was written after the full establishment of David, who was of that tribe, and before the abolition of the kingdom of Judah :—

> " Judah, thee shall thy brethren praise:
> Thy hand shall be on the neck of thine enemies
> Thy father's children shall bow down before thee;
> Judah is a young lion . . .
> The sceptre shall not depart from Judah,
> Nor a lawgiver from between his feet
> Until," etc.

The warlike vigour assigned to Judah is characteristic of the tribe under the monarchy and is appropriately shared by Benjamin, the tribe of Saul :—

> " Benjamin shall spoil as a wolf:
> In the morning he shall devour the prey,
> And at night he shall divide the spoil."

The greater portion of Benjamin remained attached to Judah at the division of the kingdoms.

Joseph is addressed as the representative of the tribes of his sons Ephraim and Manasseh, and at greater length and with more special favour; exalted for prolific fruitfulness, energy in war, though sorely pressed, and the protection and blessings of God. Ephraim is the more important and is currently referred to by the prophets as titular of the associated tribes of the kingdom of Israel.

There is only occasion to refer further to Reuben; the tradition that made him the eldest of Jacob's sons is probably an offset of the tradition that in the division of the promised Land the Reubenites were the first in possession of their portion. There was a certain prejudice against the tribe from the accusation of selfish regard for the interests of their peculiar position beyond Jordan, and generally the tribe attained to but slight influence. At the division of the kingdoms it joined the ten tribes,— or Ephraim, in opposition to Benjamin and Judah.

Whatever date after the limit indicated may be conjecturally assigned to this composition, it will not fail to be observed how evenhanded is the balance held between the types of the rival kingdoms of Ephraim and Judah. The patriarch takes a common pride in both, and both are thus reminded of the common tie by which they are united.

Throughout the story of Joseph again, we have hints by no means ambiguous, of similar reference. Judah and Benjamin and Joseph, the eponyms of the royal tribes—the tribes of Saul, of David, and of Jeroboam, have the same lead in the narrative as their tribes in history. Benjamin, the youngest son of the patriarch, aptly represents the very smallest tribe, and the spirit and pre-eminence of Judah are in like manner characteristic of the vigour and daring of the tribe. Thus read, the entire story becomes an obvious apologue inculcating mutual forbearance and brotherly affection among the tribes of Israel and especially between the groups of them that come into opposition, as Joseph and Judah, the kingdoms of Judah and of Israel. Joseph is represented as unusually affectionate towards Benjamin his own brother, though in truth the narrative implies that Benjamin was a party with the rest to the injury done him; it is by the appeal and suggestion of Judah that the life of Joseph is spared, and that slavery is substituted for death; from the mouth of Judah also at last comes the pathetic appeal to Joseph to compassionate the paternal anxieties of Jacob, and the free exhibition of unselfishness in the proposal, that he himself should be detained a slave rather than his father's heart have a final wound by loss of the remaining son of Rachel. There is some appearance of an inculcation of tolerance of a still wider scope in the assignment to Joseph of an Egyptian wife and the daughter of a priest of On, a sun-worshipper, who bore him children, the eponyms of the tribes of Ephraim and Manasseh.

The various localities that are introduced assist the application. Jacob is fixed at Hebron, the most ancient seat of David's royalty in the tribe of Judah, and as we see in the history of Absalom, a political as well as religious centre; it is also one of the cities fortified by Rehoboam. Joseph is sent to visit his brethren at Shechem, the future capital of Ephraim, of the kingdom of Israel, and follows them thence to the future territory of Manasseh at Dothan, as Jeroboam, afterwards the first king of Israel, is sent by Solomon to fortify Shechem on Mount Ephraim.

I am, then, strongly disposed to believe that the history of Joseph took the form in which we have it, of a pacificatory apologue inculcating forgiveness and forbearance between the rival tribes, and with a leaning towards Joseph, at a very early date after the division of the kingdoms;—that it was in fact designed to allay and assuage the first heats and rancour ensuing on the separation, and during the lifetime of Jeroboam and Rehoboam.

On the first revolt of the tribes, with Jeroboam at their head, Rehoboam, as we read, prepared to recover his power, as he had received it from his father, by force of arms. He assembled all the house of Judah with the tribe of Benjamin, 180,000 men, to fight against the house of Israel, and to bring the kingdom again to Rehoboam, the son of Solomon. The attempt, however, was stayed by the intervention of Shemaiah the prophet; with the authoritative formula, Thus saith the Lord; he forbade the commencement of civil war:— "Ye shall not go up nor fight against your brethren the children of Israel; return every man to his house, for this thing is from me." Conflict, therefore, was forbidden on the special ground of brotherly tie between the divided tribes, and whether by influence chiefly on the army or the king, the expedition was put an end to. The words assigned to Shemaiah are doubtless but the sum and moral of his exhortation; I can readily believe that some story of Joseph may have been employed by him to illustrate and enforce his moral with as much force as the parable of the pet lamb lent to Nathan's denunciation of David—" Thou art the man."

How much substratum of earlier tradition, not to say authentic history, may still underlie the elaboration of the story for a purpose, it is difficult—impossible, to determine. But type and antitype, as we can now compare them, fall into correspondence on this wise.

Jeroboam, of the tribe of Ephraim, was marked by King Solomon for high qualities of intelligence and vigour, and appointed superintendent of the works of fortification for the defence of Jerusalem, and in this position he so far justified the opinion of his energy as to be made in consequence "ruler over all the charge of the house of Joseph." In the words of Josephus he was entrusted with the generalship—the military command, which was probably very comprehensive, of the tribe of Joseph.

The energetic and favoured minister of such a monarch as Solomon is rarely popular, or in a position very advantageous for the conciliation of popular favour. He may endeavour, like the Wolsey—at least of Shakspeare,—to defraud his master of what credit for popular measures there may be a chance of intercepting, but it is more within the rule that he should be obnoxious to even far more odium than he deserves. The date of his appointments cannot be fixed, but from the occasion of mention it appears to have been towards the end of Solomon's reign, when the pressure on the subject overpowering by long continuance upon still decreasing strength, was beginning to be borne uneasily from the prospect that soon it must, and immediately it might, be relieved by a demise.

It was when Jeroboam quitted Jerusalem to betake himself to the scene of his extended functions that he was accosted by Ahijah of Silo, a city of Ephraim, near Sichem, who took the new garment he had on, that of his office it may be, tore it into twelve pieces, and so by a visible and sensible type, as usual with the Hebrew prophet down to the days of Paul, announced the will of the Lord, the God of Israel. Ten of the tribes of Israel he declared, symbolized by ten pieces of the garment, would the Lord take from the kingdom of the house of David, and of these should Jeroboam, after the death of Solomon the idolatrous, be king.

The same consequence, as the story goes, ensued now as when Samuel anointed David during the lifetime of Saul,—jealousy on the part of the monarch, and peril to the king designate, and plots and preparations on his part that he was necessarily committed to, whether he waited for provocation or not. This, or something like this, was of course the intention of the prophet; Solomon, however, took the alarm, and Jeroboam was obliged to fly, and took refuge in Egypt, where he was apparently received and entertained by Shishak. Later events show that he had made some way in laying the foundations of a party in the ten tribes before his flight, while his flight nevertheless, is proof equally satisfactory that the tribes at large,—possibly from the unpopularity that I have assumed and characterized, were not prepared or disposed to support him at once by open rising. It is scarcely necessary to remark that the original prophecy and promise of Ahijah was probably destitute of the deferring clauses it now contains in deference to the event, and may easily have promised the kingdom of ten, if not twelve tribes, to Jeroboam, "the mighty man of valour," as soon as he should care to strike for it.

On the death of Solomon, and accession of Rehoboam, Jeroboam invited by leaders of the people reappeared; that he was unmolested at Shechem, during the conference there of the king with his discontented subjects, may be assumed as evidence of the position he assumed at once; events were now ripe, and on the insolent refusal by Rehoboam of all hopes of redress, the people at large were evidently now as zealous as their leaders in favour of Jeroboam for their liberator from tyranny too grievous to bear; he became the first king of Israel, and the division of the tribes was completed. It is probable that the assistance he brought to the insurgents was not only his vigour of character, but also substantial support from the treasury of Shishak. The division being established, the voice of prophets, as we have seen, declared that it was ordained and sanctioned by God, and types and predictions would come in with usual abundance to prove to satisfaction, after the fact, that events must of necessity and from Divine preordinance be on such wise as it could not be disputed that they certainly were.

Shemaiah the prophet declared the divine approval of the order of events, which the stimulative words of Ahijah the prophet had so mainly contributed to bring about. Joseph was triumphant in royalty, rivalling the elder house; and Judah was comparatively humbled at the elevation of a tribe lately subject and treated with unceremonious and contemptuous harshness. Bitter feelings could not but rankle on either side; but there was some voice raised, of poet or prophet, to remind of common brotherhood, and to urge forgiveness, penitence, forbearance. It was by the will of God, and no crime of Jeroboam, that he had been marked for royalty, and announced as a future king, and thus an object of divine favour: such might be the colour of an apology. But he had been expelled and exiled, having done no wrong, even if his life was spared, and with what addition of injury to possessions or relatives is not now to be known. Does he, then, it might well be said, content with tardy recognition of his divinely sanctioned rights, forego animosity and revenge, and tender not retaliation but good offices, where good offices are wanted, with the mighty king of Egypt? It is admiration, not rancour, of which such magnanimity is properly the object, and let such brotherly affection be admitted, and in like spirit happily requited.

In the fifth year of the divided kingdom, Shishak, king of Egypt, entered Jerusalem; that he contented himself with plunder, or, we may say, with ransom, is a degree of forbearance in these times that we may not improbably ascribe to the interposition of Jeroboam, whose immunity from like mulct is very noteworthy. It is explained, if we assume his friendly connection with his former host and protector; but we must, then, give him credit for the good feeling in question to account for this connection not being fatal to his rival Rehoboam. The addition of the LXX. to 3 Kings xii. 24, states that Jeroboam became son-in-law of the king of Egypt on leaving for Judæa. The administrative talent recognized by Solomon may have also been employed by Shishak, and thus the type of Joseph is still more closely applicable.

The Joseph of the patriarchal apologue, then, is marked out in youth for future distinction and dignity by the dreams of happy omen; the sheaves and the stars of his brethren and even of his parents making obeisance to him, just as Jeroboam, viceroy of Joseph's tribe, is marked out by the prophecy of Ahijah. The robe (of office, as I have assumed) which, torn in pieces, is made the type of Jeroboam's dignity, when he is on his road to his charge, has strange coincidence with the coat of divers colours (pieces in the margin), arrayed in which Joseph travels from Hebron to Shechem and Dothan, to make survey of his brethren's proceedings, and report them—not favourably, to his father. (Gen. xxxvii. 2.) The coat, in either case, is the occasion of jealousy, and promotes the outburst prepared by too inconsiderate enunciation of prophetic hopes; and the localities correspond. Doomed to death, Joseph—Jeroboam finds refuge in Egypt, obtains favour and preferment with the Pharaoh, which enables him at a later period to rescue and protect his brethren, the ten tribes first, and afterwards the kingdom of Judah and Benjamin. The former victim of envy became the instrument of salvation, and used his power to console and preserve at the very moment that the temptation was greatest to abuse it for purposes of retaliation.

It seems to me not at all impossible that the details of the mercy of Joseph may have been devised at a time when occasion was still open to inculcate forbearance on Jeroboam by heroic and ancestral example. In fact, notwithstanding the truce effected by Shemaiah, we read, 1 Kings xiv. 29, "There was war between Jeroboam and Rehoboam all their days," and therefore continued occasion for the exhortations of the prophets to remember, not past injuries, but original brotherhood,—the common father, the common God.

Throughout the history of Joseph, there is a very discernible Egytian interest to the extent at least of a tolerance for the alliance of Hebrews with Egyptians, and the residence of Hebrews in Egypt, that contrasts with the tone assumed in large portions of the prophetic Scriptures. No doubt Jeroboam was accompanied from

Egypt by Hebrews whose relations to the country were even more intimate than his own.

A question is thus raised that is indifferent to the matter immediately in hand, but worth a notice for its own sake. What was the precise political relation of Jerusalem to Egypt after Shishak had departed with the spoils of the temple? Are we to assume that no further tribute was periodically exacted,—that Judæa was not virtually tributary to Egypt for long afterwards? The historian says nothing of such continued dependence; yet it is quite consistent with the course of political reactions to conjecture that the Egyptian invasion of Syria, and temporary occupation of Jerusalem, had taught and was considered to have taught Rehoboam his weakness, and that he was left in possession of his kingdom, in consideration of a tribute which there was little apprehension of his venturing to withhold. The policy of the Romans furnishes example of this plan of provincial administration, which has many advantages to an empire which regards and values provinces merely as contributing to revenue, and from proper constitution, or from religious or other peculiarities of the subject-provinces is beset with difficulties in an attempt to administrate them directly.

That the historians say nothing of tribute is not matter for wonder,—it is as little brought forward by Josephus that Herod paid tribute to Augustus; and there are indications of still·more considerable suppressions;—as when the defeat of Sennacherib, ascribed by Herodotus to the agency of an Egyptian God in favour of an Egyptian King, is related with Hebrew colouring, and with no reference to Egyptian concern of any kind whatever.

I have little doubt that the story of Ruth, like that of Joseph, is a moral apologue. Or rather let us say it is a poetical apologue, for though if my view of the composition and its period be correct, it had an application of the directest kind to the social circumstances of its original audience, yet is this moral so entirely unforced, while yet so forcible, it issues so spontaneously and so unconsciously, while at the same time so effectually, that we accept it not as from a teacher, but are impressed with it as from the lips of an inspired singer and poet.

The story is told of the days of the Judges; a reference to the customs of that time as antiquated in the time of the narration, dates the composition relatively, as indeed the mention of Jesse places it at least as late as the reign of Saul.

The language of the Book is said by De Wette to have certain relationship to that of the Book of Samuel, but apparently from its Chaldaisms and other peculiarities, to be distinctly later.

I desiderate more exact information as to the chronological value of the Chaldaizing impress,—in the meantime anticipate none that will materially affect my present conclusions.

Ruth, a young Moabitess, is married by a Bethlehemite who along with his father and mother had taken refuge in her land on account of a famine. Her husband dies, and her mother-in-law, Naomi, also become a widow, proposes to return to her own country alone, but Ruth affectionately accompanies her, adopting both her country and her God. "Thy country shall be my country and thy God my God."

Arrived at Bethlehem she is noticed by a wealthy kinsman of her husband's, Boaz, who is struck with her piety and marries her, and she becomes the ancestress of David.

Boaz marries her in conformity with the Levirate law or rather custom, as the nearest disengaged relative of her former husband; it is plainly implied that by doing so he evinced a fine appreciation of virtue, and as a wealthy man marrying a poor widow, much generosity of character. Yet this generosity is not enhanced by any intimation that from the foreign birth of Ruth he might without blame have avoided the match had he chosen to do so, it simply depends on the delicacy with which he proceeded and the motive—his admiration of Ruth's filial piety, which caused his attention to her. The merit of Ruth is in truth set forth by the exhibition of the share it had in inducing Boaz so readily to fulfil the obligations of the law, which it is thus implied was not in every instance embraced and admitted at once as a matter of course. Indeed this is shown by the circumstance that Naomi does not immediately on her arrival put Ruth in the way of making or having made the formal claim. She takes the more modest course of first giving her the opportunity of coming under the eye of Boaz, and not until she has received positive proof of having "found favour" with him, does she intimate the claim which she might lawfully make. The true explanation of the scene of the threshing-floor appears to be this. Ruth was entitled to claim Boaz as her husband,—probably she would have been considered, in the event of question, as already legally his wife. The step she took with her mother-in-law's advice, was therefore, simply a formal claim of recognition of rights, and the forbearance of Boaz, though he had eaten and drunk and his heart was merry, is a gratuitous addition to the dignity of his character with no disparagement of Ruth's.

Pharez, an ancestor of Boaz, was the offspring of intercourse under circumstances very similar but less justifiable. Tamar, the Canaanitish woman, the widow of two sons of Judah, was withheld from her legal claim upon the third, and vindicated herself by waylaying even Judah his father.

When Naomi tells Ruth and her sister, that in going with her they gave up hope of second marriages, she either suppresses the legal claim they would have on their husbands' kindred or recognizes the uncertainty of success in enforcing it, from flaw in their title or the irregularity of administration. Ruth, however, who braved this consequence from attachment to Naomi, is rewarded with a husband, and a rich one.

The intermarriage of Jews with Moabitish women is at one period of their history,—under Nehemiah and Ezra, very severely denounced, and traces occur earlier of like aversion; on the other hand, the earlier records of the Jews exhibit such mixed marriages on the part of patriarchs and princes of the nation with much greater liberality. Was the Book of Ruth written in an earlier and more tolerant period, when such an alliance passed as a matter of course, or was it written when it would be most distinctly forbidden, with a view to inculcate the innocence of the step, and to set forth a moral beauty in opposition to a Levitical restriction. The latter is my opinion.

When a party of Jewish exiles, by favour of the Persian monarch, obtained permission to rebuild the walls of Jerusalem, it was but a limited number that resolved to quit the ties that engaged them to their new country for the dangers and difficulties of the precarious adventure. We may conceive that the expedition comprised the more bigoted Jews, and yet among them were many who had allied themselves in marriage with women of foreign blood. The opposition to the enterprise was manifold; the Samaritans applied to be admitted and were rejected, and the strict theological character of the undertaking was declared generally in a jealous degradation and repulse of all who could not establish claim to purity of blood (Nehemiah vii. 61–64; ix.). Very shortly, as was natural in such case, an outcry arose about alien wives, and in result they were put away.

The preservation of nationality, of which the return from the captivity was such a triumph, was not unnaturally regarded as dependent on preservation of purity of blood; those who did not join in the return were probably precisely the class that had linked itself in foreign family relations. Hence genealogies were scrutinized with strictness,—populations that proffered friendship—for anything that appears with sincerity, were sourly rejected, and lastly came the divorce of the strange wives—wives of Ashdod, of Ammon, and of Moab (Nehemiah xiii. 23),—Canaanites, Hittites, Perizzites, Jebusites, Ammonites, Moabites, Egyptians, Amorites;—princes and rulers being chief in the trespass (Ezra ix. 1).

It is said (Nehemiah xiii. 3) they separated from Israel

all the mixed multitude, but whether wives of Babylonian origin, and their descendants were included, is not distinctly stated. It seems noteworthy that no account occurs of this class that could scarcely but have existed in some numbers.

No exception was made in favour of the wives who had already borne families. From the tenor of the account in Ezra, it may be doubted whether the mass of the people fell in with the scheme so heartily as its originators, and whether the plea for delay did not turn out a plan for some evasion.

In Nehemiah, the Ammonites and Moabites are mentioned with especial virulence, ostensibly on the ground of the old grudge—their opposition to the children of Israel returning from Egypt, and their hiring Balaam to curse them; the denouncement of them in Deuteronomy xxiii. with greater severity than Edomites or Egyptians probably dates here.

In the earlier historical books also, Balaam is charged with having counselled the seduction of Israel by Moabitish female charms; whether of the two, the later prejudice or the earlier dated record, was in truth the progenitor of the other it is hard to say.

I cannot imagine any occasion, and historical conjuncture when the sentiment and incident of the story of Ruth could have been more livelily appreciated. If, indeed, in the clamour for putting away the strange wives, the bigotry of the agitation did not even spare those, as it probably would not, who had not only been faithful wives in Assyria, but had freely accompanied their Jewish husbands, and renounced country and their country's faith to participate in the dangers of the great design, with what force must have fallen on their ears the story of the Moabitish girl, who adopted the religion and the sympathies of her husband, and followed her mother-in-law with filial piety to Judæa! That this trait is intended to be marked for approbation is clear by the contrast by which it is set off in the character of Orpah, who, otherwise blameless, yet fails of the full devotedness. The anecdote exhibits in fullest force the effect of marriage to induce the complete attachment of the wife to her adopted relations. The interest that is thus created in Ruth not only justifies Boaz, and might justify him to a bigoted exclusionist in Jewish caste, but at once rouses us to watch his proceedings with pre-formed principles of judgment. The natural feelings of the heart are roused, and demand that he shall treat her with respect and generosity; could even the sourest formalist denounce his tender and dignified conduct as unlawful, and an abomination? It is my impression that it was in such an apologue that some gifted Hebrew asserted, and set forth the superior beauty and value of natural piety as contrasted with the literal ceremonialism of unfeeling priests and official genealogists.

Was it a mere invention of the poet or prophet that the Moabitess Ruth was an ancestress of David, or did the traditional genealogy of the king really furnish a Moabitess ancestress, to whose name there was an opportunity of attaching a story? Perhaps the latter view is the more probable; to trace the line of David himself to such an origin was of course to give the alliance a very high sanction, and it even appears that in following the ancestry still higher up to Pharez there was an intention to protect the inference from the later incident by the parallel of an undoubted authority.

David, persecuted by Saul, placed his parents for security with the king of Moab; was this suggestive of the later Moabitish story, or was it suggested by it, a late plea for Moab?

Nehemiah's denunciation of the mixed marriages seems to challenge such a reply as the Book of Ruth affords:—"Did not Solomon," he said, "king of Israel, sin by these things? yet among many nations there was no king like him who was beloved of his God, yet even him did outlandish women cause to sin." Solomon, who married idolatresses, and fell in with their superstitions and customs, is contrasted with the son-in-law of Naomi, whose Moabitish wife adopts his country and worships his God, and practises the most engaging piety.

FINIS.

www.ingramcontent.com/pod-product-compliance
Lightning Source LLC
Chambersburg PA
CBHW021232300426
44111CB00007B/512